MAYBERRY
MEMORIES

MAYBERRY MEMORIES

The Andy Griffith Show Photo Album

KEN BECK and JIM CLARK

RUTLEDGE HILL PRESS®
Nashville, Tennessee

A Thomas Nelson Company

Dedicated to the cast,
production crew, and
writers of
The Andy Griffith Show

Additional material and compilation copyright © 2000 by Ken Beck and Jim Clark

Photographs from *Gomer Pyle, U.S.M.C.* courtesy of Ashford Productions
Photographs from *Mayberry, R.F.D.* courtesy of RFD Productions

Published by Rutledge Hill Press®, a Thomas Nelson Company, P.O. Box 141000, Nashville, Tennessee 37214.

Design by Harriette Bateman, Bateman Design.

Library of Congress-in-Publication Data

Beck, Ken, 1951–
Mayberry memories: the Andy Griffith show photo album /
by Ken Beck and Jim Clark
p. cm.
ISBN 1-55853-830-5
1. Andy Griffith show (Television program)--Pictorial works. I. Clark, Jim, 1960– II. Title.

PN1992.77.A573B43 2000   00-055260
791.45'72--dc21   CIP

Printed in Colombia
3 4 5 6 7 8 9   05 04

CONTENTS

Acknowledgments

The compilation of this book has been a collaborative effort by more than a hundred people who share a particular devotion to *The Andy Griffith Show*. The comments from more than five dozen members of the cast and production crew and from writers for the show are cited throughout the book and represent one of its two main components. We give our heartfelt thanks to all who took time to share their thoughts and feelings for this book.

The book's other dominant component is its photographs, most of which have never been published in a book and many of which have been published only once or not at all in any form. Many of the photographs have been shared by the actors, crew, and writers for the show. Their contributions are credited with each photograph.

We give special thanks to several photographic archives, collectors, and fans whose enthusiasm, knowledge, and generosity have allowed this book to present a truly remarkable collection of photographs. We are grateful to Jason Gilmore and Jim Schwenke of the Gilmore-Schwenke Archives for permitting this book to be the first published appearance of several of the spectacular photographs from their exceptional collection. We also thank David Lombard of the CBS Photo Archive for his unsurpassed professionalism and assistance with our use of several exquisite photographs (again, most never before published) from the CBS collection.

Other collectors who have shared some extraordinary photographs from their extensive collections are Phil Bowling (who also helped tremendously with key research), Bart Boatwright, Joel Rasmussen, Steve Cox, and Joshua Kessler at *TV Guide*.

Further assistance with photographs was offered by Beverly Sweeney, Bridget Sweeney, Earle Hagen, Aaron Ruben, Richard O. Linke, Ronald Jacobs, Mary Dodson, Maydale McQuain, Art Baer, Bill Idelson, Harvey Bullock, LeRoy Mack McNees, Roland White, Jeffrey Hayden, Jean Carson, George Lindsey, Ronnie Schell, Renée Aubry, Joy Ellison, Margaret Kerry-Willcox, Arlene Golonka, Kit McNear, Barbara Stuart, Donald M. Lant, John O'Quinn, Bill Jarnigan and Celia Reynolds at the University of North Alabama, Darrell Perry, Jack Hilliard, Nancy Clark, Blake Clark, Emmett Forrest, and Paul Gilkes.

We also received invaluable assistance with our research and gathering of information from David Fernandes, Dale Robinson, Donny Whitehead, Judy Murata, Sherwin Bash, Randy Bash, Dorothy Best, Mike Cramer at Pacific Trading Cards, Bill and Barbara Hartman, Paul T. Mulik, Neal Brower, Greg Kelley, Lloyd Wells, Peggy Myres, Steve Weatherby, and Drew White.

This book also never would have come to be without the licensing provided by Mayberry Enterprises and Viacom, licenser for *The Andy Griffith Show*. We are especially grateful for the support of Ressa Kessler and Phyllis Ungerleider throughout the process of compiling the book.

We also thank Larry Stone at Rutledge Hill Press for his continuing belief in Mayberry and his faith in our exuberance for the show. We're also grateful for the talents and superb efforts made by editor Geoff Stone and designer Harriette Bateman. Others at Rutledge Hill assisting with this book have been Bryan Curtis, Tracey Menges, Anne Gillem, Nicki Pendleton, Denver Sherry, and Bob Pardue.

Ken wishes to express his thanks to wife Wendy, daughter Kylie, and son Cole for their patience and support. Jim thanks his wife, Mary, for her steadfast understanding and help with all aspects of the book.

And, as someone once said, "They call it *The Andy Griffith Show* for a reason." Without the "Man Himself," Mayberry would never have existed at all and there certainly would be nothing to write about forty years after nothing in particular had happened. As much as anything, this book is a loving tribute to Andy Griffith by all of the people listed above and by all of the people who speak, are written about, and are pictured in the book.

We thank each of you for your part in making this book possible and special.

INTRODUCTION

This book has been compiled on the occasion of the Fortieth Anniversary of the first broadcast of *The Andy Griffith Show*, the television series that many people regard as simply the best television show ever produced. We hope that the comments and images within this book will be more than just a nostalgic look at a great television series. Rather, we have tried to capture glimpses of the timeless storytelling and production of the show itself.

To accomplish that effect, we have done several things in our approach to this book. First, the photographs in the book are arranged largely in the order that the show itself was originally broadcast. Whenever possible and in order to provide the best possible sense of historical perspective, we have indicated the dates that many of the photographs were taken.

Second, whenever possible, we have used photographs depicting either recognizable scenes from within episodes or rare, behind-the-scenes moments from the production of those episodes. We have made an effort to keep familiar, posed publicity shots to a minimum, except in cases where they are especially striking or show characters or expressions that are not otherwise available.

Though the vast majority of the comments in the book were made expressly for this book by the actors, crew, and writers, we have worked to carefully place those comments throughout the book in a way that, combined with the photographs, will provide the reader with a sense of *almost* being there for special moments of the show's production.

Most of all, this book is a celebration of an extraordinary television series and the people who were a part of its production. *The Andy Griffith Show* has touched the hearts of countless millions of viewers for four decades. Our goal in writing this book is to give as much of a sense as possible of the passion and professional pride felt, then and to this day, by the people who worked on the show. That feeling is, of course, mirrored by those of us who have enjoyed Mayberry exclusively from the viewing side of our TV sets.

As much entertainment and pleasure as *The Andy Griffith Show* has given us, it is only right that this book should try to give a little back. As we have with previous books about *The Andy Griffith Show*, we have designated that a portion of the proceeds from the sale of this book be donated to Court Appointed Special Advocates (CASA), an organization that identifies children in the judicial system who need the involvement and support from specially trained and dedicated advocates for their best interests. *Andy Griffith Show* producer Aaron Ruben is deeply involved in this worthwhile program. He is affiliated with the Los Angeles chapter, which will benefit directly from proceeds from this book. (For more information about CASA or to become involved in your local chapter, contact National CASA at 1-800-628-3233.)

Enjoy wandering through these pages as we salute four decades of outstanding entertainment and a world of good that continues to come from this marvelous TV show and the little town called Mayberry.

—K.B. and J.C.

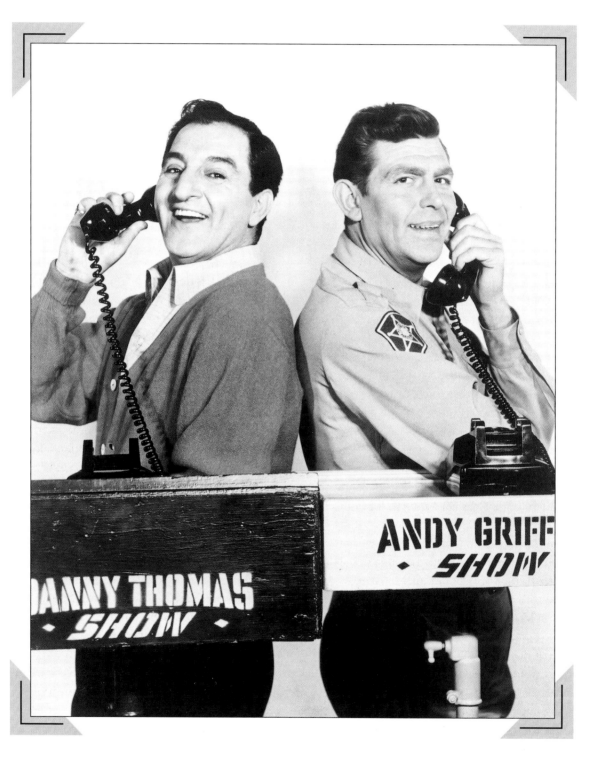

CALLS FOR LAUGHTER—*Danny and Andy anchored the CBS Monday prime-time lineup back to back for four seasons in the early 1960s.*

IN THE BEGINNING
The Pilot and Season One

The CBS Television Network officially gave birth to *The Andy Griffith Show* on October 3, 1960. But many viewers were given a sneak preview of Mayberry on February 15 of that year on *The Danny Thomas Show* in an episode titled "Danny Meets Andy Griffith." The episode was written by Arthur Stander and directed by *Danny Thomas Show* producer Sheldon Leonard.

Within a short time, Leonard, Danny Thomas, Andy Griffith, and Andy's personal manager Richard O. Linke were joined by producer/writer Aaron Ruben. Characters and story lines were developed. A strong cadre of writers, principally Stander, the team of Charles Stewart and Jack Elinson, and Frank Tarloff (writing under the name David Adler), began tapping their imaginations and their typewriters to cut an entertaining world out of the fabric of a small southern town.

On that first Monday in October 1960, American television viewers saw for the first time a boy and his father walking down a dirt road with fishing poles in hand and heard for the first time the finger-snapping, whistled theme that would become an anthem for simple living and great storytelling. *The Andy Griffith Show* quickly found a place in the hearts of millions of fans all across America.

The first line of the show is spoken by its star and the man who held everything together: "Anybody here know why these two should not be wed, speak now or forever hold your peace." Viewers may have been quiet for that one moment, but they were soon laughing and crying and thinking out loud about all of the activities in Mayberry ("Such goings-on, such goings-on!").

That first episode, "The New Housekeeper," introduces us to Sheriff Andy Taylor, his son Opie, his Aunt Bee, and his unforgettable deputy, Barney Fife. We also soon come to know Ellie Walker, Otis Campbell, Emma Brand, Mayor Pike, Floyd the Barber, Thelma Lou, and two citizens often mentioned but never seen, Sarah and Juanita. While some of the characters might be considered comic stereotypes of sorts, all have individual traits and reveal emotions that to this day give them a sincere believability not found in most situation comedies.

For the next eight years, millions of viewers paid a visit every Monday night to their favorite television town. In the following decades, courtesy of reruns and videotape, viewers have continued to visit again and again. Mayberry lives.

Several production milestones occurred in the first year of the show. First, Bob Sweeney took over directing chores after the first ten episodes and would continue in that role for three seasons and eighty episodes, about a third of the entire series. Second, the writing team of Jim Fritzell and Everett Greenbaum turned in their first script, "Quiet Sam," near the end of the season. While the two did not return to

Mayberry with a script until the third season, they would prove to be the show's most prolific pair of writers, along with the duo of Jack Elinson and Charles Stewart. (Elinson's solo efforts and other collaborations gave him the most episodes written by any one *Griffith* writer).

At the end of its premiere season, *The Andy Griffith Show* ranked as the fourth most popular show in America according to the Nielsen ratings. Capping off the season, Don Knotts won his first Emmy Award for an actor in a supporting role in a series. The following are some of the memorable images and recollections from Mayberry's first year that gave the show such a spectacular launch.

Sheldon Leonard's recollection of the beginning: "It all began back when I was doing *The Danny Thomas Show*. An agent at William Morris said they had just acquired a brand new client, Andy Griffith. They asked me to design something for him. The show was an excerpt from *The Danny Thomas Show*.

"Andy came to Hollywood and he sat down with us at a table. It was with me, Danny Thomas, and writer Artie Stander. They worked at a very high level of noise. At the end of the day, Andy said 'I'm gonna do your show for you, but I don't think I want to do a television show.'

"'Why not?'

"'I can't yell like you people do.'

"'Don't worry about that. When we make your show, we'll do it with quiet people and we'll go on with a peaceful atmosphere.' And they lived happily ever after. The success was due largely to Andy's personal charisma and appeal; and although not recognized by the cultural elite, rural subjects are very popular with the American people."

A FINE TIME—"*Woo-eee! That's quite a roll you got there.*" Big spender Danny is about to be spending more time in Mayberry than he had planned, but like most visitors, he'll be all the richer for having done so.

Sheldon Leonard

Andy Griffith remembers how he first met Sheldon Leonard and how Don Knotts happened to join the show: "In 1959 I was on Broadway in a half a hit, a musical called *Destry.* By half a hit I mean we were on 'twofers' (two tickets for the price of one and at Thanksgiving and Christmas they put a sign on the sidewalk saying 'Matinee Today'). At some point during the run of that show I went to see my agent Abe Lastfogel, then head of the William Morris Agency, and I told him I had struck out in movies and on Broadway, and I didn't want to go back to nightclubs. I asked him, 'What do you think of my trying television?' A few weeks later, I got word that Sheldon Leonard was coming to New York to see me.

Well, one Saturday night after the show we were all running to our dressing rooms, and I saw a man at the stage door I kind of recognized. When I got to my dressing room I went down the hall and asked Art Lund (also in the show) who that man was at the stage door. He said, 'Sheldon Leonard.' Well, it didn't take me a second to get back to that stage door!

Sheldon and I visited in my dressing room, then went to a restaurant there in New York for him to tell me his idea for a spin-off pilot on Danny's show. There was something about the idea I did not like, but I liked Sheldon. Some weeks after that I asked him to come to New York to see me again. He did. Something still bothered me about the idea, but I really liked

Sheldon, so I agreed to do it.

When the show aired, Don Knotts, a friend of mine from *No Time For Sergeants,* called me and said, 'Don't you need a deputy?' I said, 'Lord, call Sheldon Leonard!' He did and I did. Sheldon met with Don and hired him.

It soon became obvious to me the part of Sheldon's idea that I had not liked. My character, *Andy Taylor,* was not only sheriff, but editor of the paper and justice of the peace and 'funny man.' With Don, I became the straight man, and my only official job was sheriff of the town of Mayberry."

actors. We had the best ones in town. These ingredients and good comedy…we never deserted the integrity of the characters. Our primary backbone was the love that we had for one another as characters and as people, and that is, I think, why we were so successful. All of us knew what was funny. We had some shows that were a little sweeter and sadder than others, but some of those were really funny.

"Mayberry came from the very fertile imaginations of these people (Sheldon Leonard, Aaron Ruben, Don Knotts, Earle Hagen), and many others. We had the best comedy writers in town. We created in our imaginations this wonderful little town that people still want to go to—with all of the characters that lived there: Aunt Bee, Opie, Barney, Gomer, Goober, Howard, Floyd the Barber. Those eight years of my life are very precious to me."

WELCOME TO MAYBERRY—*Danny Williams (Danny Thomas) and wife Kathy (Marjorie Lord) and an entire nation are introduced to Mayberry and Sheriff Andy Taylor in the "Danny Meets Andy Griffith" episode of* The Danny Thomas Show. *Ronny Howard also appears as Opie. Frances Bavier portrays Henrietta Perkins, not Aunt Bee. Will Wright (later Ben Weaver in Mayberry) and Rance Howard (Ronny's father) also appear in this episode. The name of the hardware store seen here was Danny Thomas's name before he derived his stage name from the first names of his two brothers, younger brother Daniel and older brother Thomas.*

Andy Griffith reflects on Mayberry's beginnings: "One day Aaron Ruben came to see me at my house in Rye, New York. We sat in two lawn chairs and talked. Aaron became our producer. Aaron ran our show and was head writer. Aaron and Sheldon allowed me to learn to write…and Don Knotts was a key to our success and longevity.

"By the second episode we knew that Don should be funny and I should be the straight man. We added other comedy character

Ronald Jacobs, assistant to the producer (and nephew of Danny Thomas), offers his perspective: "When we did the pilot, as a spin-off on *The Danny Thomas Show*, everyone knew we had something special. Any series that starts with Andy Griffith has a big advantage. Then as all the other elements were put together, both in front of and behind the camera, it carried out its promise and went on to eight wonderful years on television. And then, please let's not forget *Mayberry R.F.D.*"

Early observations by director Jay Sandrich: "As assistant director on the pilot, how interesting it was to see Andy Griffith try to fit his style into *The Danny Thomas Show* style. Andy had come from Broadway and worked very quietly, but with such authority. I remember that you just knew this man was so talented and had so much authority, but nobody dreamed it would go on to become such a classic. My other memory is the casting of this little cute face, Ronny Howard. (Don Knotts was not on the pilot and Frances Bavier just played a townsperson.)

"Later, I was the associate producer and sort of involved in the post-production. At the time, I had two sons, who were older than Opie. I would see these shows and think, 'Darn, why didn't I think of that, why didn't I handle the situation that way?' I think it was a wonderful show that reached a broad category of human beings.

"Aaron Ruben was a brilliant writer. So it was a combination of wonderful acting and Andy's philosophy and Aaron's writing and Bob Sweeney's direction. A wonderful combination of people. Anybody who was in any way involved in the show was very proud to be a part of it.

"It was always fun to wander down to the stage. It was so creative in a nice way. Sometimes creative people can scream and yell and are under tremendous pressure. You never felt pressure on the stage. I think they all knew what they did and they all had fun and joy being with each other. And I think it came across on screen. I also remember that the theme song sort of set the style of the show with the whistling."

OUT WALKING FENCES—*With the help of his parents and the support of an ideal cast and crew, Ronny Howard, seen here in a publicity photo taken during "The Manhunt" episode, was able to maintain a well-balanced childhood in Mayberry.* COURTESY OF BART BOATWRIGHT COLLECTION.

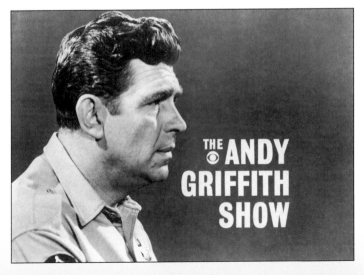

EAGLE-EYE ANDY—*If ever there was the right man to keep a watchful eye over things, Mayberry sure has him.*

SOUNDS WONDERFUL—*Sheet music for the theme for* The Andy Griffith Show *was published in 1962, by which time lyrics had been added by actor Everett Sloane, Mayberry's Jubal Foster in the second season's "Keeper of the Flame" episode. With the lyrics, the song is called "The Fishin' Hole."* COURTESY OF JOEL RASMUSSEN COLLECTION.

The show's ready to roll, but every show needs a theme song. Enter music director Earle Hagen: "Sitting at home and wracking my brains for an idea for a theme for the *Griffith* show, it finally occurred to me that it should be something simple—simple enough to whistle. With that in mind, it took me about an hour to write 'The Andy Griffith Theme.' I called my contractor, Manny Stein, who was also my bass player, and had him get Alvin Stoller, my drummer, and Vito Mumolo, my guitarist. I booked a studio for that night, scribbled out a piano part, and I went in to record the theme. I made the demo to main-title length and whistled it. I took a copy of it to Sheldon's house the next morning. He listened to it and said, 'Great. I'll shoot it this week at Franklin Canyon Lake (a lake above Beverly Hills, which became Myers Lake in the show) with Andy and Ronny walking along the bank with a couple of fishing poles over their shoulders.' He shot it later in the week using the demo for a playback and that was that. Who knew the theme I whistled for *The Andy Griffith Show* would become a piece of Americana? To this day, Andy can't go anywhere without someone starting to whistle the theme."

Producer Aaron Ruben comments about the contribution of Earle Hagen's music to the show: "Earle was talented, creative, and a real gentleman. His opening credits whistling theme was a real inspiration. One cannot think of the *Griffith* show without the theme and vice versa. Earle would check with me on where he planned to use background music and where not. And he was always right. Earle had impeccable taste. I guess one of the first things that impressed me was the fact that he had played trombone with Tommy Dorsey. Earle is one of the friendliest guys I ever knew."

Production manager Frank E. Myers on finding the perfect fishing spot: "Sheldon, Andy, Aaron, and I were sitting around trying to figure out what to do for the opening. They were afraid we'd have to go far away somewhere to get what we were looking for. I said, 'We can do it right here. I know a beautiful spot.'
"'It can't be,' they said. 'Take us up there.'
"Well, I did, and they were open-mouthed. But I knew of the spot, not far from downtown even, from some commercials I'd shot over the years and from *Lassie* episodes." And thus the fishing spot became known in Mayberry as Myers Lake.

SLICK AS A WHISTLER—*Longtime entertainment collaborators and fishing buddies Sheldon Leonard and Earle Hagen visit during Earle's 70th birthday party in 1989.* COURTESY OF EARLE HAGEN.

LEGENDARY WALK (below)—*Filming the opening title sequence on July 26,1960. This site at the Franklin Canyon Reservoir, now part of a park that is home to the William O. Douglas Outdoor Classroom, still looks remarkably similar to the scene in this forty-year-old photograph.*

"Well, now, take down your fishin' pole…

…and meet me at The Fishin' Hole."

Key *Griffith* writer Jack Elinson recalls the very early days of production: "Sheldon Leonard did a lot of organizing quickly. So we started writing scripts. When Aaron Ruben showed up, he didn't have to start from scratch. There were already some complete scripts written. Of course, Aaron did his thing on them. He's a great writer himself. He was the one that stayed with the *Griffith* show all those years. He would put his touch on the scripts. You just keep polishing and polishing."

Earle Hagen chimes in: "Sheldon Leonard built the show around Andy Griffith as the sheriff of Mayberry. I don't think in the history of TV there has ever been an ensemble cast as good as *The Andy Griffith Show*."

```
                    THE ANDY GRIFFITH SHOW

                         STAFF SHEET


EXEC. PRODUCER               SHELDON LEONARD
PRODUCER                     AARON RUBEN
ASSOC. PRODUCER              RICHARD LINKE
ASST. TO PRODUCER            RONALD JACOBS
DIRECTOR                     DON WEIS
SECRETARY                    SHIRLEY SOKOLIK
PRODUCTION MANAGER           FRANK MYERS


ASSISTANT DIRECTOR           BRUCE BILSON
2ND ASSISTANT DIRECTOR       JOHN GREENWALD
SCRIPT SUPERVISOR            HAZEL HALL
CAMERAMAN                    SID HICKOX
OPERATOR                     HARRY WEBB
1ST. ASST. CAM.              SHIRLEY WILLIAMS
2ND. ASST. CAM.              BOB KING
EDITOR                       JOE GLUCK
ASST. EDITOR                 JERRY JAMESON
MIXER                        DAVE FORREST
BOOM MAN                     JIM DUFFY, JR.


CABLEMAN                     JOE BRISSINGER
GAFFER                       FRANK JENKINS
BEST BOY                     HARRY ESTIN
PROPMASTER                   REGGIE SMITH
ASST. PROPMASTER             LEW WILDEY
KEY GRIP                     HARRY STONE
2ND GRIP                     JOHN NICHOLAS
DOLLY GRIP                   ROSS CANNON
MAKE UP                      LEE GREENWAY
HAIRDRESSER                  BETTY B. PEDRETTI
WARDROBE                     ANN HELFGOTT
WARDROBE                     HARALD JOHNSON
WELFARE WORKER               CATHERINE BARTON
STAND-IN                     TOM JACOBS
STAND-IN                     MARVEL LAWRENCE
STAND-IN                     GEORGIE SPOTTS
STANDBY DRIVER               BOB THETFORD
CASTING                      RUTH BURCH
ART DIRECTOR                 KEN REID
SET DECORATOR                BOB PRIESTLEY
LEAD MAN                     SAM HARRIS
CRAFT SERVICE                BOB TANNER


WILLIAM MORRIS AGENCY
BENTON & BOWLES
MUSIC - SPENCER-HAGEN
MSI

DESILU-CAHUENGA

DESILU-GOWER
DESILU-CULVER
TRANSPORTATION
FRANKLIN CANYON              Herb King
LUNCHES                      Rolly Harper
```

WORTHY OF SALUTE—*"Reliable Barney Fife" has knocked his own hat off with enthusiasm in this scene from "The New Housekeeper."*

ROLE CALL—*Production staff sheet from the first season.* COURTESY OF RONALD JACOBS.

FATHER AND SON CHAT—*Andy persuades Opie that running away from home because of Aunt Bee is maybe not the best idea.*

Production Manager Frank Myers recalled his first meeting with Ronny Howard: "Jean (Ron's mother) brought Ronny to my office so we could meet. Ron wasn't quite six years old. I asked him how tall he was and he didn't know. I stood him against the door frame of the office and made a mark. That mark was forty-six inches from the floor. He was absolutely the greatest kid in pictures, and I worked with a lot of them—Mickey Rooney, Judy Garland, Lana Turner, Margaret O'Brien, Liz Taylor. Ronny had great parents. Rance and Jean made sure everything was handled correctly."

Rance Howard shares his first impressions about allowing his son to work on the show: "Our impression was immediately that it was a wonderful family atmosphere and that we were greatly relieved…the calmness, the wonderful atmosphere with Andy and Don and Aaron Ruben and Sheldon Leonard, Frances Bavier. It was like a wonderful ensemble group and it felt like a family. We were, to begin with, skeptical, to a degree, about going into the business. But just right away we both saw that this was going to be really a healthy kind of experience for Ron. And it was. You just couldn't have found a better climate, better atmosphere, and better surroundings for a boy Ron's age. He did the pilot when he was five. By the time they started doing the series; he was six. Those are very formative years. I think they were very healthy in every respect for Ron."

NOT THE KIND OF BATTER SHE'S USED TO—*"Uh, Aunt Bee, I think you've got it wrong. I believe…I believe you hold it with the little end, see, and you hit it with the big end."*

Aaron Ruben talks about Sheldon Leonard: "Sheldon Leonard was my guide and mentor. All I ever needed to know about producing a TV sitcom I learned from Sheldon Leonard. I had written and directed but never produced, and Sheldon was the perfect teacher. His cool unflappability together with his extraordinary management style made him a perfect role model, not just for me but for a number of other writers whom Sheldon instructed in the art of TV producing. He was fair and reasonable, and in the ten years we worked together on *Griffith* and *Gomer*, there was never an argument having to do with a script.

"I remember one time he had suggested to our editor cutting a scene from one of the episodes and I didn't agree. I confronted him with my reasons for keeping it, and he simply said: 'Do you feel very strongly about it?' 'Yes, I do.' 'Then leave it in,' was his reply. Sheldon's organizational skills and his ability to plan ahead were what made the *Griffith* show the smooth operation it was. In the 150 shows that I produced, I don't recall a single time that we worked far into the night as did many of the shows of that time. I will always be grateful to Sheldon for his tutelage, and above all, for bringing me in to produce *The Andy Griffith Show*, my best five years in the business. He remained right up to the end my good friend."

Jack Elinson, who, with partner Charles Stewart, wrote nearly half of the episodes for the first two seasons, recalls the reception when *The Andy Griffith Show* first aired: "The biggest memory I have is the very beginning when we finally got on the air. We weren't treated too kindly by the critics out here, the hip Hollywood people. The cast and everybody was just a little glum. The critics compared it to some of the other shows that they shouldn't have compared it to, some of the country shows, but what cheered everybody up was after we read the bad reviews, we got the ratings. They were through the roof. That calmed everybody down and we went and did our work and the show stayed right up there all the time it was on.

"None of us had any idea, when we were doing it, what the show would become. For Chuck Stewart and me, it was a job and we'd do it and move on. But everybody says they're just amazed at the staying power of this show. It's forty years and it's still going. Everybody feels so good about it and now they consider it one of the best-written shows. The writing was great and the acting was great. It's a classic."

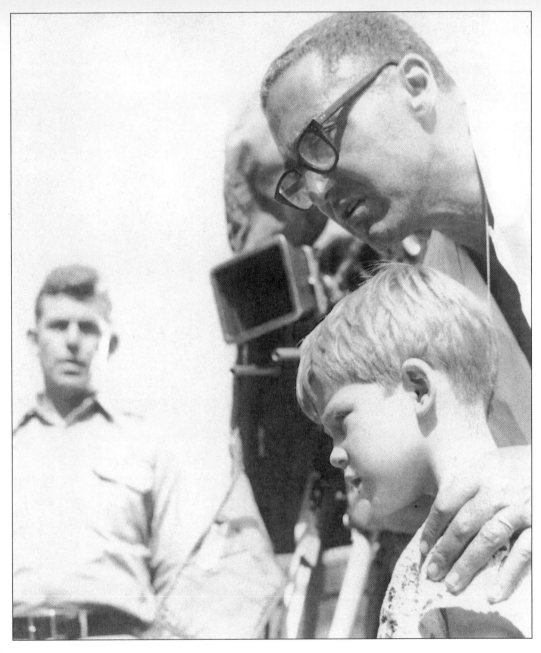

A DIRECT HIT—*Sheldon Leonard discusses the closing scene in "The New Housekeeper" with Ronny Howard. The first episode was one of two episodes that Sheldon Leonard directed during the eight seasons. (He also directed the series pilot.)* COURTESY OF GILMORE-SCHWENKE ARCHIVES.

"DON'T LEAVE ME, AUNT BEE!"—*Only one person can convince Aunt Bee to stay, and he's about to come running to the rescue in his pajamas.*

"One of my favorite episodes is when Aunt Bee first comes to take care of Opie. I love that. I cry every time I see that at the end."—Betty Lynn

"When Ronny was first starting out, it was hard to believe. He couldn't even read yet, just five years old. He was already acting so wonderfully. You could get any emotion you wanted, sad or happy or whatever. I can't say enough about him."—Don Knotts

ON TOP OF MAYBERRY—*A view of downtown Mayberry during the filming of "The Manhunt."*

Ron Howard gives credit: "My dad gave me a lot of confidence. He really made sure that I was prepared, but privately, without being a cheerleader. He just very honestly, matter-of-factly, would tell me that I was really a good actor and that I could really do this. And then he helped prepare me in such a way that I really was good. I'd get this positive feedback from grown-ups who were impressed, but so much of it had to do with the fact that my father had really thoroughly prepared me."

Writer Jack Elinson comments on the episode that won him and partner Charles Stewart a Writers Guild of America Award for best writing in a comedy or variety series: "'The Manhunt' is my favorite script because it sort of helped flesh out the character they had in mind for Barney Fife. We created a lot of the little things that would stay with him, like Andy would only give him the one bullet. Winning the award was a thrill. You're getting an award from fellow writers."

STUMPED—*Andy rescues Barney in "The Manhunt."*

Ronald Jacobs has fond memories of "The Manhunt," too: "I have way too many favorites to mention. But one of the earliest shows, 'The Manhunt,' gave us all the feeling that there was no way this series would not be a big hit. To this day the interaction between Andy and Don Knotts still makes us all laugh."

And from Richard Linke: "'The Manhunt' set the whole future role for Don Knotts. It's still my favorite. In my mind, that episode is very important."

Aaron Ruben talks about the immediate contributions of Don Knotts: "Usually when you start a new series, the writers, in defining the new characters, will introduce bits of business, gestures, mannerisms, etc. If the character does them well, he has established for himself a persona, and the writers can now feed on that. With Don it was the other way around. Don was the one who came in with the idea of a 'by-the-book' deputy who was a bit arrogant, self-assured, proud of his cap, his uniform, his gun, and his one bullet.

"And it was Don who came up with the 'memorization' bit, in which he has to memorize a passage from the Sheriff's manual or a historic document. And with Andy holding the document to test him, it turned out that he never knew a single word of the text. There is no doubt that the character of Barney Fife was Don's invention, just as surely as his famous 'nervous speaker' was his. You would think an actor who won five Emmys would get a bit difficult to deal with. Not Don. If anything, he was even more modest and humble. He was a delight to work with, and he was one of the main reasons the *Griffith* show was my happiest five years in the business."

CHECKERED PAST—*One of the signature pastimes in Mayberry is playing a good game of checkers. In this photograph, taken during the filming of "The Manhunt" on August 1, 1960, Judd Fletcher (Burt Mustin, left) and a fellow town loafer (Frank Chalee) receive pointers from Andy and Opie.* COURTESY OF GILMORE-SCHWENKE ARCHIVES.

ELLIE COMES TO TOWN—*Pharmacist Ellie Walker proves to be generous and caring almost from the moment she arrives in Mayberry, as Emma Brand and Barney witness for themselves here.*

Elinor Donahue was impressed on the set right away: "I remember how taken I was, immediately, with Ronny Howard. He was a real boy who just happened to be a good actor. And what made him so good was that 'real-ness.' Doing a scene with him was a transporting experience. No cameras, no lights it seemed (though in reality they were there); just the two of us talking. I adored him."

Elinor tells how designer "Mr. Burt of Encino" made it into some of the early *Griffith* credits: "I was having dinner one night at a restaurant in Encino with my mother and three-year-old son Brian when a man came up to introduce himself. Thinking he was a fan, I was polite but eager to return to the quiet time with my family.

"It turned out, though, that he was the manufacturer of a clothing line that I wore in real life, and he was offering to provide my wardrobe for the series. Taking his card, I put

the costumers in touch with him and that is how Mr. Burt came to have clothing credit on the show.

"I never did justice to his line, however, because I was in a weight-loss kick. I'd get thinner; he'd send a smaller size. If that fit, I'd decide I needed to be thinner, and so on. Smaller, thinner, smaller, thinner. By the end, I weighed ninety-eight pounds, but his clothes were gorgeous."

IN A CHORD—*Andy and Ellie stay in tune with Mayberry.* Courtesy of Gilmore-Schwenke Archives.

Music was always an important part of *The Andy Griffith Show*. Earle Hagen comments: "I always enjoyed the live musical moments on the show. Whenever Andy had to sing a number (usually in the tag of the show while sitting on the porch with Ronny Howard and Frances Bavier), I would cover the recording. Andy was always concerned that his pitch be right on, and it always was. I don't remember ever having to make a second take."

DEEP THINKING—*Andy Griffith and Danny Thomas visit on the sound stage (with the front porch area of the Taylor home in the background) during a break in production of "Runaway Kid" in August 1960.* COURTESY OF CBS PHOTO ARCHIVE.

QUICK-DRAW ARTIST—*Barney thinks he has done a pretty good rendering of the missing George "Tex" Foley in "Runaway Kid," but Andy knows Barney's drawing is sketchy at best.*

SET TO MUSIC—
Legendary makeup artist Lee Greenway and Andy, seen here during the production of "Irresistible Andy" on September 8, 1960, would play guitars or whatever musical instruments might be handy whenever an opportunity presented itself on the set. COURTESY OF CBS PHOTO ARCHIVE.

A comment from Mrs. Lee Greenway: "Lee and Andy were very, very good friends. Both were from North Carolina and they enjoyed the same things and had fun in that relationship. They used to go trapshooting and go riding motorcycles together. Andy did the eulogy for my husband. He titled it 'My Friend.'"

IT'S NOT FROM THE SNAPPY LUNCH, BUT IT'S NOT BAD—*Miss Rosemary (Amzie Strickland) has brought one of her homemade pies by for Andy in "Andy the Matchmaker," the only episode to mention the now world-famous Snappy Lunch. Amzie Strickland says about her Griffith work, "I have an all-over happiness about it. I remember Andy playing his guitar and my listening. I wish I could start over and do it again."*

TIME OUT—*Joining Don Knotts and Andy Griffith for a break during the filming of one of the first ten episodes are script supervisor Hazel Hall and director Don Weis.*

Right on target:

ANDY: Now, you know how folks in these parts feel about their feudin'. Now, what if it was to get out that we had a eighty-seven-year-old feud a-goin' on here with nary a killin' to show for it? Now we'd be the laughing stock of the state. Yeah, now I believe, I believe that we can get done in just a few minutes what you boys ain't been able to get done in eighty-seven years....Good luck now, fellas, and goodbye. I reckon you'll see one another in that great feudin' country beyond.

A FEUD IS A FEUD—*Andy presides over a duel between Mr. Carter (Chubby Johnson, left) and Mr. Wakefield (Arthur Hunnicut). Not only does Andy make sure that nobody gets hurt by unloading both shotguns before the men step off for their duel, but, apparently for extra safety, Andy also gives each man the other's shotgun, which neither nervous feuder seems to notice.* COURTESY OF GILMORE-SCHWENKE ARCHIVES.

A GRINCH PINCHIN' A BENCH—*Ben Weaver (Will Wright) is not (yet) in the holiday spirit when Mayberry's finest nab him for carting off public property.*

Rance Howard shares a special memory about Frances Bavier, including a Christmas visit:
"Frances was really a great lady. She was a consummate actress. Frances was very warm and comforting. She was like your favorite aunt, someone you idolized and respected and loved. But you didn't want to get caught with your hand in the cookie jar.

"I recall on Christmas Eve during the first year the show had been running, it was raining and Frances came to our door. She brought gifts for Ron and for Clint and, because Jean and I had spent quite a lot of time in New York, she thought some roasted chestnuts would be appropriate. So she brought us a bag of fresh roasted chestnuts and stayed and chatted for a little while and then was off to deliver Christmas cheer somewhere else."

IT'S BEGINNING TO LOOK A LOT LIKE CHRISTMAS—*First-season stars posed for this official holiday portrait on August 27, 1960.* COURTESY OF CBS PHOTO ARCHIVE.

BELLE OF MAYBERRY—*Bess Muggins (Margaret Kerry-Willcox) probably hadn't planned on spending Christmas at the Mayberry jail, but the cheer of the season will prevail. Margaret Kerry-Willcox also plays Helen Scobey in "Andy Forecloses."* COURTESY OF MARGARET KERRY-WILLCOX.

Margaret Kerry-Willcox (who was also the model for Disney's animated Tinkerbell) played Bess Muggins in the "Christmas Story" episode and Helen Scobey a few episodes later in "Andy Forecloses." She has happy memories about her Mayberry work: "There seemed to be two scenarios going on when I was on *The Andy Griffith Show*. One was, of course, the script itself, and the other was the cast and crew and how they worked together. What I mean is that everyone knew where they stood in the scheme of things, even when we were just setting up.

"Easygoing Andy was the anchorman, so to speak. Conversation, creative decisions, and most things whirled around him. Bob Sweeney, the brilliant comedian, now turned director, was working as the leader of a smoothly running team. He would briefly consult with Andy, they'd smile and agree, or talk it over, and then they'd smile and agree. Andy seemed to be always available and approachable during the filming.

"The regular cast members would sort of fan out away from the set when we weren't shooting. They'd stand or sit on the periphery chatting quietly and watching intently for their voice cue to step into the scene.

"The nonregulars (I was a part of that group) stayed behind the regulars in the cast and then we would take our place as we were called. Now, during most of this activity, Don Knotts was perched on this tall director's chair waiting (usually) silently.

"The minute Don was called on the set, his introspective manner changed. He became the jokester setting up camaraderie with his fun banter. Although Andy really enjoyed Don's lighthearted talk, looking back, it was as if on cue, Don was there to bring a Mayberry mood to everyone on the set and on the crew.

"It seems that we all knew our comfortable places. The regular cast members, the nonregular actors, the crew, and especially Don Knotts, who held down both his jobs as Barney Fife and as the performer who delighted Andy with his humor while priming the pump for that good ol' Mayberry feeling.

"It was a blessed time for me to see real professionals at work and having a 'purty' good time while doing it. And the fact that they all included me in the camaraderie as if I had been a regular for years, well, I shall never forget that."

SAMPLE SAM—*When the holiday spirit finally consumes Scroogey Ben Weaver, Sam Muggins (Sam Edwards) and his family end up with a nice Christmas after all. Sam Edwards returns as Lester Scobey when "Andy Forecloses" and as other townspeople through the seventh season.* COURTESY OF JIM SCHWENKE.

Margaret Kerry-Willcox shares this story about working with Sam Edwards, who appeared as various townspeople in a total of five episodes during the first seven seasons: "I have been working in show business since I was four years old, appearing in four of the *Our Gang* comedies. Growing up, I was on a three-year run as host on *Teleteen Reporter* on Channel 13 in Los Angeles and on the ABC-TV network as the teenage daughter on *The Charlie Ruggles Show* for five years. Then I went on to performing for Mark Davis and the Disney animators as the live model/dancer/actor for the Tinkerbell in Walt Disney's *Peter Pan*.

"Now, these were fascinating assignments. However, I bring them up to point out that never was I cast in the part as a spouse with a husband of my own. The first time on TV I was cast in that role was opposite that wonderful actor Sam Edwards in *The Andy Griffith Show*.

"I must say that to be convincing as a married couple, it is really better to have met your actor/spouse a minimum of two or three hours before you work in a scene. The tight schedule just didn't give us that luxury.

"Sam and I were introduced on the set. 'This is Sam Edwards, your husband.'...'This is Margaret Kerry, your spouse.' Within fifteen minutes we were playing our first scene as concerned 'husband and wife.'

"Sam, who had played a husband many times over, sensed that I was not quite as comfortable as I might be in my role. Sam, the consummate actor, 'fed' me the appropriate attitude as we rehearsed three times before the camera and crew. He then built upon my re-acting to him. He was wonderful.

"By the time we were called to do the scene where Sam is 'behind bars' and I rush in to see him, I was comfortable enough to simply open my arms and hug him. Well, after two days 'married' to Sam, I surmised that he was a huggable guy. And I was right. Sam reacted and we had a lovely moment for the show.

"The director came over and said, 'I like that hugging bit, Sam. Good idea.' Sam said softly, 'It wasn't my idea. It was my wife Margaret here who came up with the bit of business. She does good work.'

"Anyone who says that actors are not gracious people will get a strong argument from me. I'll tell them about working with Sam Edwards."

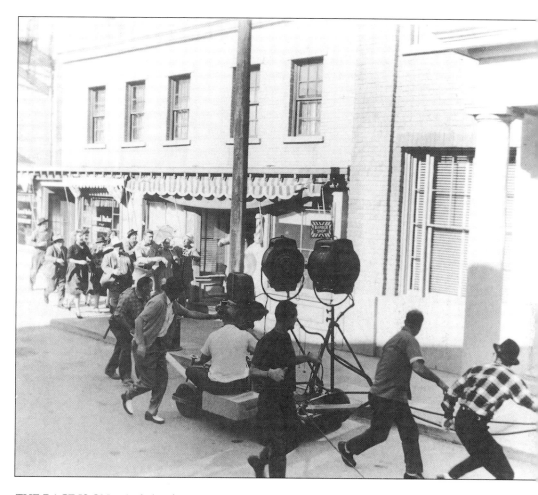

THE RACE IS ON—*Andy hot-foots it away from townspeople with suggestions for the Founders Day Beauty Contest as he keeps production crew members on their toes, too.* COURTESY OF GILMORE-SCHWENKE ARCHIVES.

Opie has his own ideas about who should win "The Beauty Contest":

OPIE: I know who ought to win if you want to choose the prettiest girl in town.
ANDY: Who?
OPIE: Mary Wiggins.
ANDY: Mary Wiggins?
OPIE: Yeah. She's got freckles and braids and a bandage on her knee and a tooth out and all the boys in the first grade are crazy about her.
ANDY: I can understand that. She sounds wild!

"I CROWN THEE MISS MAYBERRY JUNIOR"—*As Opie's first sweetheart, Mary Wiggins (Joy Ellison) is definitely "the cat's." Earlier, Joy Ellison appeared as Effie Muggins at Christmastime, and later as Mary Scobey, she and Andy "gum us another cookie" when Ben Weaver forces Andy to foreclose on those poor Scobeys. As a teenager, Joy appears as both Betsy and Iris, friends of Opie's.* COURTESY OF JOY ELLISON.

Though Joy Ellison was usually among the youngest actors on the Mayberry set, she has fond memories of her days working on *The Andy Griffith Show*: "It was great. It was a really warm, happy kind of set. It was great for kids because it was such a family kind of feeling. There was such a great chemistry with everyone that any newcomer was openly embraced. Yet, even though Ron Howard and I were usually classmates or boyfriend-girlfriend, he and I were sort of at that age where boys and girls kind of hated each other, so we didn't really get to hang out or get to be pals. It was always just a warm atmosphere and they were great to kids. It was really a high point whenever I got called."

ALCOHOL AND OLD LACE—
Andy is about to bust up a still full of "special occasion" elixir made by Morrison sisters Clarabelle (Gladys Hurlbut) and Jennifer (Charity Grace). Filmed in December 1960, this episode premiered during the week of the 1961 TV Guide on the following page.

MAYBERRY COVERAGE—*The 1961* TV Guide *features a photograph that director Bob Sweeney also had hanging in his office for many years.* TV Guide FURNISHED BY JOEL RASMUSSEN COLLECTION. REPRINTED WITH PERMISSION FROM TV GUIDE MAGAZINE GROUP, INC., PUBLISHER OF TV GUIDE MAGAZINE; COPYRIGHT © VOLUME 9, ISSUE 4, 1961, TV GUIDE INC. TV GUIDE IS A TRADEMARK OF TV GUIDE MAGAZINE GROUP, INC. LARGER PHOTO COURTESY OF BOB SWEENEY COLLECTION OF TAGSRWC ARCHIVES.

MAYBERRY ON RECORD—*Performing on the barbershop set with Andy Griffith are the Country Boys (a.k.a. The Kentucky Colonels). From left to right, the Country Boys are Roland White on mandolin, Eric White on bass, Clarence White on acoustic guitar, Billy Ray Latham on banjo, and LeRoy Mack McNees on resonator guitar.* COURTESY OF LEROY MACK MCNEES.

Country Boys member LeRoy Mack McNees (now performing with the California-based Born Again Bluegrass Band) tells how he and the band made it to Mayberry: "The telephone rang and I picked it up to hear someone say, 'This is *The Andy Griffith Show* calling and we would like to book your band to be on the show.' I almost could not believe my ears. This was 1961, and *The Andy Griffith Show* was one of the top shows and my personal favorite. After the shock wore off, I must have stammered for a moment, and then I said, 'Why, yes, I think we can fit you into our schedule.'

"Actually, our schedule was quite open, as we were a struggling bluegrass band in the Los Angeles area—doing mostly local gigs. We had, however, just released a single record, 'Head Over Heels in Love with You,' which was being played on the local country station. It seems Andy heard it and told his producer to contact us and have us on the show.

"The big day came for us to go to the studio. What a thrill it was to see and meet the cast of the show, Aunt Bee, Barney, Floyd, and all the folks who made up Mayberry. I remember looking at the sets and thinking, 'So this is really what it looks like.' I felt a little like the hick from the sticks myself. I could have said, 'Well, gollllleee!'

"We had two scenes in the show. One was recording our songs in Floyd's Barbershop and then listening to the recordings with Andy, Hugh Marlowe (who played Mr. Maxwell, the record producer), and others. The other was when we were recording in the hotel, where we were. I had a one-line speaking part; I'll never forget it: 'We appreciate you letting us buy stock in your record company, too.' Andy had to coach me on the way I said 'appreciate.' He said to say ''preciate,' not to sound the 'a.' So this California-born Country Boy used his best North Carolina accent and delivered his big one line.

"Andy really liked the band and asked us to record some songs with him for his next album (*Songs, Themes and Laughs From The Andy Griffith Show*). Well, gollllleee yes! We sure would. It was the first time for us to record at such a prestigious studio as Capitol Records. The studio had a huge control room with the latest, state-of-the-art equipment.

"The studio itself was large enough to record a full orchestra, and in the center was an isolation booth where Andy would sing his part. Before we started, I remember Andy stepping out of the booth and saying, 'Boys, if we don't get 'er right the first time, we'll just do 'er again.' Andy must have known we were a little tight, and this really helped us to get relaxed.

"After the show aired, I remember people asking me all the time, 'Is Andy as nice a guy in person as he is on TV?' My answer was always, 'Yes, a genuine, nice guy.'

"Well, it has been nearly forty years since we were on the show, and my brown hair is now gray—and there is a lot less of it. But I do weigh about thirty pounds less, so that's a blessing. Being on *The Andy Griffith Show* was a real highlight in my life—providing some wonderful, lasting memories. It's like a happy, recurring dream every time the episode is rerun. Congratulations on forty years of smiles."

"We'd go into Desilu Productions and once you get inside the main gate, it's like a city. We were all totally 'Oh, wow' with everything. They were very respectful. Andy really liked the music. His style of music is guitar strumming and singing. There weren't any problems playing along the way he wanted us to do. They were very respectful and they treated us really nice.

"I'm just a fan. That little bit of work we did happened so fast. As a fan, I think the show is truly educational and very good for young children to watch. It's a family show, a show for adults and children, all ages. I've loved all the characters on there. I still sit down and watch it whenever I can."

THEY MUST HAVE TAKEN A WRONG TURN AT ALBUQUERQUE—*Members of the Country Boys pose with Frances Bavier on location at the "Forty Acres" lot in Culver City during a break in filming "Quiet Sam." Country Boys (left to right) are LeRoy Mack McNees, Eric White, Billy Ray Latham, and Clarence White. Country Boy Roland White is not pictured here and did not appear in this episode because he was going through admissions examinations for the Air Force during filming.* COURTESY OF LEROY MACK MCNEES.

ANDY SAVES BARNEY'S MORALE—
While Andy's away on business, Barney has arrested the whole town including Mayor Pike. Wearing the white hat with the dark band in the middle of the crowd is frequent extra Tom Jacobs, older brother of Danny Thomas. This photo was taken on November 15, 1960. COURTESY OF CBS PHOTO ARCHIVE.

"VAGRANCY AND LOITERING? THE MAYOR?!"—*Mayor Pike listens intently as Andy holds a hearing for the townspeople Barney has arrested while Andy was away. The tall man in the background is, once again, Tom Jacobs.*

BUT WHERE'S BARNEY WHEN THERE'S REAL LOITERING GOING ON?—*Relaxing on the streets of Mayberry are* Griffith *regulars Tom Jacobs (stand-in and often-seen townsperson), Assistant to the Producer Ronald Jacobs (nephew of Tom Jacobs and Danny Thomas), and wardrobe man Harald Johnson.* COURTESY OF RONALD JACOBS.

JUANITA WHO?—*Already a big fan of the* Griffith *show, Betty Lynn was herself welcomed to Mayberry as Thelma Lou in the episode "Cyrano Andy." About working with Don Knotts, she says, "How glorious it was to work with him. He's so special and unique. I don't think there's anyone else like him. I felt very privileged to have the opportunity to work with Don. Besides, he's a wonderful person."*

"LAND SAKES ALIVE!"—Andy and Opie
prepare to assault the mountain of dishes
they've made for themselves while Aunt Bee is
away in "Andy and Opie, Housekeepers."
COURTESY OF GILMORE-SCHWENKE ARCHIVES.

A breathtaking situation with "New Doctor"
Robert Benson (George Nader):

DR. BENSON: Take a deep breath, please. Uh,
go ahead and take a deep
breath.
BARNEY: I did.

A PLAQUE FOR MAYBERRY—*It's a proud day for Otis (Hal Smith) and Rita Campbell (Dorothy Neumann) when Otis is honored for being a descendant of Mayberry's Revolutionary War hero Nathan Tibbs. Hal Smith later recalled the scene earlier in the episode, in which Barney was giving Otis a sobriety test (which Andy called "The Barney Fife Peter Piper Nose-Pinching Test for Drunks") and Otis pinched Barney's nose: "That was an accident when we got that nose. I put my fingers together and my eyes were closed, and I got his nose. They said, 'Leave it in, leave it in!'"*

When Barney organizes local menfolk to save Andy in "Quiet Sam," Floyd and the boys eventually arrive ready, willing, and, well, they arrive:

> ANDY: Floyd, what are you all a-doin' up here with guns?
> BARNEY: Uhh. Oh, they're just some boys from an old posse I was organizing there for a minute.
> ANDY: A posse?
> FLOYD: I'm sorry if we're late, Barney. Nate lost the keys to his car. My missus wouldn't let me take her stick and then on top of that …
> BARNEY: Uh, drop it, would you, Floyd?

TO THE RESCUE— *Has anybody checked to see if Floyd is kin to Ernest T. Bass?* COURTESY OF BART BOATWRIGHT COLLECTION.

Kit McNear shares thoughts about his father and his work as Floyd the Barber: "My dad worked with a lot of people in the business and I can remember him saying this show was almost like working with family. It was very relaxed, not pressured, fun, and just a really sincere, great bunch of people. It was really a favorable place for an actor to work.

"The working style of the *Griffith* set, before my dad was ill, was really favorable and positive, something he looked forward to going to. I never, ever remember him saying there were problems with people on the set. There never seemed to be tremendous egos and personality clashes.

"Typically my dad was, in a lot of his characters, very much a fidgety guy who a lot of times acted before he thought about it. He was very intelligent. He wasn't a whole lot different than some of his characters off-camera."

Kit adds: "I have always been an avid sportsman and I'm in the fishing business. I shoot competitively sporting clay targets. When I was a teen-ager and was involved with the NRA, I shot competitively (.22s, targets, etc.) with a high school club. My dad used to take me and a couple of my friends out to the desert and we'd shoot rabbits and things. He would take carrots and vegetables to put out to feed them. I'd shoot at 'em and he'd put stuff out for 'em.

"Another example of what a caring, sincere person he was has to do with the fact that he didn't like boats in the ocean because he got seasick. But he was willing, before I started driving, to take me on to boats and barges. He'd take his scripts and he'd be sick with motion sickness, a horrible thing. He would do that for me because he knew there was an ingrained thing with me and boats and fishing and the ocean."

James Best describes how he got the part of Jim Lindsey:
"The agent called and said, 'Would you like to do *The Andy Griffith Show*?' And I said sure. The casting woman, Ruth Burch, said, 'Jimmie, do you play the guitar?' And I don't lie. I said, 'I have *two* guitars.' So I got on the set and they said, 'There is the music.' I said, 'The music for what?' And they said, '"Rock 'n' Roll Rosie From Raleigh."' I said, 'Wait a minute. I can't read music. I play by ear'. They said, 'You said you could play the guitar.' I said, 'I said I *had* two guitars.'"

POLICE LINES UP—*Bob McQuain and Andy Griffith study the script during the filming of "Barney Gets His Man," on March 14, 1961. Bob played Sgt. Johnson.* COURTESY OF MAYDALE MCQUAIN.

MAKING NOTES—*Director Bob Sweeney goes over points in the script with guest star James Best and Andy Griffith during filming of "The Guitar Player Returns."* COURTESY OF GILMORE-SCHWENKE ARCHIVES.

"LET THAT MIDNIGHT SPECIAL SHINE ITS EVER-LOVIN' LIGHT ON YOU"—*Jim Lindsey, wearing his "set of threads," plays the blues for Andy, Barney, Aunt Bee, and Ellie after having his little red sports car repossessed in "The Guitar Player Returns."* COURTESY OF GILMORE-SCHWENKE ARCHIVES.

More good Mayberry memories from James Best: "It was like old home week. Andy fit like an old shoe and Don was a sweetheart. The whole cast was great. Opie was a little boy at that time and I loved children. Lee Greenway, the makeup man, played the banjo and Andy played the guitar and I'd get Don and we'd get back there. The director would have a hard time getting us back on the set because we'd be back there singing spirituals, just having a good time.

"I think all the shows were entertaining. I see a lot of reruns right now. I've never been disappointed with an *Andy Griffith Show*. They had a flawless combination of writers and talents on that show that absolutely was priceless. That's why it's legendary. They had a winning combination. I don't think they've ever been beaten as far as portraying a good home and family tradition."

HAPPY MOMENT—*Frances Bavier and Elinor Donahue, on the last day of shooting Elinor's final episode (March 22, 1961), share a jolly scene during the filming of "The Guitar Player Returns."* COURTESY OF GILMORE-SCHWENKE ARCHIVES.

Elinor Donahue reminisces: "I remember how much I liked Frances Bavier, who, from what I'd heard was a 'pistol.' But she was so kind to me during my all-too-frequent bouts of insecurity. We'd sit in our canvas chairs near the set waiting to be called and she'd just chat about 'stuff,' relaxing me. She was very supportive."

The last word about the first season goes to one of its leading writers, Jack Elinson, who also wrote the last words of the season's final episode: "I've written an awful lot of shows and when people find out that I'm a writer and what shows I've worked on and mention *Griffith*, they say, 'That's my favorite.' It's got such staying power, it could go on and on. It just

blows everybody away now. It's a one-in-a-million shot that a show would last this long.

"It was a pleasure to write for Barney Fife. Andy became the Solomon of the town, the wise one, and everybody else in town became the characters, the funny ones, like Floyd the Barber. Outside writers who wrote scripts for us would come in for stories. Let's say they had five stories. Each of them was a Barney Fife story. We'd have to explain to them, 'Well, we have four Barneys coming up. And we could really use something on Aunt Bee.'

"I think the show could live forty more years. This show is so clean and so sweet and funny that people love it. Rather than watch a new show, they'd rather turn on an *Andy Griffith Show* rerun. It's sure made its mark."

TAYLOR MADE FOR MAYBERRY—Photo by Gabor Rona. Courtesy of Bob Sweeney Collection of TAGSRWC Archives.

HITTING FULL STRIDE
Season Two

1961-1962

During the second season of *The Andy Griffith Show,* most of the characters found their comfortable niches, with the notable exception of pharmacist Ellie Walker (Elinor Donahue), who had quietly left town.

Several new characters begin strolling the sidewalks and country roads of Mayberry. Farmer Rafe Hollister shines in Mayberry for the first time (though actor Jack Prince had appeared earlier as other characters), and Clint Howard pops up as a little cowboy who never speaks (though he doesn't acquire his trademark sandwich and a definite name until the third season). County nurses named Mary (played by Julie Adams and Sue Ane Langdon) add a spark to Andy's romantic life, and actor Allan Melvin makes the first two of his eight memorable guest appearances (as eight different characters, usually heavies).

There are other important firsts in the second season. Writer Harvey Bullock notched his first credit on *The Andy Griffith Show* with the script "Opie's Hobo Friend." He would go on to write a total of twenty-six solo episodes of the series and he teamed with longtime partner Ray Allen (a.k.a. Ray Allen

Saffian and R. Saffian Allen) for five more episodes. This season also brings the first "Nip it in the bud!" from the lips of Barney Fife, the classic "Pickle Story" about Aunt Bee's kerosene cucumbers, and Andy and Barney's first foray into the big city of Raleigh as they check in with the Esquire Club and nab a jewel thief in a hotel.

One of the most dramatic moments in the show's history comes in the episode "Andy on Trial," as Barney gives riveting testimony about how Andy doesn't go so much by the book as by the heart. Don Knotts also won his second Emmy Award for his work this season.

Behind the camera, Bob Sweeney directed every episode of the second season, and the show finished the year seventh in Nielsen's prime-time ratings.

Betty Lynn talks about beloved director Bob Sweeney: "One thing I remember is that he could play all the parts—Andy, Barney, Aunt Bee, Opie—just for a minute and give you exactly what he was looking for in a particular scene. He related to all of us so well and had a wonderful temperament and so much energy. You're so grateful to have the chance to work with someone like that. He always made the time and helped so many people—on and off the set."

FUN ON THE SET—*Don Knotts and Andy Griffith have a good time going over a script with director Bob Sweeney.* COURTESY OF BOB SWEENEY COLLECTION OF TAGSRWC ARCHIVES.

Ron Howard talks about Bob Sweeney: "Bob was the first director I was really aware of. Then when I found out he had been an actor also, that was the first signal to me that there was this job called 'director' that was different than acting and it was really fun. And between watching my dad direct plays and working with Bob Sweeney for those first three seasons, I think I developed the real sense that actors would make good directors. Later working with Lee Philips and Richard Crenna and later on *Happy Days* with Jerry Paris, this idea kept getting reinforced–that actors could make good directors. It was inspiring for me."

Adds Aaron Ruben: "The fact that Bob was half of the successful comedy team *Sweeney & March* was a big plus for the show. Nobody had to point out where the comedy was. Bob knew. His instincts were exactly right, and he really dug the off-center characters of Mayberry. And he had what is a must for any good director. He had excellent rapport with the actors, whether it was Andy or Don or a bit player. And he was fun to work with."

WANDER BY THE FISHIN' HOLE— *Andy and Opie return from Andy's secret fishing spot in "Opie and the Bully," which was originally broadcast on October 2, 1961, as the first episode of the second season.* COURTESY OF BART BOATWRIGHT COLLECTION.

TAKING A BREAK—*Betty Lynn and Andy Griffith visit between scenes.* COURTESY GILMORE-SCHWENKE ARCHIVES.

ENFORCING THE LAW—*Barney writes former deputy Bob Rogers (Mark Miller) a ticket for illegal parking in front of the Courthouse in "Barney's Replacement." This photograph was taken during filming on July 18, 1961.*

ANDY AND THE WOMAN SPEEDER—
Elizabeth Crowley (Jean Hagen) is held at the Mayberry jail after she is in just a little bit too much of a hurry to make it back to her magazine in Washington, D.C. But like most people who mistakenly try to speed through Mayberry, she learns the benefits of slowing down to a Mayberry pace.

PORTRAIT IN CONTRASTS—
A relaxed Andy appears to be enjoying getting Barney a little riled by being, as Barney would say, "purposely obtuse."

Ronnie Schell, later to appear in two episodes of the show (as well as to portray Duke Slater on *Gomer Pyle, U.S.M.C.*) remembers his first visit to the set: "It was Dick Linke who introduced me to Andy and Don Knotts on the set of *The Andy Griffith Show* in 1962. I was so thrilled. My folks were there and they met them. It was a thrill seeing them in color for the first time."

ESQUIRE COPS—
A rare shot of Andy wearing not only a gun, but a necktie.

THE PERFECT FEMALE—*Andy's fishing rod may be called Eagle-Eye Annie, but when Thelma Lou's cousin, Karen Moore (Gail Davis), proves to be as good a skeet shooter as, well, Annie Oakley herself, Andy finds that he has just finished in second place in the battle of the sexes. But as Andy observes, "Maybe second ain't so bad."* COURTESY OF GILMORE-SCHWENKE ARCHIVES.

PROUD PUBLIC SERVANT—*There's nothing to worry about as long as this confident lawman is on duty.*

Harvey Bullock comments on his experience writing for the show:

"It was joyous to write for Barney Fife. Don Knotts made every writer look great. Sure, we worked long hours getting stories down on paper. Don's genius was in being able to lift the words and scenes off the paper and imbue them with his own very special blend of Fife's follies, foibles, and fantasies.

"I have written for over thirty TV comedy shows. Usually I include guidelines with the dialogue to be sure the performer gets the spin of the scene.

"Example: BARNEY
          (THE RAFFISH ROGUE)
          'Thought we might check
          out the duck pond.'

"Actors dislike this device intensively. They insist they are professionals and can best determine the sense of a scene without spoon-feeding. But I continued inserting them to make sure. Except in a Barney Fife script. We soon learned we were dealing with a truly gifted comic with his own special timing and mugging that always worked. We didn't have to remind him he was the raffish rogue. He would lean back at his desk with his phone to chat with Juanita and knew instinctively every nuance of any scene."

GREEN WITH ENVY?—*It's doubtful that Clara would ever need to be jealous of Aunt Bee's homemade pickles, even though Bee's "kerosene cucumbers" will likely make anyone who eats one turn green.*

Don Knotts usually says that his two favorite episodes are "The Pickle Story" and "Barney and the Choir" (both from the second season). He comments: "They just stood out in my mind. There's another one I should mention: "Barney's First Car." There were so many—it's really hard to pick out a favorite, but those have stood out in my mind."

What is "Pickle Story" writer Harvey Bullock's favorite episode that he wrote?: "'Opie's Hobo Friend.' I suppose this is special to me since it was the very first *Griffith* show I wrote, and its acceptance or nonacceptance would determine whether I would get further assignments. My other favorites: 'The Pickle Story,' 'The Bed Jacket,' 'The Loaded Goat,' 'Mr. McBeevee,' and 'Opie the Birdman.'"

Rance Howard shares his impressions of Andy Griffith:

"Andy is a real gentleman. He's a hard worker and an ambitious actor. Here's a man that the industry as a whole has underestimated. Even though he has done very well on television and has had some very respectable films, the industry has overlooked Andy because here is a man who, if the Hollywood film industry had taken him a little more seriously, would have been a huge film star, probably even much beyond the television star that he is. Of course, he's done very well as is.

"Andy stands for what is right, just as he plays Sheriff Taylor. He is so much like that in everyday life. You don't really want to mess with Sheriff Taylor. Guys like Sheldon Leonard and Danny Thomas found that out when they tried to impose certain things on the show that they thought might draw a bigger audience. Andy could dig in his heels pretty well. Andy is a very instinctive actor and instinctive person. He listens to his instincts and abides by them."

Ronald Jacobs, assistant to the producer, offers his perspective:

"*The Andy Griffith Show* can't be forty years old. I mean, I can still see it at least once a week, every week, on my television set. It's still as entertaining, still as well done, still has those wonderful performances we all enjoyed when we were doing the show. It was a wonderful run with a good crew, fine writers and directors, an excellent cast (what a fine guy that Ron Howard was and is). Stages 1 and 2 at Desilu Cahuenga and Franklin Canyon Reservoir, where *The Andy Griffith Show* was filmed, and the back lot at Forty Acres in Culver City, were the scenes of many, many, many happy memories, and the scenes of many great shows."

A SOLO MAN—*The sage of Mayberry.*

A VIEW OF MAYBERRY FROM THE HEAVENS—*This early 1960s aerial photograph of the legendary Forty Acres lot in Culver City provides an interesting overview of the set used for downtown Mayberry. Look for the buildings used for the Courthouse, Floyd's Barbershop, the grocery store, hotel, movie theater, drugstore, and bank, as well as the church and the Taylors' neighborhood. All of the buildings seen here are no longer standing.* COURTESY OF JOEL RASMUSSEN COLLECTION.

GREAT CONCENTRATION—
*Andy Griffith and Don Knotts are in
deep thought while going over a
script.*

COLORFUL CHARACTERS—
*This coloring book was one of the
few* Andy Griffith Show *products
licensed during the show's original
prime-time run. Though the show
itself was still in black and white,
kids could use their imaginations
to give Mayberry all kinds of
dazzling colors—back in the days
before you might have to explain
to some kids that just because
somebody's name is Barney
doesn't mean he should be
colored purple with a green
belly.* COURTESY OF JOEL
RASMUSSEN COLLECTION.

"JUBAL, JUBAL, JUBAL, JUU-BAL"—When Barney accidentally discovers moonshine kept by Jubal Foster (Everett Sloane), Andy knows that it was Jubal and not Opie who burned down Jubal's barn in "Keeper of the Flame." The multitalented Sloane also penned the lyrics to "The Andy Griffith Theme" when he found out that the popular tune didn't have words.

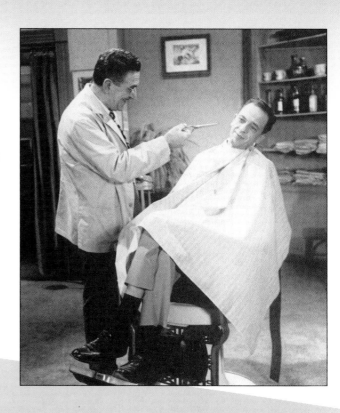

BARNEY: *Floyd, are you giving me a haircut or trying to make the mark of Zorro?!* COURTESY OF GILMORE-SCHWENKE ARCHIVES.

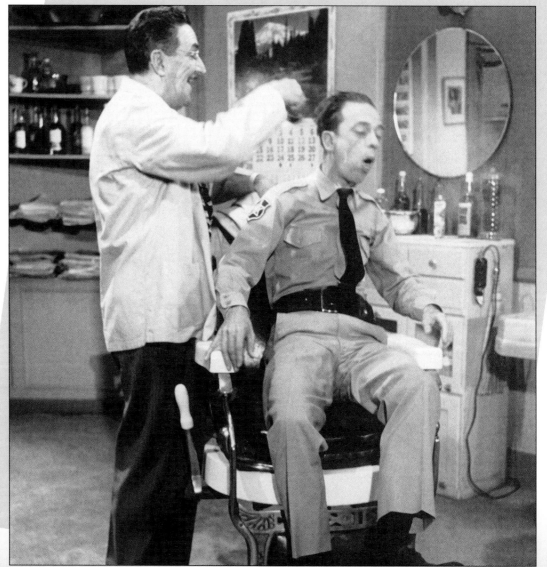

BARNEY: *Floyd, do you have to dust me like that? I'm not a diseased crop!* COURTESY OF GILMORE-SCHWENKE ARCHIVES.

WINDOW TO THE WORLD—*The local menfolk can't believe their eyes and apparent good fortune when manicurist Ellen Brown (Barbara Eden) gets off the bus in Mayberry.* COURTESY OF GILMORE-SCHWENKE ARCHIVES.

The bus bringeth:

> BARNEY: Hey, will you look what's getting off that bus!

The men in the barbershop all stare.

> BARNEY: Ring-a-ding-ding.
> MAYOR: That is what I call a female.
> OTHER MAN: Me too.
> FLOYD: Yeah, that's a female all right, right Andy?
> ANDY: Yep, that's definitely not a boy.

"OH, STOP YOUR BLABBERIN'!"—*Not everyone in Mayberry is pleased about Ellen Brown's arrival, especially aspiring manicurist Emma Watson (center).*COURTESY OF GILMORE-SCHWENKE ARCHIVES.

ALL'S WELL THAT ENDS WELL—*It is at about this moment, as Ellen Brown thanks Barney for welcoming her to Mayberry, that Barney would most certainly agree with Andy's pronouncement, "Ain't we lucky to be living in such a friendly town!"* COURTESY OF GILMORE-SCHWENKE ARCHIVES.

Kit McNear reminisces about his father: "In 1961 or 1962, he had bought a small boat, about a sixteen-footer with an outboard, basically for me. He didn't like boats. Somewhere on the boat it needed to be spray painted. He had a pretty good temper at times. He had his glasses on and we're standing on the back porch, and the gizmo on the top of the can wouldn't work, so the spray paint wouldn't squirt out. So he says, 'We'll fix this.' He got a can opener and proceeded to open the spray can. It squirted all over him. It covered his face. My mother about had a heart attack. But that was typical Howard McNear stuff. His face was completely black except for where his glasses were."

Don Knotts laughs just talking about Howard McNear: "Howard was one of those guys who would make you laugh. When you're working with him, you have a hard time keeping from laughing. He came up with these sudden, unusual body movements or takes or readings that would just put you away. He was very funny. In my book, I listed him right up there with Tim Conway as one of the funniest people I've ever worked with."

A SPECIAL PERSON—*The universally beloved Howard McNear, Mayberry's extraordinary barber.* COURTESY OF STEVE COX COLLECTION.

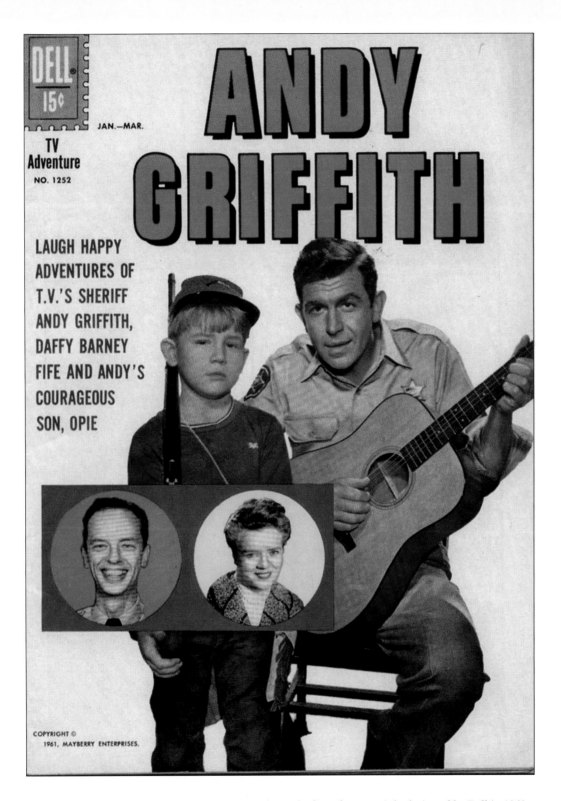

"YOU BELONG IN THE FUNNY PAGES"—*This is the first of two comic books issued by Dell in 1962.*
COURTESY OF JOEL RASMUSSEN COLLECTION.

SO, JUST HOW MANY FOLKS DOES IT TAKE TO CATCH A FISH?—*This scene from "The Jinx" was filmed at a pond on the Forty Acres lot in Culver City. Besides "Jinx" John Qualen, Andy Griffith, and Don Knotts (back to camera) in the front rowboat, some of the other people in the photograph are assistant director Bruce Bilson in the other boat; "stand-ins" for John Qualen and Don Knotts (both wearing hats*

and standing in the middle of the picture); script supervisor Hazel Hall (standing next to the front of the truck and holding an open script book); director Bob Sweeney (seated with his left arm resting on an open script book); and cameraman Sid Hickox (wearing a cardigan and cap and standing with arms crossed at far right). There likely are fifty more crew members off camera. Courtesy of Bob Sweeney Collection of TAGSRWC Archives.

DEDICATED CHOIR MEMBER—*Singer Renée Aubry was a regular in the Mayberry choir.* COURTESY OF RENÉE AUBRY.

Renée Aubry provides a library of information about her fellow Mayberry choir members in "Barney and the Choir": "I did work onstage with most of the singers in the Mayberry Choir. All of the singers were principal performers and well known locally.

"Delos Jewkes (the bass singer Glen Cripe, who sings for Barney) and I appeared in *The Student Prince* for San Bernadino Civic Light Opera. Also, we worked on the movie version of *Music Man* with Ronny Howard. Delos died in 1984.

"Enrico (Ric) Ricardi owned The Horn, the club in Santa Monica frequented by Andy Griffith, Don Knotts, and Dick Linke, and where they discovered Jim Nabors. If I remember correctly, Ric did not appear on camera, but got credit.

"Barry O'Hara was an Irish tenor discovered by George Jessel. Barry and I were featured in *Twist Around the Clock*, a Columbia picture. Bill Parsons, another operatic tenor, and I toured the United States and Canada with Yvonne De Carlo as part of her nightclub act.

"Marjorie McKay, a wonderful mezzo soprano, was married to Harper McKay, who played piano at The Horn. Jean Determine was married to Tommy, the bartender at The Horn. Tom Peters was a song-and-dance man. We worked together in the Los Angeles and San Francisco Civic Light Opera productions of *Carousel*.

"The Horn in Santa Monica was known for having the best singers and entertainers in town. Many celebrities and Hollywood notables visited the club and many of them would get up and entertain. Because of my age at the time of Mayberry, I was not allowed to sing at The Horn. However, Ric and Margaret Ricardi knew my agent and my parents. Therefore, I was given the opportunity to work with their wonderful coaches and pianists, Carlos Noble, Harper McKay, and Carl Brix, in the studios behind the club.

"As for the Mayberry family of actors, they were just that. I'm glad they included me."

BEN WEAVER MAKES HIS POINT—*But score another one for Andy in "The Merchant of Mayberry."* COURTESY OF GILMORE-SCHEWNKE ARCHIVES.

LOADING UP—*The famous bullet!* COURTESY OF JOEL RASMUSSEN COLLECTION.

Ben Weaver can't believe the outstanding stand Andy has built for meek peddler Bert Miller:

BEN: What is this? What, what is this?

ANDY: Well, Ben, What in the world you complaining about now? You said the man needed a roof. He got a roof. You said he needed a proper structure. He's got hisself a proper structure. What else, Ben?

BEN: All right, all right. I tried to get you to stop. I gave you the proper reasons and I've been nice.

ANDY: Oh, you've been nice, you've been nice. Hasn't he been nice, Barney?

BARNEY: Oh, he's been a real sweetheart.

ANDY: He sure has. Would you say he was nicer about the stand than the umbrella or was he nicer about the umbrella than the stand?

BARNEY: Oh, I dunno. I'd say he was nicer about the stand.

ANDY: 'Cause it's bigger! Ben, you know you're smart. You're smart! To make people believe that you're a skinflint and a mean old tightwad. 'Cause if they ever found out how sweet and kind you *really* are, they'd take advantage of you.

BEN: You'll be sorry.

"JUST HAD TO HAVE AN APPLE"—*Bob McQuain and Andy Griffith enjoy a snack on the set. This photograph was taken during filming of "The Merchant of Mayberry" on January 15, 1962. Bob portrayed problem parker Joe Waters for the second time in this episode. ("Trained noticers" might sense something askew between this photo and the actual episode. If so, it's probably that in the actual episode, you can see the neck of a white T-shirt under the plaid shirt Joe Waters wears, but it's not visible here. Better make that* obsessively *trained noticers.)* COURTESY OF GILMORE-SCHWENKE ARCHIVES.

COMMANDING PRESENCE—*Mayberry's fearless leader.*

ANDY GET YOUR GUN—*Bob McQuain and Andy Griffith set their sights for big game on the home front.* COURTESY OF MAYDALE MCQUAIN.

Bob McQuain appeared as various characters in about a dozen episodes during the first three seasons, but mostly in the second season. He died at Christmastime in 1999, but his widow Maydale describes his connection to Mayberry: "How Bob came to be on the show was that he did *The Lost Colony* outdoor drama in Manteo, North Carolina. Andy Griffith had done that show, so his manager, Dick Linke, would come to the theater, and he met Bob there because Bob did the lead while he was going to college. Bob signed with Dick Linke and went to New York and didn't really do anything there and then went to Hollywood. Dick was actually grooming him as more of a leading man for a sitcom or whatever, and he did bit parts for *The Andy Griffith Show* just to have income.

"Usually he was disguised. He would have the beard, a cigar, or be wearing a baseball cap. He didn't have a running character, but played different characters. He played police officers. He drove into town in one episode and parked wrong and got a ticket from Barney. He did quite a few of them, but he just wasn't a regular, but his name was in the credits. He spent a lot of time on the set and got to know everybody. He worked in a film lab at night, so he could act during the day.

"To be on Andy's show, he had to be a character that didn't stand out, but he was handsome and he was tall. Everywhere he went people paid attention to him.

"It was a wonderful thing in his life. He really treasured his memories of all of the things about the show. He got to know the people on the set and got to know Andy really well. He would watch the marathon reruns. We just felt Andy Griffith was part of our family."

SEE IF YOU CAN SPOT THE ENTERTAINING DINNER GUEST—*"Gravy is no joke, no siree. Takes a lot of work to get it cleaned off proper, a lotta good spottin'. People just don't realize." And so it goes when dry cleaner Fred Goss (Fred Sherman) visits.*

Jack Prince talked about working with director Bob Sweeney:
"Bob spoiled me. Ah-h, he was good! We had a great rapport. I could read his face and he could read mine."

Julie Adams describes what it was like for her on the set:
"'Friendly' and 'homey' are the words that first come to my mind in describing the atmosphere on *The Andy Griffith Show*. All the players enjoyed and appreciated each other. This was especially true of Andy and Don, who created a uniquely comic relationship with delicious charm and subtlety."

THE COUNTY NURSE—*Andy tries to help Nurse Mary Simpson (Julie Adams) persuade stubborn Rafe Hollister (Jack Prince) to get his tetanus shot. This photograph was taken on January 29, 1962.*

SO IT REALLY IS A JUNGLE OUT THERE!—*Barney keeps an eye out for a suspected jewel thief at the hotel in "Andy and Barney in the Big City."* COURTESY OF BART BOATWRIGHT COLLECTION.

TWO'S COMPANY—*Nurse Mary Simpson (not to be confused with Mayberry's other Nurse Mary Simpson) and Andy share a pose in this photograph taken on February 26, 1962.* COURTESY OF STEVE COX COLLECTION.

Sue Ane Langdon reflects on her work in the "Three's a Crowd" episode: "I was having a really great time on *The Andy Griffith Show* set. Everyone was just so wonderful to work with. The show has endured as something really so positive in our life that we don't find today.

"Don and I had worked together on *The Steve Allen Show*, and in the future would work on *Three's Company*. He's such a fine talent, a master at the kind of character he created. His and the *Griffith* show's humor is sadly not seen anymore. Just watching Don and Andy bounce off of each other really made it all a great experience.

"Granted, I was playing one of the few rather 'genteel ladies' of my whole career. Up to that point and pretty much after that, I was usually not too 'genteel.' Quite the opposite. I was usually more of a character and therefore felt I contributed more to the comedy, which I like to do. The 'Three's a Crowd' episode was certainly one of the funniest on *The Andy Griffith Show*, due mainly to Andy and Don and the script and the story concept. It was great to be a part of it. I had been told from the get-go that this might develop into a regular as Andy's girlfriend, and since all was going so well and we all were having such a good time, I felt 'Hey, I guess I'm gonna be a lady!'

"But then, along toward the end of the shoot, possibly after Andy and Nurse Mary Simpson's kiss up at the lake at the end of the episode, Andy seemed a little withdrawn, not quite so affable. O.K. So we finish shooting, say our fond farewells, and I go home.

"As we all know, I didn't become a regular as Andy's gal. Being an actress, these kind of things come with the territory. For whatever reason, you don't or do get the part. You accept it and go on to the next show. At the time, though, I kind of did wonder, 'Where did I go wrong? Maybe I don't kiss good enough, maybe I kissed *too* good, maybe I ain't no lady?'

"It is now the fortieth anniversary of *The Andy Griffith Show* (you understand I was born shortly before shooting that episode) and way back in my mind I still wonder 'Wha' hoppen?' Well, I found out just recently.

"One of the adorable *Andy Griffith Show* fans asked me to sign Richard Kelly's *The Andy Griffith Show* book. I thumbed through it before giving it back and found a section entitled 'The Trouble with Women.' Kelly quotes Andy as saying, '…because of my peculiar nature, and my personal relationship with women, and the difficulty I've always had with them, it became even more difficult for us to write for women.' Kelly quotes Richard Linke, 'Andy…is not really a lady's man….He didn't know how to hug and kiss on screen romantically.' Kelly quotes Don: 'He's (Andy) very shy with women.'

"Boy, if I'd have known this when we started shooting, so I could have become a regular as Andy's girl, I would have told Andy, 'Hey, relax, not to worry…I'm a guy!'"

AND, YES, THREE'S A CROWD—*Barney may not have his bongos at the moment, but that doesn't mean that someone's not just about ready to beat him like a drum.* COURTESY OF GILMORE-SCHWENKE ARCHIVES.

BE THE BOARD—*Part of Ronny Howard's strategy in playing checkers backstage with father Rance might be to camouflage himself as a checkerboard in order to maintain the element of surprise and confuse his opponent.*

Ron Howard proves he was indeed a real kid: "I'll never forget one time when I was cutting up, getting a little out of line, and pushing the envelope, and my dad said, 'No, don't do this and don't do that,' and warned me a couple of times for something. I don't remember quite what it was, and finally, right in front of everybody, he spanked me–gave me a spanking. And I was so shocked that on the set in front of people he would spank me. He was right. I was clearly getting away with something, trying to exploit the situation. The fact that we were not only in public but on the set—boy, everybody got quiet. My dad always did three quick swats right on the butt, and they never hurt as much as they just stung, but it was more the idea. I remember looking around, and my dad said, 'Anywhere you are–I don't care who's watching, I don't care what's going on–I have only one job and that's to be your father and that's to teach you right from wrong. And nothing about that job embarrasses me.'

"And there's something about that that I've never forgotten, because he was completely willing to do what he had to do, and it was family, and it was the idea that my being raised properly was more important than anything else on the planet. That meant a lot to me, even though I didn't like getting a spanking."

Ruta Lee guest-starred in two episodes, including the funny and poignant "Andy on Trial," in which she played reporter Jean Boswell. Some of her reflections from her first episode: "I think that Aaron Ruben set the pace. It was light and fun and joyous. And then, beyond what the producer had created, you've got stars like Andy Griffith, who looooves to laugh and who smiles through everything he says and does, and you've got the rest of the wonderful characters, all of whom did exactly the same thing. I just found it a joyous, joyous experience at all times. I remember everything that I ever did there with only one superlative—that is the sweetest and the funniest. That's two superlatives."

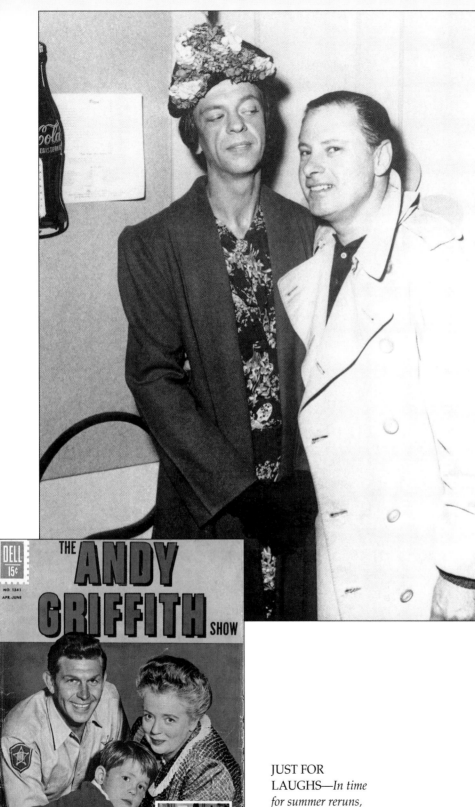

MAYBERRY THOROUGHBREDS— *Don Knotts visits off-track, uh, that is, backstage with producer Aaron Ruben during a break in filming "The Bookie Barber."* COURTESY OF AARON RUBEN.

JUST FOR LAUGHS—*In time for summer reruns, the second (and final) Andy Griffith Show comic book was issued by Dell in April 1962.*

"SUCK IN THAT GUT!"—
*Barney supervises Otis's
training to be a proper deputy.
This photograph was taken on
March 28, 1962, during the
filming of "Deputy Otis," the
final episode of the second
season.*

**Don Knotts has fond memories of
his pal, Hal Smith:** "Hal Smith was
fun to work with, a nice man, and
very able–a great actor. He put all of
his years of skill and experience into
Otis. That was a wonderful
character. He was always up."

HAT'S OFF TO A GREAT ONE—*There's not a more easy-going and lovable person in all of Mayberry than
Otis Campbell.* PHOTO BY GABOR RONA.

PEERLESS FIFE—*The photograph from the cover of this* TV Guide *is another one that once hung in director Bob Sweeney's office.* TV GUIDE *FURNISHED BY JOEL RASMUSSEN COLLECTION. REPRINTED WITH PERMISSION FROM* TV GUIDE *MAGAZINE GROUP, INC., PUBLISHER OF* TV GUIDE *MAGAZINE; COPYRIGHT © VOLUME 10, ISSUE 19, 1962, TV GUIDE INC.* TV GUIDE *IS A TRADEMARK OF TV GUIDE MAGAZINE GROUP, INC. LARGER PHOTO COURTESY OF BOB SWEENEY COLLECTION OF TAGSRWC ARCHIVES.*

GATHERING AT THE CEMENT POND—*This publicity photograph was taken on August 18, 1962. It features many of the kids on CBS TV series. First in Mayberry hearts is Ronny Howard, but also look for Jay North (Dennis the Menace), Donna Douglas (Elly May Clampett), Max Baer Jr. (Jethro Bodine), Lucie Arnaz, and Desi Arnaz Jr., among others. Floating in front of Ronny Howard is Keith Thibodeaux (Mayberry's Johnny Paul Jason). The man standing at the far end of the pool is Keith's father, L. J. "Thibby" Thibodeaux.* PHOTO BY GABOR RONA. COURTESY OF STEVE COX COLLECTION.

The last word again goes to writer Jack Elinson, who, along with partner Chuck Stewart, wrote the most episodes in the second season, as the pair also did in the first season. It's fitting that Jack mentions Jim Fritzell, Ev Greenbaum, and Harvey Bullock because they are the writers for most of the episodes during the next two seasons. Jack comments: "I didn't have to go to school to know 'southern' because in each script you could be sure Andy had his say on language. Between Aaron and Andy, they had the control of the southern thing. Also, Jim Fritzell and Ev Greenbaum and Harvey Bullock were wonderful. They had such a feel for the show. It was just easy; it just happened."

GIDDY-UP!—*Ronny Howard appears ready to ride the range.*

RINGING TRUE—*Opie visits with Mr. McBeevee (Karl Swenson), the magical telephone lineman who eventually makes a believer out of Andy. This photograph was taken during location filming on July 30, 1962.*

NEW FACES IN THE CROWD
Season Three

$$1962\text{-}1963$$

The third season of *The Andy Griffith Show* introduces many of Mayberry's most memorable characters. It brings back the writing of duo Jim Fritzell and Everett Greenbaum. Among so many classic episodes, they were at the peak of their writing when they crafted "Man in a Hurry," an episode that is beloved by fans and epitomizes the spirit of Mayberry.

Among the characters to arrive are Peggy McMillan, who supplies Andy a romantic interest for four episodes and Helen Crump, Opie's schoolteacher, who becomes Andy's steady girlfriend for the rest of the series, until they eventually wed in the first season of *Mayberry R.F.D.*

This season also brings the first encounter with the "fun girls" from Mt. Pilot, Daphne and Skippy, who furnish big-city romantic twists for Andy, Barney, Helen, and Thelma Lou.

Gomer Pyle is introduced as Wally's hired hand at the filling station, and he utters his first "Shazam." The character proves so popular that when he is recruited by the Marines, they stationed him to his own TV series.

In town we meet for the first time Mayor Roy Stoner, security guard Asa Breeney, and the Reverend Tucker. We meet Opie's pal Johnny Paul Jason and learn Leon's name. From England comes jolly Malcolm Merriweather, and down from the hills come Briscoe Darling, his four sons, daughter Charlene, and the irascible rock-throwing Ernest T. Bass.

By the end of the season, Don Knotts earned his third Emmy Award, and the show ranked sixth in the Nielsen prime-time ratings.

Harvey Bullock recalls "Mr. McBeevee": "'Mr. McBeevee' was fun to write. You had the central figure described in two wildly different styles. Opie talks about Mr. McBeevee's twelve hands, his silver hat, and how he jingles when he walks through the trees. The scene was written by finding ordinary objects that could be accurately described in extraordinary fashion. Barney, in contrast, tries in vain to get a formal ID.

"There has been a mild controversy over whether or not a boy Opie's age would believe such fancies. However, Ronny carried it off masterfully. These vivid descriptions powered the story and added to Andy's deep struggle to believe them."

"IT MUST BE THE LIGHTING"—*Andy Griffith and Don Knotts wait for lighting to be adjusted before shooting the scene in "Mr. McBeevee" where Barney discovers that Opie's horse Blackie is "a little on the invisible side."*

WHITTLE, BIG MAN—*Ron Howard watches as father Rance fine-tunes a slingshot on location during the filming of "Mr. McBeevee."* COURTESY OF GILMORE-SCHWENKE ARCHIVES.

MAYBERRY TRIUMVIRATE—*Andy Griffith poses in late 1962 with producer Aaron Ruben (center) and director Bob Sweeney.* COURTESY OF AARON RUBEN.

High praise for Aaron Ruben from Harvey Bullock: "Aaron, like other producers, listened to possible stories pitched by freelance writers. But there was a difference. Some producers would dwell on the negatives in a proposed story; Aaron looked for the positives. He was a collaborator, not an antagonist.

"Aaron also made sure that there were no discrepancies between how the dozen or so writers at work portrayed the Mayberry characters. Some discrepancies still got by. In one story Gomer was a completely unskilled mechanic who just pumped gas, but in another episode soon after he was portrayed as a whiz at fixing engines. Call it artistic license.

"Aaron also was the watchdog to see that Mayberry didn't become just a fount of hick humor. Whenever a joke per se appeared in a script, it seldom survived the first reading. Aaron was a gifted writer himself; his experiences made him uniquely sympathetic to the lonely plights of sitcom writers. He was always available. If a writer needed help, Aaron was the good uncle who lent a hand.

"Furthermore, he had a unique gift of making the lonesome writer feel like he was a vital part of a glorious undertaking. When changes were made in the script, copies of the changes went out to the writer. So we all felt we were an important cog in *Griffith* show success...and I'm sure subconsciously we all polished a *Griffith* script a touch more than other assignments."

Beverly (Mrs. Bob) Sweeney and daughter Bridget share their feelings about the Sweeney family's association with *The Andy Griffith Show*: "The whole company was like a family working in an atmosphere of common goals and affection. Our family was very proud to be a part of the Mayberry family. That time was very special to Bob and us. The values espoused on the show were so true and the writing so fine that it was inevitable that the show would become a worldwide symbol for how Americans would like to be perceived.

"Our favorite episodes were the one about the boys fixing Ernest T. up to present him at the social tea and the episode about Opie, the slingshot, and the bird."

It is noteworthy and likely a sign of the true generosity and sense of sharing among the Mayberry crew that neither episode singled out by the Sweeneys happens to be one directed by Bob Sweeney.

SOMETHING'S FISHY—*"That's my lunch. I usually have tuna fish, but today I thought I'd have trout."* Newly-elected Mayor Stoner *is not amused by this explanation and proves to be a real bear (and, as it turns out, he's not the only one in Mayberry this week). This photograph was taken on August 20, 1962, during the filming of "Andy and the New Mayor."* COURTESY OF GILMORE-SCHWENKE ARCHIVES.

LET'S PLAY BALL—*This coloring book is one of the few licensed* Andy Griffith Show *products issued during the 1960s.* COURTESY OF JOEL RASMUSSEN COLLECTION.

POPULAR COUPLE—*Andy and Peggy make a good picture together.* COURTESY OF JOEL RASMUSSEN COLLECTION.

PEGGY TO THE RESCUE— *With Andy and Opie fending for themselves while Aunt Bee's away in "Andy and Opie–Bachelors," Miss Peggy offers to help out. Floyd, on the other hand, makes a pain in the neck of himself (as a close examination of this scene demonstrates) by telling Andy that Peggy has matrimony on her mind.*

"ANNNDY, WHAT HAPPENED TO YOUR EYYYYE?!"—*Andy didn't know he was going to be in for such a rocky romance in "Barney Mends a Broken Heart." But then, he hadn't expected to meet the "fun girls" from Mt. Pilot or Daphne's boyfriend, Al. All in all, Andy would have been better off just staying home by himself and watching "that George Raft movie on TV."* COURTESY OF PHIL BOWLING COLLECTION.

Music director Earle Hagen comments about working on "The Mayberry Band" episode: "We did quite a few shows with a musical story line. One of them involved the Mayberry Marching Band. The town of Mayberry existed on the back lot of Hal Roach Studios in Culver City. I assembled a band of first-class musicians to play the parts, and we recorded on one of the stages at Hal Roach. We did a version of 'The Stars and Stripes Forever.' It was supposed to be bad, as most small town volunteer bands are, but not *too* bad.

  "The hardest thing for a group of really good musicians is to try to play 'bad.' Invariably they will overdo it and the result is exaggerated. The trick is to get it bad while the band visually is trying to play good. Andy was the tuba player in the band. I ran the piece down without telling the band what I wanted. We then went for a take and I asked them to make it bad, not horrible, just not good. When we made the take, the first trumpet player started one bar late and stayed there. When the band came to a finish, he had one bar left to play. It was perfect and so darned funny that Andy and the rest of us wound up on the floor laughing."

GET A BOTTLE OF POP—*Though veteran character actor Norman Leavitt appeared as other characters in five earlier episodes, he makes his first of two appearances as filling station owner Wally in "Lawman Barney."*

A WARM RECEPTION AND A COOL DECEPTION— *Things get pretty rich when Floyd meets lonely hearts club pen pal Madeline Grayson (Doris Dowling) in "Floyd the Gay Deceiver." This photograph was taken during filming on September 11, 1962.* COURTESY OF GILMORE-SCHWENKE ARCHIVES.

Oh what a tangled web...:

MADELINE GRAYSON: Floyd, Floyd Lawson. How perfectly marvelous to meet you.

FLOYD: Yes, how marvelous to meet me. Hello, how are you, Mrs. Grayson?

MADELINE GRAYSON: Mrs. Grayson? So formal? We do better in our letters, don't we?

FLOYD: Oh, the letters?

MADELINE GRAYSON: Aren't you going to introduce me to the nice young man?

FLOYD: Mrs. Grayson, Madeline, I'd like to have you meet Andy. And Andy, this is Miss Madeline, Mrs. Grayson.

MADELINE GRAYSON: Hello.

ANDY: How do you do?

MADELINE GRAYSON: Who is Andy?

FLOYD: Andy, oh, he's my son. He's a big fellow isn't he? Hello, son?

ANDY: Hi, Pop. Dad wanted me to meet you. Didn't you, Dad?

FLOYD: Yes, I did.

ANDY: Dad's told me an awful lot about you.

FLOYD: Oh, excuse me, Mrs. Grayson, Madeline, this is Aunt Bee.

MADELINE GRAYSON: *Aunt* Bee?

ANDY: Oh, she's been with us so long, we come to think of her as one of the family. Right, Beatrice?

A CLEAN GET-AWAY BEING MAID—*Though we're still waiting to see Aunt Bee's "mean left jab," we do get to see her "fancy footwork" as she whisks Opie into the kitchen.* COURTESY OF GILMORE-SCHWENKE ARCHIVES.

HAPPY DAYS AHEAD—*It's hard to believe a kid this cute could ever cause the trouble between Andy and Miss Peggy that Opie does in "Opie's Rival." But not to worry, cuteness prevails again in the end.* COURTESY OF BART BOATWRIGHT COLLECTION.

"BLOOD BROTHERS"—*Andy enjoys himself while camping with his son in "Opie's Rival." If there's a lull in the conversation, Andy and Opie likely can find just the right words to say in the open book that's resting on the squad car hood.* COURTESY OF GILMORE-SCHWENKE ARCHIVES.

"BETTER PHONE HIM, AL"— *These are definitely not "fun girls" or even "Girl Campers of America" that Floyd and Barney have encountered in "Convicts-at-Large." "They're cons!" With Big Maude as their leader, Naomi (Jean Carson, left) and Sally (Jane Dulo) keep a close watch on their hostages. (This was Howard McNear's last episode before suffering the stroke that would keep him off the show for more than a year.)*

SHAKIEST GUN IN THE SOUTH—*Bank guard Asa Breeney (Charles Thompson) would be a disgrace to his uniform. That is, if he had a real uniform. This photograph was taken on November 6, 1962, during the filming of "The Bank Job." The episode also marks the first broadcast appearance of Gomer Pyle, though "Man in a Hurry" was written and filmed earlier.* Courtesy of Gilmore-Schwenke Archives.

Time for a security check:

BARNEY: What are those green things in your cartridge belt?
   ASA: Bullets.
BARNEY: They're *moldy*! Asa, let me show you what a bullet oughta look like.

Barney reaches into his left shirt pocket and pulls out his single bullet.

BARNEY: Now, there's bullet maintenance.
   ASA: Oh, Barney, that's beautiful. I've heard about your bullet, Barney. Beautiful. I like for things to be nice and shiny. One of these days I'll bring over my ball of tin foil.

CHOW TIME AT THE OL' CORRAL—*As Andy Griffith studies his lines for a Jell-O commercial about to be shot during filming of "The Bank Job," Clint Howard is fully armed and ready to face whatever the pudding can dish out. But don't worry that Leon has given up his prized peanut butter and jelly sandwiches. There's one ready right there on the table for a quick-draw when needed.* COURTESY OF GILMORE-SCHWENKE ARCHIVES.

Future Miracle Salve salesman (Richard) Keith Thibodeaux recalls his work on the show: "I remember my dad saying that I had the part of Johnny Paul. It wasn't a big part, but anytime you're gonna be on *The Andy Griffith Show*...well, I really, really looked forward to it. I looked forward to Ron and being with him. He was one of the nicest kids in Hollywood that I knew. The set was so relaxed. It was professional. I think Andy and the cast and crew gave it that feel of Andy being from the South. Ron seemed like he was a good old southern boy, too.

"Seeing the guys in the makeup room playing checkers and Andy taking hold of his guitar and singing some songs back there as the guys were playing, it kind of made me feel at home."

And a vote from Keith for "One-Punch Opie": "My favorite episode is the first one I was on with the bully and the apples. That was my introduction to the show, but there was also one about the guy descended from Wyatt Earp. It was just fun. I didn't think much of it at the time. It was still a job, but it was a very pleasant oasis in Hollywood."

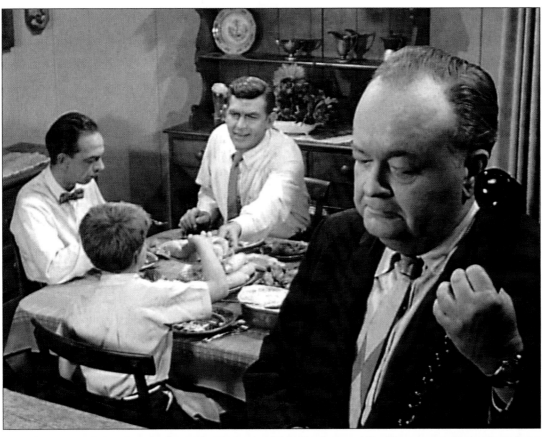

MAN IN A HURRY—*Malcolm Tucker (Robert Emhardt) gets an earful about sore feet from the Mendelbright sisters in the episode widely ranked as a (if not, the) favorite episode of the entire series.*

NO PHONY LINES TYPED HERE— *Everett Greenbaum (left) and Jim Fritzell were key writers for the show. (Eight of their episodes are listed in the Top Twenty as voted by fans in a recent poll.) On top of the bookshelf behind them is their award from the Television and Radio Writers Association honoring their script for "Barney's First Car."*

Writer Everett Greenbaum described how he came up with the character Gomer Pyle: "I had recently had an experience with a garage attendant who couldn't think of anything to do to fix my car except add more gas to the tank. The name came from a writer named Gomer Cool and from actor Denver Pyle."

And Everett's remarks about writing with partner Jim Fritzell: "Jim and I had a real affinity for small-town life. If we had both been from New York City, we probably couldn't have written for the show as effectively. It was great having Andy Griffith around too. He sometimes would come by when we were writing. He's very creative and smart."

Writer Harvey Bullock talks about friends Jim Fritzell and Everett Greenbaum: "They were truly the Odd Couple. No two other people on earth could be more disparate. Jim was a stoic Viking, totally dedicated to watching all sports on TV, day and night. He was single, and his bachelor apartment was in such sorry shape he could easily qualify for hurricane relief.

"Everett was married and had a daughter. He also had a workshop and turned out museum-quality kinetic sculptures. An ex-Navy pilot, he flew a single-engine sport plane for relaxation. He had been tossed out of MIT, and then went to the Sorbonne instead.

"Everett had a vast imagination. And he knew everybody in town…and they also knew him. At his memorial service, friends told Everett stories over and over. A favorite was when Everett was stopped in a traffic jam en route to an acting audition. He had sparse hair, so he opened his briefcase, took out his hairbrush and started to use it.

"A huge truck driver, in a rage over the stoppage, pulled his eighteen-wheeler up next to Everett's car and bellowed, 'Hey, Buddy, you gonna drive that car or brush your *#@! hair?'

"Everett looked calmly at the fuming trucker, paused, then deliberately asked, 'But don't you want me to look my best?'"

At the dawn of the fortieth anniversary year, *The Andy Griffith Show* Rerun Watchers Club conducted one of its periodic polls of the favorite episodes of fans. Here are the top twenty episodes as tallied in the poll:

1. "Man in a Hurry"
2. "The Pickle Story"
3. "Convicts-at-Large"
4. "Opie the Birdman"
5. "Barney's Sidecar"
6. "Mountain Wedding"
7. "Three Wishes for Opie"
8. "Opie's Charity"
9. "Christmas Story"
10. "The Haunted House"
11. "Barney's First Car"
12. "Citizen's Arrest"
13. "Mr. McBeevee"
14. "The Manicurist"
15. "Barney and the Choir"
16. "The Sermon for Today"
17. "The Fun Girls"
18. "Dogs, Dogs, Dogs"
19. "A Date For Gomer"
20. "The New Housekeeper"

Harvey Bullock echoes the poll results in picking his favorite episodes among those that he did not write: "Heading the list would be the favorite of every poll, 'Man in a Hurry,' written by Jim Fritzell and Everett Greenbaum. Others: 'Barney and the Choir,' 'Barney's Sidecar,' 'The Christmas Story,' and 'Mountain Wedding.' I also admired the writing skills of Bill Idelson in 'Barney's Uniform.'"

FILL 'ER UP—*Portrait of Gomer.* Photo by Gabor Rona. Courtesy of Bob Sweeney Collection of TAGSRWC Archives.

Richard O. Linke on the discovery of Jim Nabors: "Andy had already caught Jim's act at The Horn nightclub. Andy told me, 'I don't know what this guy does but what he does he does well. You better go see him.'"

Jim Nabors reflects on Andy Griffith and his time in Mayberry:
"My memory of Andy is that I was very grateful to him for giving me a break. That's the first thing I think of. My main memory of Andy is the incredible talent he has. He always led a good show. He set a tone of real professionalism for anybody who worked on the show. He let you know exactly what he expected. It was pretty much a learning experience for me. I was incredibly appreciative of the whole effort.

"It was a real pleasurable experience to me to work with everybody I worked with on that show. I have no bad memories or frustrations of it whatsoever. Looking back on it for me, probably it was the nicest part of my career because I did not have to carry the show and it was a learning period for me. And I knew I couldn't wait to go to work every day because I knew I was going to laugh all day and have a good time and learn a lot. Everybody was very nice. Andy set a high standard for us and it worked well.

"There were several episodes that meant a lot to me. The first one, 'Man in a Hurry,' really established my character. But I liked them all.

"In retrospect, in looking at all the TV shows of that period, I think it was the best one for a situation comedy—real Americana. I think it was exceptional. I don't think we knew it at the time. We knew it was a good show, but time proves a lot of these things out."

GOT YOUR GOAT?—*When Jimmy the goat eats a bellyful of dynamite, Andy and Barney are quickly down to the last straw handling the matter. (And yes, as Andy points out, with Otis around, one loaded goat at a time is enough!) This photograph was taken during the filming of "The Loaded Goat" on December 4, 1962.*

GOAT BUSTER—*It's too bad that Andy and Barney didn't know that the solution to their "loaded goat" problem was as near as Opie, their very own "goat whisperer."* COURTESY OF GILMORE-SCHWENKE ARCHIVES.

"CAREFUL. A CLINKER MIGHT SET HIM OFF"—*The Mayberry crew prepares to shoot the scene where Andy and Barney escort Jimmy out of town in "The Loaded Goat." Discussing the scene with Don Knotts is director Bob Sweeney. Wisely keeping a safe distance in the background is that familiar face around Mayberry, Tom Jacobs.* COURTESY OF GILMORE-SCHWENKE ARCHIVES.

GLASS REUNION—*Barney has his hands full but apparently needs different kinds of glasses in order to recognize old classmates at the Mayberry Union High reunion.*

THE CLASS OF '45—*When Andy's high school sweetheart Sharon DeSpain (Peggy McCay) shows up at the "Class Reunion," everybody is all smiles.* COURTESY OF JOEL RASMUSSEN COLLECTION.

Peggy McCay shares memories about her "Class Reunion" in Mayberry: "Of all the shows that I have done, it remains a favorite. People really remember that episode. What I remember is that Andy was very shy about doing a romantic scene. I believe I'm right that, while Andy might have done 'screen' kisses prior to our scene, this was the first one that was intended to be truly romantic, as opposed to being played for comedy. Well, we just relaxed and said 'Let's just do it and not worry about it.' And I must say it was the best kiss I ever had. And good kisser or not, Andy is truly one of our great actors and a very nice person."

A REAL PRINCE OF A SINGER (below)—*Rafe Hollister (Jack Prince) sings "Look Down That Lonesome Road" for the Ladies League Musicale.*

Jack Prince commented about his work on the show: "The ambiance of that show was so great–such pride in what they were doing. Everybody in the whole crew, from the writers right down to the lighting men, was proud of the work. And I'm proud to have been even a small part of it.

"The reason I left Broadway was that I'm a singer. I'm not an actor–unless it's something really simple or if something like *The Andy Griffith Show* comes along where you're working with all of these talented people, like Andy and Don and Bob Sweeney. I have so much admiration for Don. It's hard to come into a comedy and do a scene exactly the same on every take or make exactly the changes you're asked to make by the director. He is by far the best actor I ever worked with. People are always asking me, 'what's Andy really like?' I'll tell you what Andy's really like. He's what you see."

At one point Richard Linke talked to Jack about joining the cast as a regular. Jack's response: "Naw, fellas, I'm a singer. When I can't sing anymore, I'll see about acting."

HISTORY TROOP—*When Andy shows Opie and pals (left to right) Johnny Paul (Richard Keith Thibodeaux), Whitey Porter (Joey Scott), and Howie Pruitt (Dennis Rush) that history can be an exciting subject, Barney is as fascinated as the other boys.*

"Andy Discovers America" introduces Aneta Corsaut as "Old Lady" Helen Crump. Aneta Corsaut recalled the experience: "It was supposed to be just a guest shot, a one-shot thing, but it melded into six years. My first day on the set, Andy and I got into a bit of a battle about women's lib or something. I was for it and he was against it. We were battling like old buddies. I think he respected me for standing up for what I believed in, and it may have surprised him. Anyway, by the end of the week, we were good friends and have remained so ever since."

Keith Thibodeaux shares insight worthy of Johnny Paul: "I just loved anything that Don Knotts had a big part in. I loved it when we had the history lesson and he gets locked in jail, that same old classic predicament he finds himself in. I liked it when we were all standing in front of the jail and Barney's behind us like a kid. That was just so hilarious, even as a kid. I also loved any of the shows that Ernest T. Bass was in, just hilarious."

And Dennis Rush shows that he really is a student of history: "Almost forty years have passed since I visited Mayberry, but all I have to do is hear that whistle or see Andy and Opie walking along that dirt path and I am flooded with fond memories. I was one of those very lucky kids that can claim to be one of Opie's pals. 'Andy Discovers America,' was Miss Crump's (and my) debut on the show.

"I worked in Hollywood for almost a dozen years and had over a hundred credits by the time my child acting days were through, but nothing compared to my time on *The Andy Griffith Show*. This was by far the most enjoyable show to work on. The cast and crew were honestly one big family. They took you in and made you feel like one of the family. Andy was certainly the boss, but to me he was more of a gentle giant. Don Knotts made you laugh for no reason at all. He just had a way. Ron Howard was a really nice guy. So many kid actors took advantage of their position as stars and were really a pain. Not Ron. It was always a thrill to go to Mayberry, and Ron seemed to really enjoy having some kids to work and play with."

On the other hand, Ron Howard himself confesses that he wasn't always the model kid actor: "One time we were in a classroom scene–an episode where there was a scene with a lot of kids in it, a big classroom scene–and I was kind of cutting up and not behaving very well, and I was always shown a lot of respect for my concentration, even at an early age, and for my professionalism.

"But in this classroom situation, there were a lot of kids around, and I was a little distracted, I guess. And I was kind of cutting up and being a wise guy. Bob Sweeney took me aside (my dad wasn't around; he was working on something else that week), and said, 'I'm really disappointed in you. You're not concentrating and I don't feel you're really paying attention to this scene and these are important scenes.' It really took me aback because I so respected Bob, and I also prided myself in being a professional and being above average in that way and not like a kid, but rather being somebody who could really sort of function as a young adult. And I'll never forget that. He did me a world of good by sitting me down and giving me a little stern talking-to there."

THE DARLINGS ARE COMING—*Andy makes acquaintance with Briscoe, Charlene, and the boys. (But Andy forgot to warn Briscoe to watch out for that microphone cord snaking around at his feet—especially while dipping hatfuls of water.)* COURTESY OF GILMORE SCHWENKE ARCHIVES.

Mitch Jayne, bass player for the Dillards, tells about the creation of the Darlings:
"The Darlings were an invention of Jim Fritzell and Everett Greenbaum and an example of their comedic genius. With Sheriff Taylor being the ultimate 'good guy' problem-solver, the writers had to come up with problems that were uniquely Mayberry's for him to straighten out by using logic and his own good-natured native intelligence. The Darlings were ideal because they were bizarre, funny, and entertaining, a nearly perfect foil for Andy's patient handling of human situations. They were also a good way to remind the audience that Andy was quite a musician himself and that he could identify with this strange family with its musical boys, their flirting sister, and a father who was the absolute ringmaster of this circus. The Darlings, like Ernest T. Bass, were patently nuts. Having Andy dealing with them, showed that he could cope with any sort of human behavior."

Mitch adds: "I think my favorite, and longest-lasting memory of the six shows we did was the first one–watching the way Andy Griffith eased the Darling family into his Mayberry world. He showed utmost respect to Denver Pyle as a fellow actor, a warm and helpful kindness to Maggie Peterson as a promising actress, and a totally hospitable sense of belonging there to his greenhorn fellow musicians, the Dillards. Since he believed in us, we could too, and all of us could relax enough to learn about the other people on the set. Andy had a way of making you feel that you were a valuable asset to his show, but more than that, a person he would like to know. It was a feeling that lasts to this day and has brought me through many a hard time. To be valued by Andy Griffith, you had to really be good at something, and since he wouldn't forget it, you couldn't either."

DIP OF THE HAT—
Not that we were counting (O.K., we were), but Briscoe didn't dip the full eleven hatfuls.
COURTESY GILMORE-SCHWENKE ARCHIVES.

Oh, my...Darlings!:

CHARLENE: Sure is boiling, Pa.
    BRISCOE: This machine is half mad with thirst.

He gets water from the David Mendelbright Horse Trough ("Let No Horse Go Thirsty Here") as he dips his hat.

CHARLENE: How much she gonna take, Pa?
    BRISCOE: She's always good for eleven hatfuls.
      ANDY: Hidee.
    BRISCOE: Hidee.
CHARLENE: My!
    BRISCOE: Now that's enough, Charlene, back in
           the truck.
CHARLENE: Aw, Pa, can't I look at the pretty man?
    BRISCOE: Back in the truck!

Dillards' guitarist and lead singer Rodney Dillard describes his ride to Mayberry: "We usually came into town on the truck and left on the truck. Well, when Denver Pyle was driving that truck and we would pull in, he would always pop the clutch and everything to make it give an extra little dramatic jump. You had to hang on tight when he did that, and if you'll look closely we were hanging on dearly.

"With my being the young kid from the Ozarks, the show was my first introduction to Hollywood and the television scene. They made us feel so comfortable. Andy was so considerate of us. He was always concerned that we were happy with the way the music was presented.

"I think, because of the excitement and newness, our first episode, 'The Darlings Are Coming,' is my favorite. Being able to see the set and where they shot it was fascinating to me."

SHINING BRIGHT—
Andy Griffith enjoys a light moment next to the Darlings truck as director Bob Sweeney makes preparations to shoot the next scene in "The Darlings Are Coming."

And this from Dillards' mandolin player Dean Webb: "They couldn't have been friendlier to us. The very first show was the best in the bunch, 'The Darlings Are Coming.' Maggie Peterson was a real sweetheart. You couldn't ask for anybody to play your sister that would have been more likable. It was one of those lovely places we all really identified with, that we wished we could live in. That's why everybody still watches it on TV. Everybody still longs for that, a part of the past. People are sorry that it is a part of the past in a way."

One "Other" thing from Dean Webb: "Andy found out that 'Other' was the makeup man Lee Greenway's middle name. So my name became Other. 'Where's Other? Other's not here.'"

Mitch Jayne shares a story about Denver Pyle: "Denver said to me one time, 'Most people are too busy memorizing their part to tell you what the story's about. You watch Andy. He never forgets the story and plays it all the way through.' Denver told me that because, he said, 'I think most of us can learn something from that. It's not just your part you have to learn, but what's the story all about.'"

"THERE'S DUD"—*Everybody seems excited to see Dud (Hoke Howell) arriving home after "fulfilling my country's needs" in "The Darlings Are Coming."*

Maggie Peterson describes her road to Mayberry and beyond:
"Forty-plus years ago in Estes Park, Colorado, I was spending the summer vacation working at the old Stanley Hotel with my brother's Dixieland group, the JaDa Quartet. It was quite the perfect setting. We were kids with lots of energy and the locals and tourists packed the place every night to see us. That summer Capitol Records held their convention at the Stanley Hotel. Dick Linke was an executive with Capitol and that is how I met Dick. (I believe he had recently signed a country boy named Andy Griffith and recorded 'What It Was, Was Football' on Capitol.) He loved the group and just casually mentioned if we were ever in New York to look him up.

"That was all I needed to set my sights on New York. The day after graduation we hit the road. At the time, it seemed normal. But from my

view today, we were incredibly fortunate. Indeed fortunate to have Dick Linke, who got us some wonderful opportunities. We were guest stars on *The Perry Como Show* several times and regulars of *The Pat Boone Show*. And we traveled all around the U.S. working in the best nightclubs.

"It was in New York that I first met Andy Griffith. He was doing the Broadway show *Destry Rides Again*. We became good friends from then on. Later, after several years, when Andy was doing the series, the part of the hillbilly girl, Charlene Darling, came up. Dick Linke, Aaron Ruben, and Sheldon Leonard came to see me perform and decided to give me a chance at the part.

"Talk about being fortunate. The entire experience was delightful. Of course, I couldn't know at the time how really special it was. The Desilu

GETTING READY TO ROLL—*Andy relaxes between shots with Denver Pyle and Maggie Peterson.* COURTESY OF GILMORE-SCHWENKE ARCHIVES.

Studios were small and friendly. If Mayberry had had a television studio, it would have been Desilu. Everyone was so kind and encouraging.

"The first script reading of 'The Darlings Are Coming' was magic to me. To have the words on the page come alive. Denver Pyle as Briscoe, Don, Frances, Hoke, Andy, and the silent Darlings. It went so well and was so much fun. After the reading, Andy grabbed his guitar and the Dillards started playing and it was hard to get any rehearsing done. Andy always loved it when the Dillards were on the show. They would all play in the makeup room, play during set changes, play during lunch hour. Andy loved it.

"Being a true fan of the show, I have my favorites. 'The Pickle Story,' 'Opie the Birdman,' 'The Mayberry Band.' But I would have to say personally the first Darlings show meant the most to me as it introduced me to Mayberry, where my heart has remained for forty years. Talk about magic! We can turn on TV Land, and, lo and behold, we are all there, back in Mayberry, forever young and innocent"

And Richard Linke has this to say about "discovering" Maggie Peterson: "Maggie was always my little charm bracelet. I found her at a Capitol Records convention in Greeley, Colorado. I thought she was fabulous. She reminded me of a young Doris Day."

Dillards' banjo player Doug Dillard remembers Frances Bavier and picks his favorite Darlings episode: "The neat thing was Aunt Bee making candy for us and bringing it down to the set for us. We were really thrilled. She'd make it at home and bring it down to the set for us.

"I'm partial to the first one of the Darlings and 'Mountain Wedding.' I think I like 'The Darlings Are Coming' probably the best."

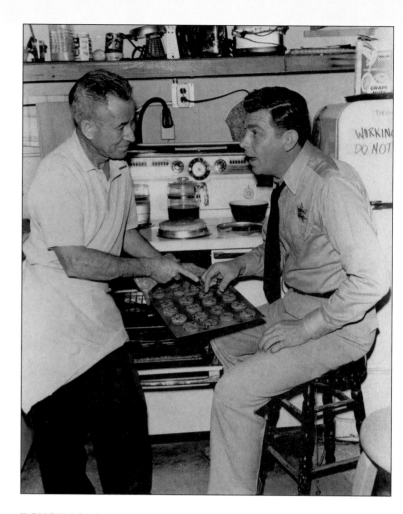

NOT A TRUCK, BUT STILL QUITE A DARLING VEHICLE—
Maybe it's just coincidence that tidy Malcolm Merriweather (Bernard Fox) traveled to town immediately after the rustic Darling family's visit. Or perhaps Malcolm intuitively knew there might be some cleaning up to do.

DOUGH BOYS—*It would be hard for Malcolm Merriweather or even Aunt Bee to top the fresh-baked goods being offered here by prop master Reggie Smith. On the top shelf in the background are some toasters apparently waiting for Emmett Clark to repair. (Their timing is off; they'll need to wait a few more years to get fixed.)* COURTESY OF BART BOATWRIGHT COLLECTION.

Bernard Fox reminisces about his experience in "Andy's English Valet" and other Mayberry adventures: "That first episode is my favorite. The whole setup of working in Hollywood was so very different from the British system that I was used to. (We rehearse for a week and then shoot the whole thing in one day.) In fact, I was so naive that my first morning on location, I attempted to pay the catering truck for my breakfast.

"I recall that everyone was pleasant (I was probably the first 'Englishter' to arrive in Mayberry!), and I enjoyed the atmosphere at the first script reading when any input in the way of Britishisms that I could offer was welcome.

"Harvey Bullock, of course, was wonderful, so very friendly and sensitive when he asked me if I played any instrument (yes, a penny whistle!), or anything that might make Opie go, 'WOW!' Obviously the penny whistle didn't impress, and I began to think, 'Here goes the job.' Harvey seemed to sense my panic and calmed me down saying something like, 'It's nothing to worry about; we will come up with something.' And then I remembered the magic paper tearing routine that I was taught to do in the Irish Fit Ups, and that was how the paper tree arrived in the script.

"Then came the waiting until it aired, wondering if I would ever work again. Well, the episode was hardly over when the phone rang and it was Andy being very complimentary. And I do believe he hinted that there would be other shows for me to do. Harvey called, of course, and Harvey's partner Ray Allen. All in all, it cheered me up considerably."

"THIS CAR'S JUST BEEN SITTING ON A VELVET PILLOW"—*"Hubcaps" Lesch (Ellen Corby) prepares to unload a lemon on "the sucker of the world." This photograph was taken during the filming of "Barney's First Car" on February 25, 1963.*

Aaron Ruben talks about Jim Fritzell and Everett Greenbaum: "Jim and Ev wrote such wonderful stories that you might have thought they had been raised in Mayberry. Their inventiveness and their off-the-wall brand of humor is what made Barney and Floyd the Barber and Otis and Gomer as funny as they were. They wrote some of our more outstanding scripts. They were a perfect team and a thorough delight to work with."

"Barney's First Car" is often cited by Andy Griffith as one of his favorites. It was also one Everett Greenbaum favored among the ones he and Jim Fritzell wrote. The memorable scene where the steering column snakes up at Barney was inspired by an incident that happened to one of Everett's friends, who, while working at a gas station, put too much grease into a steering column.

"DON'T TOUCH THE DOOR, OPE"— *"This just happens to be a very delicate piece of machinery that's been treated with kid gloves and I intend to continue to give it that same kind of care."*

Barbara Perry has special memories of her Mayberry episodes: "The first *Andy Griffith Show* I did was the day after my husband and I decided to divorce. It wasn't a usual divorce. I had a six-month-old child and wanted her to have her own father despite anything. Thus, this particular morning I was filled with conflicting emotions, on the verge of tears but with a Pagliacci smile on my face.

"I confessed to the makeup man, Lee Greenway, my distress in hopes he could cover it up with his wizardry. I did not know that he was such a dear friend of Andy's, and I could swear that he, Andy, and Don Knotts went out of their way to be amusing around me as I laughed most of the day and got to hear Lee and Andy play bluegrass music. Andy on the guitar and Lee on the banjo–what a memorable treat that was. They were both marvelous musicians.

"Maybe I am imagining this because it was always a happy set, but since I know Don Knotts knew about my distress, I like to think a little bit of the jollity was to help me through a terrible day.

"My second favorite memory was watching a scene on the front porch between Andy and Don. I forget what it was about, but it was a quiet and contemplative moment in the script. (What great scripts they were!) It was the time when 'the method' acting technique was prevalent–not the stand-up comic, anything for a laugh, sitcom style we see today.

"Although I was from Los Angeles and the Actors Studio was not available to me at that time, I audited every seminar that came this way—Lee Strasberg, Stella Adler, Bobby Lewis, Jeff Corey—and loved them all. But as I sat there on the set watching Andy and Don (who can be touching in a quiet moment), I thought to myself that these two geniuses of comedy could teach all the Stanislavsky gurus what 'expression, thought, feeling, sensation, behavior' (I quote the great Lee Strasberg), and especially timing really is. It was simple, real, rich, and very moving and I have never forgotten it.

"Another memory I have that is rather charming is about Frances Bavier. By the second show, we were on a rather warm and friendly basis, although I was very careful not to intrude on her life except at lunchtime or when she was not working. She told me that

"PUT THAT IN YOUR SMIPE AND POKE IT"—*Barney was supposed to be finding the right woman for Andy in "A Wife for Andy," but appears to have gotten sidetracked. At far right is Lavinia (Barbara Perry), who like the other Mayberry women seen here, is a potential recruit for a ladies' softball team that Barney ends up organizing.*

she loved Gilbert and Sullivan and admitted to being a bit of a Savoyard (the English expression used for a Gilbert and Sullivan fan). When I told her that my dearest friend Gwyneth Cullimore had been leading lady with the Savoy in London for eight years and on Broadway with the company on tour, she showed such interest that I had a tiny luncheon for her. It was Frances, Mary Jackson (also on *The Andy Griffith Show* and best known for *The Waltons*), Gwyneth, and me. Gwyneth regaled us with all the

backstage news of the Company when she was with it and would burst into song at moments to elucidate her story. More than once Frances joined her if only for a moment but word perfect. Yes, Frances knew her Gilbert and Sullivan!"

CHEERS?—*As Andy points out, Otis wasn't too particular about what he was drinking the night before, so he should have no reason to balk at Andy's "fixer-upper" the next day in this shot from "Dogs, Dogs, Dogs."*

Ron Howard talks about Don Knotts: "Don always impressed me, first and foremost, as an incredibly gentle, wonderful man. And he would sort of turn on this comic energy and be hilarious, but that wasn't the zone that he lived in. To me it was the first real example of a performer's energy and what an actor could really do to create a character.

  "The other thing was that he was just a lot of fun but generally he kind of laid low, and Andy would prod him into doing one of his routines or they'd start improvising something together or they'd start singing some hymn and doing a harmony and having fun with that, and Don would go into a preacher routine or something. Andy was Don's greatest audience, but every once in a while you'd find yourself front row and center for ten minutes of Don Knotts's genius."

"NOT MY MISTER COOKY BAR"—*A "slender, high-spirited person" is about to miss out on his "sugar pick-me-up" when he has his sinking spell later this afternoon.*

Otis, on the other hand, knows it's every dog for himself:

  OPIE: He looks hungry, Pa. Can't we feed him?
  ANDY: Hum, he does look a mite underfed there.
  OPIE: I think he's starved. We got anything?
  ANDY: Otis, you got anything left?
  OTIS: (hurriedly gobbling down last bite of sausage): Sorry, Andy. Just finished everything.

PACKING IT IN—*Otis may have gotten the last bite of sausage, but what he doesn't know yet is the little dog (the "trembler") that he denied that last bite to is going to be coming back with a real pack of trouble for Otis to deal with.* COURTESY OF GILMORE-SCHWENKE ARCHIVES.

Everett Greenbaum credited producer Aaron Ruben with adding Barney's classic "Boy, giraffes are selfish" speech to "Dogs, Dogs, Dogs." Though Aaron Ruben has refused to take the credit Everett gave him, he shouldn't worry because Everett also said, "It was one of the few times I ever liked it when somebody added stuff to one of our scripts."

ARMED AND READY—*It's about time to, well, pump Ernest T. Bass for some answers about the trouble he has been causing the Darlings in "Mountain Wedding." Barney seems ready to come at Ernest T. with both barrels. (Briscoe, however, would do well to put away those eyeglasses in his hand before the rock-throwing commences.)* COURTESY OF GILMORE-SCHWENKE ARCHIVES.

Darling boy Doug Dillard recounts a scene regarded by many as one of the funniest of the entire series: "The scene with the Darlings all snoring was just too funny because the director, Bob Sweeney, would crack up and even Andy did. It was hard to get through the scene. They finally broke for a while to get their laughs out and they started up again and still couldn't finish, because we were all doing the actual snoring. What was really funny—what really cracked us up—was when Briscoe gets up out of bed and puts his hat on. They finally had to shut down for lunch and then we went back to the scene and still couldn't get straightened up. By the way, I can recognize my own snore in that scene."

TYING KNOTTS?—*Won't Don Knotts make a lovely bride once the wardrobe specialist works her magic? Veteran actor Dub Taylor (in background) must have seen it all before. This photograph was taken during the filming of "Mountain Wedding" on March 26, 1963.* COURTESY OF GILMORE-SCHWENKE ARCHIVES.

IT MUST BE THE SHOES—*Dud Wash (Hoke Howell) helps Andy and Barney pull off one of the few deceptions ever to rock Ernest T. Bass.*

Howard Morris recalls how he became Ernest T.: "When I was called by Aaron Ruben to look at this person, Ernest T. Bass, and see if I wanted to do it, he had no hint of what it was going to become, nor did I. I said, 'This is an interesting part. Let me play with it.' And he did let me play with it.

"Now, I'm a kid who was born and raised in the Jewish neighborhood of the Bronx, New York, and what have I got that has any connection whatsoever, intrinsically, with Mayberry? But it's there and I can call on it in a second and I loved the guy. He's nuts! We know that and that's been attested to by many people, including the American public, which is why they adore him. He does things that everybody would like to do and gets away with it, including throwing rocks. If he could lift up a car and throw it, he would. A rock was the handiest thing he could find."

Suited to *T*: According to Everett Greenbaum, Mayberry's favorite rock thrower got his name from Saul Bass (whom Everett's brother had worked for) and from Frank T. Whip, Jack Warden's character on *Mr. Peepers*. "I always liked that *T*.," Everett commented.

Aaron Ruben talks about casting for Ernest T.: "We needed someone really offbeat and somewhat manic. I had worked with Howie on the *Caesar's Hour* show and recalled how off-the-wall he was back then, both on and off screen. The part of Ernest T. Bass was tailor-made for him. I can't think of anyone who could have played this loopy leprechaun, this wild woods creature, better than Howie. Talk about an actor adding to the written word and direction. We have remained friends to this day…and he's still manic."

TO KNOW A VEIL—*Ernest T. has met his match in trickery this day, but one thing's for sure: "You ain't heard the last of Ernest T. Bass!"*

HERE AT THE ROCK—*Andy signs in prisoners Doc and Tiny to the Mayberry jail as his crack team of deputies prepares to assist. This photograph was taken during filming of "The Big House" on April 2, 1963.* COURTESY OF GILMORE-SCHWENKE ARCHIVES.

Y'ALL COME—*Andy visits with the Dillards during production of "The Big House," which was filmed the week after "Mountain Wedding." The Dillards (from left: Rodney Dillard, Doug Dillard, Mitch Jayne, and Dean Webb) might have come back this day to record some of the music for the previous week's episode, which would air in less than a month. But it's just as likely that they came over simply to visit and pick and sing with Andy.*

Rodney Dillard recalls:
"Some of the best things that happened were between scenes. We would get back somewhere away from what was going on and with Andy we'd pick, sit around, and play music."

BULL'S EYE—*Darts was a popular game backstage. The impression of this photograph (taken during the filming of "The Big House") notwithstanding, Don Knotts reportedly was the better darts thrower of this pair, though Hal Smith may have been the steadiest of all.* COURTESY OF GILMORE-SCHWENKE ARCHIVES.

"SWEEN SONG"—*This photograph of Andy and Bob Sweeney singing "The Big Rock Candy Mountain" likely was taken around the time that the Dillards were visiting during the filming of "The Big House," the last episode Bob Sweeney directed. As "Sween" himself always said after a job well done, "Cut and print."* COURTESY OF GILMORE-SCHWENKE ARCHIVES.

Sweet songs, sour notes: Many people remember that Bob Sweeney was a bad singer. Don Knotts recalls, "Andy would egg him on to sing anything because Bob was tone deaf. He always sounded so funny when he tried to sing." Mitch Jayne specifically remembers Bob trying to sing "The Big Rock Candy Mountain," which Mitch believes was Bob's favorite song.

TICKLE ME OPIE—*Mayberry made the cover of* TV Guide *again at the end of the 1963 regular season.* TV GUIDE FURNISHED BY JOEL RASMUSSEN COLLECTION. REPRINTED WITH PERMISSION FROM TV GUIDE MAGAZINE GROUP, INC., PUBLISHER OF *TV GUIDE* MAGAZINE; COPYRIGHT © VOLUME 11, ISSUE 19, 1963, TV GUIDE INC. *TV GUIDE* IS A TRADEMARK OF TV GUIDE MAGAZINE GROUP, INC.

"HANGIN' AROUND, TAKIN' OUR EASE"—*Andy and Opie doing what Mayberrians do best...relaxing.*
COURTESY OF STEVE COX COLLECTION.

$\mathcal{S}$TAYING THE COURSE
Season Four

$\boxed{1963\text{-}1964}$

$\mathbf{T}$he fourth season of *The Andy Griffith Show* opens without the guiding hand of director Bob Sweeney, who had departed for other ventures.

Sharing the duties behind the camera this season were the able talents of directors Earl Bellamy, Dick Crenna, Jeffrey Hayden, and Coby Ruskin. And a new pair of writers, Bill Idelson and Sam Bobrick, contributed marvelous scripts beginning this season.

Three major cast happenings affected the series. Fans of Howard McNear on both sides of the TV set cheered his return to the show after more than a year's absence while recovering from the stroke that had sidelined him. George Lindsey makes his debut as Goober, Gomer's mechanically gifted cousin, as he is introduced in the "Fun Girls" episode. And Jim Nabors marches off to a series of his own as Gomer Pyle leaves his hometown to serve his country in the U.S. Marine Corps.

Among Mayberrians seen for the first time this season are Barney's landlady, Mrs. Mendelbright; Opie's pal Trey Bowden; butcher Foley; and stag line perennial Mr. Schwamp.

The season could not have gotten off to a better start than with the landmark "Opie the Birdman." By season's end, *The Andy Griffith Show* ranked fifth for the year among prime-time series.

What is Aaron Ruben's favorite episode?: "That's like asking a parent to name his favorite child. I loved them all. However, there is one that does stand out—'Opie, the Birdman.' It had everything: a 'crime,' guilt, penance, redemption. Above all, it was a wonderful lesson in a father's approach to a problem that did not involve a 'whipping,' which Opie fully expected, but a way of redeeming oneself and being a better person for it. Thumbs up and four stars.

"Harvey Bullock was one of the best writers we had. If he had written 'Opie the Birdman' as his one contribution, he would have established himself as one of the best. Thoughtful, compassionate, Harvey undoubtedly drew on his own experiences as a father to write those gentle and meaningful scripts."

"OPIE'S JUST BECOME A MOTHER"—Filming the scene in "Opie the Birdman" when Opie is preparing breakfast for his feathered friends.

Harvey Bullock talks about perhaps the single most revered of his scripts: "Almost every time somebody does a retrospective of *The Andy Griffith Show*, they show a clip of 'Opie the Birdman.' Aaron Ruben even used this show to start the season. Usually they will show a clip of the program's ending, which seemed to define the thrust of the series. It was just two lines between Opie and Andy, which were so effective. I received a lot of flattery…which is always nice.

"But the hard fact is, I didn't write that scene.

"After you write several episodes for sharply etched characters like Barney Fife, Floyd Lawson, Aunt Bee, etc., you can almost temporarily assume their persona and seek what they would say or do in a situation. So even though they rarely intermix, there is a closeness between the cast and the writers.

"I was working on the last page of the 'Birdman' script, wherein Opie and Andy come out of the house, and Opie sadly releases his birds from their cage. They fly away to freedom. I came to a stop, seeking inspiration. These final words would be crucial.

"Then I noticed something really weird.

"My fingers hadn't stopped typing. I looked at the paper totally puzzled. Opie's next line appeared of its own accord:

OPIE (wistfully): Cage sure looks awful empty, don't it, Pa.
   ANDY: Yes, son, it sure does…But don't the trees seem
     nice and full.

"The perfect ending, and seemingly…it literally wrote itself."

CAGEY CHARACTERS—Winken, Blinken, and Nod are about to fly away to once again be creatures of the wild.

Director Earl Bellamy talks about how he came to direct seven episodes, including "The Haunted House:" "I'd be doing one show and then my agent would know when that one was finishing and then he'd line me up for some more and that's the way it happened. Sheldon Leonard knew me very well because I'd been around there at the same studio. I think Bob [Sweeney] was getting ready to go and there was about to be an opening and so I went on there. I'd do a block of three or four episodes.

"The Andy Griffith Shows were wonderfully pleasant to work on. Really, everybody concerned with it was just top-drawer, and of course the little guy was so great. Opie. And, you know, it's a thrill to see what he's become. I get the biggest thrill from that, as if it were my own son. He was something in remembering lines, no question about that. [His father] Rance was great with him, and so was his mother. If one couldn't be on the set, the other one would be there. There was never any hanky-panky with him. I mean, he walked in in the morning and you'd say, 'Ronny, we'll do so and so.' That's it. And he'd do the scene and he never blew a line. Everything was right there. And Mom and Dad were there in the wings and all business. What a treat.

"The one with the haunted house was a gem. It was so funny with Don Knotts being scared. He would do things and the whole crew would break up. We'd just fall apart and then try to get back together to get the show going. It was just a super script and everything about it just worked. I liked working with Harvey [Bullock]. He was a really good writer. When I got a script, the first thing I'd look at was who wrote it, and when it was Harv, boy, that was great. You were home free. Everything worked."

The feeling is mutual. Harvey Bullock says of Earl: "When I saw an episode Earl directed, it always seemed very well done. I was very pleased to learn he would be directing one of my stories. Whenever we did meet, we always had some good laughs. Both of us had a genuine respect for the other. He's a real prince."

Aaron Ruben adds: "Earl was very easy-going and very thoughtful. It was a joy to work with him. He was a fine director and a gentleman."

PORTRAIT OF FEAR—*Andy, Barney, and Gomer are not exactly having a ball with Old Man Remshaw umpiring the situation.*

BE STILL—*Otis and moonshiner Big Jack Anderson (Nestor Paiva) think they're encountering different spirits than they're used to.*

Since it's about this time that "Ernest T. Bass Joins the Army," Howard Morris discusses what makes Ernest T. Bass tick: "He's got a lot of anger. He wants and needs things, but they're always a little bigger than most things we want. He wants a uniform. But he's not entitled to a uniform. 'But I want a uniform. Give me a uniform.' He wants a girl and he wants this and he wants that. He gets in jail. He gets out. I don't know how he gets out, but he gets out. I can go South and I will get a standing ovation in a hotel lobby. The people absolutely adore this man. I get mail every day requesting photographs and signatures. It is amazing…for five episodes! But I find it a privilege to count working on *The Andy Griffith Show* among my cherished memories."

IN CONCERT—*Andy and Barney had better hurry up and enjoy relaxing now because they're about to work really hard at being relaxed when Aunt Bee prompts them to take "The Sermon for Today" to heart.*

Andy and Barney sitting on the front porch after Sunday dinner in "The Sermon for Today":

BARNEY: Yeah, we really packed her away, didn't we?
  ANDY: Yeah, boy.
BARNEY: (Pats tummy) Fortunately, none of mine goes to fat. All goes to muscle.
  ANDY: Does, huh?
BARNEY: That's a mark of us Fifes. Everything we eat goes to muscle. (Pats his tummy) See there?
  ANDY: I see.
BARNEY: My mother was the same way. She could eat and eat and eat.
  ANDY: Never went to fat, huh?
BARNEY: (Shaking head) Know where it went?
  ANDY: Muscle?
BARNEY: Yeah. That was a mark of us Fifes…
  ANDY: Good…You know what I believe I'll do? Run down to the drugstore and get some ice cream for later.
BARNEY: You want me to go? I'll go.
  ANDY: No, I'll go.
BARNEY: Well, I don't mind.
  ANDY: I don't either. I'll go.
BARNEY: You're probably tired…Why don't you let me go?
  ANDY: No. I'm not tired. I'll go.

BARNEY: Well, I sure don't mind going.
  ANDY: You sure?
BARNEY: Uh-huh.
  ANDY: Why don't we both just go?
BARNEY: O.K.
  ANDY: You ready?
BARNEY: Uh-huh.
  ANDY: Well, let's go.
BARNEY: Where we goin'?
  ANDY: Down to the drugstore to get some ice cream for later.
BARNEY: O.K.
  ANDY: Come on.
(Both slowly rise as Aunt Bee comes out on the porch.)

AUNT BEE: Andy, where are you boys going?
  ANDY: We thought we'd run down to the drugstore and get some ice cream for later.
AUNT BEE: Well, why do you want to *run* to the drugstore, as if it couldn't wait?
  ANDY: Ma'am?
AUNT BEE: Well, that's just what the preacher was talking about this morning. It seems as if nothing can wait. Everything is rush, rush, rush!
(Andy and Barney slowly sit back down.)

ANDY TRIES TO REIN IN THE CROWD—*Gomer doesn't really have strong feelings about the sign he's holding while waiting on the gold shipment to come through town. As he tells Andy, "I'm just minding it for Regis." This photograph was taken during the filming of "A Black Day for Mayberry" on September 4, 1963.*

Clint Howard says "A Black Day for Mayberry" is his favorite episode (maybe because he got to splash around in mud puddles on location for that episode), but it's not particular episodes that Clint likes the most: "More than the episodes, the characters are the things I like about the show. I thought Jim Nabors did a wonderful job of playing Gomer. The way all the characters kind of melded together. Jim, in particular, played such an offbeat, wacky character, but I don't know quite how he did it. I believed him and I liked him.

"The same with Barney, but we got to know Barney a whole lot better than Gomer. Don was just really, really good. I believed those characters. I feel when we watch them now that they're real human beings and not just an extension of some comedy writer trying to get a joke. The team was always fighting for quality material. Andy and Don and everybody and Dad—they were always fighting for honesty. It was a good show and proved to me if you do a good show with good stories, the work will hold up."

YOU CHARACTER—*Bernard P. Fife enjoys a laugh about his claiming to be the author of his old eighth-grade history book,* The History of the United States of America.

PREAMBLE TO A CLASSIC MOMENT—*"There's things right there in that book that I learned that I still remember to this day."* Oh, yeah? *"Sure. I'll show you. Hold the book on me."* Uh-oh, here we go…

"ESTABLISH JUST…"— *Oh, just whatever. The important thing is that "once you learn something, it never leaves you. It just stays locked up tight in the old noodle."*

For the record here's what Barney "remembered": "We the people of the United States, in order to form a more perfect Union, establish Justice, insure domestic Tranquillity, provide for the common defense, promote the general Welfare, and secure the Blessing of Liberty to ourselves and our Posterity, do ordain and establish this CONSTITUTION for the United States of America."

The "Preamble" scene is often cited by fans as one of the funniest of the entire series. But close observers often wonder how it came to be that Barney's hair keeps going back and forth from combed to mussed up. Director Jeffrey Hayden has the answer: "About the hair mis-match on 'Opie's Ill-Gotten Gain,' we shot the master (two shot) and then did the closeups. Don got a little too carried away in the closeups, but it was too late to go back and re-shoot the master. (We never went over the three-day shooting schedule.) I figured the editor would stay in the closeups once he established the scene—and I sure learned my lesson."

Jeff Hayden continues: "It's hard to believe, after all these years, how terrific and funny episodes of *The Andy Griffith Show* are. Those writers were terrific. John Whedon was wonderful. We did many *Donna Reed* shows together and they were always sweet stories and very funny—and fun to do. Jim Fritzell and Ev Greenbaum were terrific too. When I saw their names on the scripts, I knew I was in for a good time and a good show. And producer Aaron Ruben was one of the best in the business."

WHO'LL EVER NOTICE?—*The fellas in the editing room probably never dreamed that, four decades later, folks would be sitting around critiquing the position of the hairs on Barney's head. Seen here are Alfred Glazer (seated) and assistant editor Jerry Jameson, both with well-groomed hair.* COURTESY OF GILMORE-SCHWENKE ARCHIVES.

"SHE'S NICE!"—Mary Grace Gossage (Mary Grace Canfield) is the perfect "Date for Gomer."

Mary Grace Canfield speaks about her Mayberry days. "I felt comfortable. The atmosphere was relaxed but disciplined. I think it is the finest series ever seen on television. I would like to have been in more than one episode. It was constantly good—real love, real humor. Jim Nabors is funny. I wish all men could cut loose and dance like that! I'm eternally grateful to Everett Greenbaum, though I think I was miscast. I was not a dog (dawg)–just shy and nice."

Jeff Hayden reminisces: "Andy and I were undergraduates at the University of North Carolina and did a couple of shows together—my only acting credits. He was very talented and had a great singing voice. Many years later, we met up again, totally by coincidence, on his show. I had been doing *Donna Reed* and was very pleased to be asked to do his show. He was surprised to see me and we had a nice reunion. I had a great time and don't think (with the exception of *The Donna Reed Show*) I ever enjoyed a cast as much as I did that group.

"It wasn't too long after *Andy Griffith* that I left the sitcoms and moved into dramas. *Peyton Place* was next and then a succession of private eyes like *Mannix*, *Ironside*, *Quincy*, and all the way up to *Magnum, P.I.*, *Heat of the Night*, and *Cagney and Lacey*. But I must say, of all the hundreds of shows I've done, *Andy Griffith* was one of my favorites. To this day, when people learn I directed it, they get excited and practically stand up and cheer. (My grandson, 15, whistles the theme song. When I told him I directed the show, he looked at me with new respect.)"

BRAVO!—*Director Jeffrey Hayden around 1963.* COURTESY OF JEFFREY HAYDEN.

UP IN BARNEY'S
ROOM—*Barney may leave
a clean wash basin at the
boarding house, but he's still
in hot water with Mrs.
Mendelbright for cooking on
his hot plate.*

Writer Everett Greenbaum once recalled part of the inspiration "Up in Barney's Room": "I lived in a rooming house in New York. The little old landlady there wouldn't let us have more than a twenty-watt bulb and we weren't supposed to cook. 'Mr. Edison is rich enough,' she'd say." That lightbulb of an idea became Mrs. Mendelbright, Mayberry's beloved bulb-snatcher and hot-plate hawk.

Ron talks about the preparation he and Clint received from their father: "The thing that I understand in retrospect that I didn't at the time (but I really appreciate his result) was that he was really teaching Clint and me how to act, not just how to perform. There's a difference because a lot of kid actors can perform. They've got their little bag of tricks and they look kind of cute and they can do some things that are pretty entertaining to watch, but they're not really learning how to be thorough, creative, thoughtful actors. My dad was teaching us, at a very early age, really, really good fundamentals. As I matured as an actor, I wasn't developing a lot of bad habits on the show. I was really learning how to do something, develop something that I could carry on with me. I have so much respect for that because it takes a lot of patience."

CAMERA, MEN—*Rance
Howard poses with sons Ronny
and Clint backstage during the
filming of "Up in Barney's Room"
on September 18, 1963.*

"CITIZEN'S ARREST?"—*Or maybe just cardiac arrest as Barney seems to be pretty fed up with Gomer, much to Andy's glee.* COURTESY OF PHIL BOWLING COLLECTION.

Jim Nabors reminisces: "The episode I remember most is 'Citizen's Arrest' for a number of reasons. First of all, about that time, they had decided to keep me on as a regular. The other thing was that it was the episode that really got Barney and me going. I just remember I kept breaking up in some of the scenes there when Barney would get so worked up after I stopped him on the street and all the townspeople came out and said, 'Get him, Gomer, get him!'"

"WHO LOOKS SILLY NOW, SHERIFF?"—
*This photograph has the look of a man who'd
rather do the time than pay the fine after being
arrested for making an illegal U-turn.*

"HOORAY!"—*This is a front page worthy of framing and
hanging on the wall in the back room of the Courthouse. That is, if
Barney happens to round up an extra copy.*

GUESS WHICH ONE IS THE NIT-
PICKING PICNICKER—*If you think
Barney's no fun on a picnic, just wait until he's
asked to go in a cave with the bats and moths
laying eggs in your hair and making you go
crazy. But he does rise to the occasion in
"Barney and the Cave Rescue."*

PRISONER OF LOVE—*When a jewel thief (Susan Oliver) is booked at the Mayberry jail, she immediately starts stealing precious glances with guards Andy and Barney. With Barney working on the case, she eventually breaks out, but Andy comes back for the "collar" at the end. (Though the beautiful prisoner is never mentioned by name, Harvey Bullock named her Angela Carroll in his script.)*

Earl Bellamy, who directed "Prisoner of Love," also has fond recollections of working on the episode he directed the next week, "Hot Rod Otis" (another high-octane Harvey Bullock script). The script is unique in that only three characters appear: Andy, Barney, and Otis. What is it like directing just three actors for an entire episode?: "Well, it's a relief. Otis used to tickle me so because he was funny when he would do the drunk scenes. He was so funny and, well, you had three real pros when you had that show to do and it worked. Everything worked with them and especially with Otis and the new car."

SIDECAR SIDESHOW—*Town loafers, led by Jase (Joe Hamilton, white-haired and no hat), are falling down with delight at the success of their gag, which results in Barney's failed effort to take Andy to the diner by "Sidecar Express."*

Howard Morris says about Earl Bellamy, who directed him in "My Fair Ernest T. Bass:" "He's a lovely man. A real old-timer in the good way of, well, old-timers. He was a good director."

It so happened that "My Fair Ernest T. Bass" was the episode being prepared for production on November 22, 1963, when President John Kennedy was assassinated. Everyone was gathered for the script read-through and getting ready to rehearse later that day. Howard Morris recalls the day:

"I was devastated. It was a time of panic, a time of depression, a time of bewilderment, a time of having been deceived, as it were. We were reading a script, a table reading, which we had every show. We would read the script and it would be discussed, in minutia if necessary, and it would be fixed and we would come back the next day and start blocking it out for camera.

"We were having this reading and in came Bob Saunders, the assistant director, white as a sheet. He said, 'Gentlemen, I have an announcement I must make. Our president has been shot and killed in Dallas.'

"Sheldon Leonard had a meeting in his office with whoever wanted to drop by. We more or less milled around for a while, but there was no more work being done."

HARLEY HAR-HAR—*"You know something I found out? If you ride in the wind with your mouth open, and you put your tongue up on the roof of your mouth, it's impossible to pronounce a word that starts with the letter 'S.'"*

THE SONGFESTERS—*Barney is shocked when he hears that Gomer really hasn't lost his voice at the Chorale Concert. The singers seen here with Don Knotts and Andy Griffith are Delos Jewkes as Glen Cripe (left) and John Guanieri as an unnamed tenor. (The identity of the man on the boom is not known.) Choir member regular Renée Aubry (also in this episode) recalls, "John Guanieri was a fabulous operatic tenor. We worked together at the San Diego Circle Arts Theatre in a production of* New Moon.*"*

In Neal Brower's *Mayberry 101,* **Everett Greenbaum revealed this nugget:** "I first heard the word 'songfester' from *Griffith* director Alan Rafkin. I liked the word and thought it would be a good title for a script that featured music."

Earle Hagen comments on the music: "We did a couple of shows about the Mayberry Choir. In all of the musical shows, Don Knotts was outstanding. He has a pleasant voice, which on necessary occasions, he could make as raspy as an old file, and he has a great ear for harmony. He and Andy did songs together that were absolutely natural."

"On the choir shows, I hired Ric Ricardi, a vocal coach previously at Fox, to contract the singers, rehearse, and conduct them. Ric had a nightclub called The Horn and invited Andy to come down and hear a new comic from Sylacauga, Alabama, by the name of Jim Nabors. Nabors wiped Andy out. After a flock of 'Gah-leeh' jokes, he started to sing. Andy was so impressed with him, he brought Aaron and Sheldon down to hear him and the part of Gomer Pyle was invented."

Bill Idelson describes how "The Shoplifters" became part of Mayberry: "In 1944 I was lying on my bunk in a Quonset hut on Guam, and a funny idea occurred to me. What if a nerdy clerk in a department store dressed as a store dummy in order to catch some shoplifters? Twenty years later, Sam Bobrick and I were shivering in the cold of a California winter, standing outside the rear entrance to Aaron Ruben's office at Desilu. Sam and I had just become partners and hadn't written a show together yet. As a matter of fact, Sam had not yet written a show of any sort. We were standing there because I'd told Sam I knew where Aaron parked his car in the mornings. Sam, a nervous Jew from New York, was heavily doubtful that I really knew where Mr. Ruben parked his car.

"But at nine-thirty on the dot, a black Lincoln turned swiftly into the small lot across the street from us, and Aaron Ruben got out. He was a small man but he looked like Goliath as he crossed the street, frowning at these two jerks blocking the entrance to his office. As he came up, I blurted out, 'Aaron, we've got an idea for Barney that we think is funny.'

"He looked us over. 'Come in at eleven tomorrow morning.' He unlocked the door and disappeared.

"The next morning we were there promptly at eleven. I presented the notion and Aaron jumped on it. He began pitching scenes and we took notes furiously. A couple of hours later, we emerged from the office with a rough but complete outline. 'Does this mean we got a job?' asked Sam.

"'Of course, dummy.'

"'Well, we got to do this perfect. It's got to be funny. It's our big chance.'

"We turned in the first draft and didn't hear a word for over a week. Sam was beside himself. Then, one night, I was at a party. Sheldon Leonard was also there. As he walked by me, he said quietly, 'Good script, boys.' We were in!

"Later that year, 'The Shoplifters' won the Writers Guild Award for Outstanding Comedy Script for the 1963–1964 season."

GOODWILL, HUNTING—*Though Leon's quiet, he's certainly no dummy and immediately recognizes a man akin to Barney at Weaver's Department Store. Barney, however, must refuse Leon's generous offer of a sandwich bite and keep his eye on the little old lady who's concealing, not sporting, goods that she doesn't intend to pay for. This photograph was taken on January 8, 1964, during the filming of "The Shoplifters."*

GOT MILK?—*If Barney doesn't want a bite of sandwich, that's just all the more for Leon. Oh, but wait—here comes a hand from above that maybe he can feed a bite.*

Clint Howard talks about the mystery of Leon's name. Maybe Mr. Schwamp knows the answer: "Somebody must have seen me with peanut butter all over my face and thought that was cute. Maybe somebody somewhere had an uncle or a friend, Leon, who ate like that and they named my character after him. I've never heard where the name Leon came from, but I would love to find out."

DUMB AND DUMBER?—
Guess who lost their prisoner? But Gomer and Barney are hot on his trail, so "Andy's Vacation" is bound to end up with a capture.

SHERIFF, DARLING—*Andy is wrapped up in another encounter with the Darlings when he has to find a way to get Charlene to take husband Dud back in "Divorce, Mountain Style."*

Darling boy Mitch Jayne shares some thoughts about everybody's "darling person," Maggie Peterson: "Maggie is wonderful and complicated and real. She very honestly loves people and hurts for them when they hurt, is glad for them when they're glad. Maggie makes us all wish we could be like her, putting her whole heart into anything she does. You could do worse than spend your life trying to be like Maggie—hoping that the world will shine back at you. She is our sister."

GETTING COLD FEET—*Charlene says an "incant" to help Andy's foot feel better on the way to the preacher's house: "Pain of heel, ache of toe, vanish now from my sweet beau." With Charlene, Andy, and Briscoe are the Boys (clockwise from bottom left) Doug, Mitch, Rodney, and Dean.*

Mitch Jayne offers this "take" on Andy Griffith: "Andy has the kind of respect for excellence in anything that inspires people he works with. We soon found out that if a cast member's 'take' bothered them, Andy would redo the thing until the actor was happy with his or her work. Andy wanted, more than anything, to satisfy people's urge to do their best, because that was what he was after, too.

"Anytime that Rodney, who was our quality-control expert, felt that something was wrong (like Briscoe's jug distorting our music in the first episode), Andy made sure it was fixed. He also saw to it that we got to do our own songs on the show, when possible—knowing that this would make us future royalties. Andy takes great pleasure in making people feel good about their work. It's probably one of the reasons so many people feel good about his."

Mitch adds: "My best memories of the show are based on the small exchanges between characters that brought viewers into the Mayberry state of mind. Like the scene where Andy plays the patient prompter to Barney's attempt to recite the 'Preamble to the Constitution' or the dialogue on the Courthouse bench where Goober and Andy discuss the best place and time to eat lunch. The interplays between these self-made Mayberry characters, which often happened in the intros or in the wrap-ups, often exceeded the plot in expressing what the town was all about.

"My very favorite of these was the small scene in 'Divorce, Mountain Style' where Andy and Barney discuss the pros and cons of a bicycle kit made of clear plastic. Barney says, 'One look and you know what you've got.' And Andy says, 'What I keep in my tool kit is my business.' It was a writer's show, a place where inventive wit could utilize people who understood the magic and could carry out the concept. *The Andy Griffith Show* was, after all, a magic act, taking us wherever we wanted to go in wishful memory. There is no best *Andy Griffith Show*, because the magic act goes on, and will, forever."

NEWS FLASH—*Floyd doesn't have a problem with Barney's being dressed in black and riding by his house on a white horse trying to go east to west under a full moon. It's just that he wasn't expecting it is all. "Divorce, Mountain Style" was Howard McNear's second episode back in Mayberry ("Andy Saves Gomer" was the first) after suffering the stroke that kept him off the show for over a year.*

Kit McNear shares his memories about his father's return to Mayberry: "After he got sick, I believe it was Andy Griffith, primarily and principally, that asked him to come back because the show was lacking something. But I had never heard of any show that would take an actor back and work with him like they did with my dad. I mean, that to me was amazing, and it not only helped him mentally. Like most actors, he didn't have retirement. My mother only had Social Security. It was a real financial blow to the family as well as to him physically and mentally when he was off the show. I believe Andy Griffith was the driving force, the catalyst that made it happen. It was fabulous for my dad and my mom, for us."

MAKING GOOD MARKS FOR EFFORT—*Salve salesmen (left to right) Trey Bowden (David A. Bailey), Opie, Johnny Paul Jason (Richard Keith Thibodeaux), and Howie Pruitt (Dennis Rush) are in search of a miracle cure of their own.*

Dennis Rush describes how he liked Mayberry: "Getting a call to be on an upcoming episode was one of the best phone calls you could get. Most television shows in the '60s took five days to produce a half hour episode. *The Andy Griffith Show* took three. That is how smoothly this show operated.

"On the set, Opie's pals would get three hours of schooling, while sets and lighting were being readied. We would get the call for the 'Fearsome Foursome' to get on the set. The four of us—Ron, Richard Keith, David Bailey, and I—would dash on the set, knock out a quick scene, and head back to school or better yet to play. Ron had a basketball hoop set up that was modified for our heights on an adjoining sound stage. We also had fierce Ping-Pong battles and always enjoyed a game of

catch football or baseball, depending on the season. Quite often in between scenes or during lunch breaks, Andy and some of the crew would stage a brief folk concert in the sheriff's office. They really did know how to pick those banjos and strum those guitars.

"Two episodes came back to back. 'Opie and His Merry Men' was filmed at Franklin Lake in the Hollywood Hills. (No, we never made it back to North Carolina.) The next call came about a week later for just a one-day shoot that introduced Trey Bowden to our gang. He replaced Joey Scott as the fourth member of our foursome. I'm not sure what happened, but I recall Joey as a little 'too Hollywood' for this show. Some kid actors and 'Hollywood moms' liked to count how many lines they had. Others would try to upstage other actors. I think this

was noticed. Whitey disappeared and in came Trey.

"My favorite episode was 'Opie and His Merry Men.' One of everyone's favorites with us kids seems to be 'A Deal Is a Deal.' We had a great time trying to sell Miracle Salve. I can still see Dr. Pendyke and Opie Taylor, Sr., and the cases of salve piled high in the Taylor house."

FINDING A WAY TO CURE THE MANGE—*Yes, claiming that Miracle Salve treats the mange is sure to help jar sales. Dr. Pendyke also says that Miracle Salve is good for poison ivy, prickly rash, athlete's foot, the complexion, spring itch, and crow's feet. All that Opie Taylor, Sr. seems to care about is, "How do you do that with your voice?"*

Jim Nabors says that Don Knotts was a miracle worker: "It was always such a pleasure working with Don Knotts. He's one of the finest character actors, comedic actors, that there's ever been. The reason that I used to say 'Shazam' and all of that was I wanted the audience to realize that Gomer thought that Barney was the most sophisticated thing that ever came down the pike."

Jim Nabors talks about fellow Alabamian George Lindsey: "I met George when we were doing a pilot at Universal, *Butterball Brown*. He'd come over on the *Griffith* set and visit me. I think that's where Aaron got the idea for the episode, and it worked out very well for him, because I was leaving."

George Lindsey relates that the Pyle family tree almost branched out in another direction: "I had auditioned for the part of Gomer. They said, 'You got it, but there's one more person we've got to look at this weekend.' And so I didn't have it, after all. It was supposed to be just a one-time part, as far as I know. But you can't keep a good Pyle down."

"ANDY, SAY HEY TO MY COUSIN GOOBER!"—In the only episode with both Gomer and Goober, "The Fun Girls" is a wild experience for Andy. In addition to the Pyle boys (and for Goob measure, Cary Grant, Edward G. Robinson, and Chester on Marshal Dillon), fun girls Daphne and Skippy also have invaded. Do we also learn that Goober always says "yo" for "yes"? Yo!

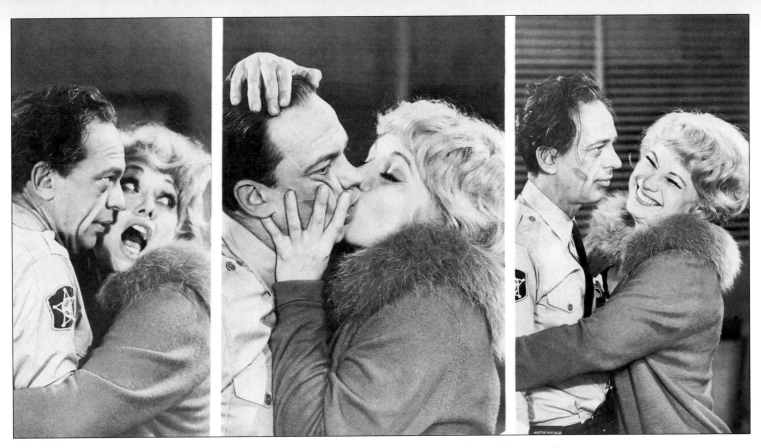

ENFORCED BUSSING—*Mt. Pilot "fun girl" Skippy (Joyce Jameson) seems to handle "Bernie" pretty well.*

Aaron Ruben talks about "fun girls" Jean Carson and Joyce Jameson: "Jean and Joyce were the perfect combination to face off with Andy and Barney. Wildly out of place in Mayberry, they were quite aggressive in their attitude toward Andy and Barney, two very proper clean-living chaps to whom the 'Fun Girls' were both challenging and bizarre. The 'Fun Girls' were always fun to work with."

FROM WARDROBE TO WARPATH—*These two shoppers will not be pleased when they find out that Andy and Barney have been entangled with the "fun girls" from Mt. Pilot.*

SALT AND PEPPER WITH
SUGAR AND SPICE—*It's
looking like a recipe for disaster
for a man who's supposed to be
taking Thelma Lou to the big
dance. This photograph was
taken during the filming of "Fun
Girls" on February 24, 1964.*

**Jean Carson (Daphne) comments
on her time in Mayberry:** "It was
the most prepared TV show I ever
worked on. The atmosphere was
always a happy one. I loved all of
the episodes, but I agree with the
public: 'Convicts-at-Large' and 'The
Fun Girls.' It still amazes me that a
TV show can have a forty-year
popularity.

 "I didn't get to know Joyce
Jameson as well as I'd like to have,
but I adored her—and what a pro.
Also, no one seems to notice that
cinematographer Sid Hickox on the
show was the best ever. I don't ever
remember being photographed
better. Also Lee Greenway was the
best makeup man ever, besides
being a perfect southern
gentleman."

MR. SCHWAMP TAKES IT ON THE CHIN—*Whether it's raw animal magnetism or some other secret, the sociable Mr. Schwamp gets the nod from Daphne at the big dance.*

Betty Lynn remembers that Jim Nabors was a real trouper in a scene in "Barney and Thelma Lou, Phfftt": "There was the scene where Thelma Lou was going after Gomer and kissed him and scared Gomer to death. Jim had a high fever and was so sick that day, and here we all were worried to death about him. But he was brave enough to keep going, and I kept thinking, 'Poor thing,' because I really was worried about him. But poor Jim—he had to finish that and he was so sick and so miserable."

"BACK TO NATURE"—*Of course, Barney would like to keep hiking, but if Andy wants to stop and set up camp here to keep the boys from getting tired, Barney'll go along with the group.*

EVEN BETTER THAN A PRESTON FOSTER MOVIE—*Gomer can practically taste that wild pheasant bird ("perhaps the most difficult species of all to ensnare") that he and Barney are going to catch using good old "pioneer moxie." Even so, Gomer lacks the raw courage to eat the bird without first having it "heated a touch." It's just a good thing that Barney the Pioneer knows that "any fire started pioneer-style is bound to be hotter than a fire started with just ordinary matches."*

HAPPY CAMPER—*Barney's confidence as an outdoorsman is rekindled when he and Gomer begin successfully "living off the land," with a little help from Andy and from Aunt Bee's kitchen.*

READY TO ROLL—*Sgt. Carter (Frank Sutton) gives Gomer his marching orders in* Gomer Pyle, U.S.M.C., *the final episode of the season. (The last episode Jim Nabors filmed was "Back to Nature.")*

ALL IN THE FAMILY—*That is, eventually.*

STRONG MAYBERRY LINKE—*Huddling for a 1963 fundraiser for the Richard O. Linke Scholarship for the School of Journalism at Ohio University are (at center) Maggie Peterson and Andy Griffith and (clockwise from far left) Ernie Mariani, Woody Woodruff, Norman Diamond (Maggie's fellow members of the Ernie Mariani Trio), Ronnie Schell, Richard O. Linke (an Ohio University alumnus), and singer Tommy Leonetti.* COURTESY OF RONNIE SCHELL.

A final note to wrap up this season from author Stephen Spignesi, who writes: "Mayberry is my 'spiritual home town.' *The Andy Griffith Show* has always been a port in a storm for me, a respite from the fast-paced life we all seem to live these days, and a balm for the stresses this kind of life invariably causes. There is nothing to compare with the peace and calm that comes from watching a black-and-white episode of *The Andy Griffith Show*. I'm grateful that the town and all its wonderful denizens are there, tucked away in their quiet corner and waiting for me whenever I choose to visit. And isn't that what a home town is all about anyway? Long live Mayberry: proud waves her banner in the sky."

MEN IN UNIFORM—When Gomer leaves town to join the Marines, he becomes Mayberry's most visible ambassador to the outside world.

C APPING A LANDMARK ERA
Season Five

$$\boxed{1964\text{-}1965}$$

The fifth season of *The Andy Griffith Show* is another one rich with classic episodes and the antics of Barney Fife. But it ends with a touch of sadness, as we say farewell to Barney as a regular character.

This season also sees the coming of age of Goober Pyle as he fills up the vacancy left by his cousin Gomer. Coby Ruskin directed the most episodes this year, although Howard Morris was also behind the camera for eight episodes, which is more than he acted in as Ernest T. Bass. Alan Rafkin, who would go on to become "TV's most prolific sitcom director" directed the first of his many *Andy Griffith Show* episodes this season.

The Andy Griffith Show finished its final black-and-white season ranked fourth in prime-time television ratings.

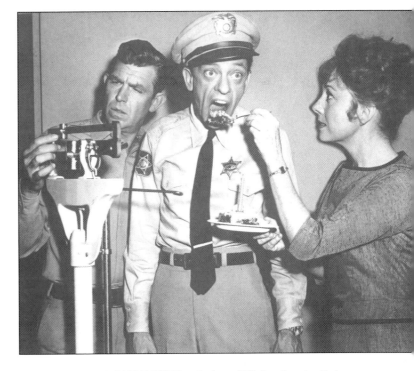

THE WEIGHT IS NOT OVER—*Andy and Thelma Lou try their best to help Barney gain weight. Through a clever chain of events, they will succeed. This photograph was taken during the filming of* "Barney's Physical" *on July 28, 1964.* COURTESY OF PHIL BOWLING COLLECTION.

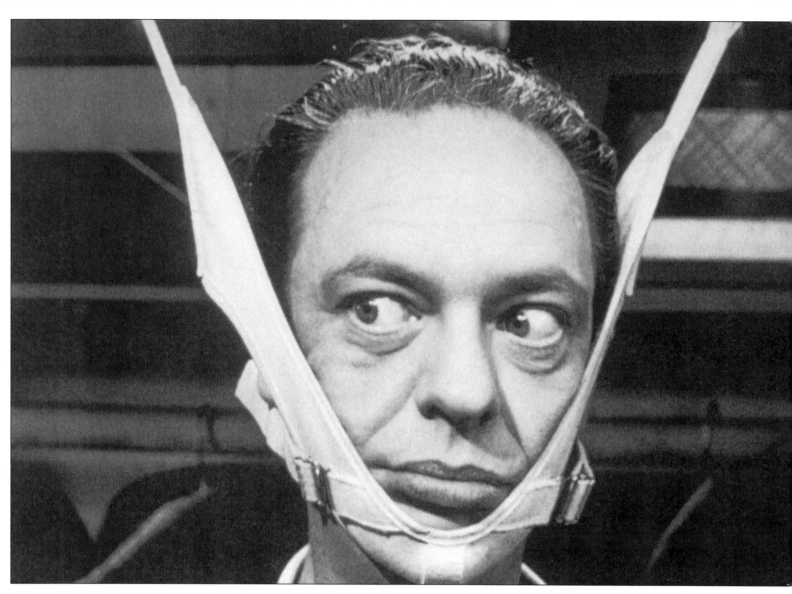

GOOD DAY FOR A-HANGIN'—*Not only does Barney have to gain weight to meet the new civil service requirements, but he also has to become taller. It's a stretch, but he's obviously braced for the challenge.*

FAMILY VISIT—*When Andy's Uncle Ollie (James Westerfield) and Aunt Nora (Maudie Prickett) come to stay with the Taylors, it's a wrenching experience. Of course, things might have been better for Ollie if Nora hadn't forgotten his goose down pillow. This photograph was taken during the filming of "Family Visit" on July 15, 1964.*

"Family Visit" director Howard Morris shares a memory about Ron Howard: "When I directed Ron Howard, he was ten years old. He was a kid. There was one scene where he was in the back of a car with four or five other people, and I said, 'Are you comfortable?' And he, said 'No.' I said, 'Get used to it, kid. That's what it's gonna be like for the rest of your life.' And I forgot that I said it, until maybe twenty years later we met under some circumstances. It may have been in the film *Splash*, but he quoted that line to me as if I had said a wise, wonderful thing, which is, 'You're gonna be uncomfortable as an actor for the rest of your life.'"

THE EDUCATION OF ERNEST T. BASS—*It's a proud day for everybody when Miss Crump awards Ernest T. a diploma "for learning."*

Don Knotts talks about Howard Morris: "As an actor, Howie's always funny. You can't tell what he's gonna do either. He's just remarkable—the way he could just wrap himself around you."

And Howard Morris talks about Don Knotts: "Having the joy and the voluptuous experience of knowing this incredible man and relating to him as a friend–he's wonderful, he's inspiring. The joy of working with him is a very special taste of life. It blows out into all kinds of detours and side roads. It's a wonder and a joy to be his friend and life would be less joyous without him."

EARNEST DISCUSSION—*Don Knotts and director Howard Morris discuss an upcoming scene in "Barney's Bloodhound." This photograph was taken on location at Franklin Canyon Reservoir (a.k.a. Myers Lake) on July 6, 1964, the first day of filming for the fifth season of the series.* COURTESY OF CBS PHOTO ARCHIVE.

Howard Morris likes the direction of Mayberry: "It was about people in real situations. You put two guys, Andy and Don, in two chairs on the front porch just talking, and you've got a wonderful, real scene. These two human beings relating to one another. And there is a sense of man's revelation to man. I don't mean one man to another, I mean Man in general. That's why one camera was better than three with all the business that goes with it, and you get involved in the technique of shooting rather than doing a scene. Aaron Ruben was absolutely right to insist on us being a one-camera show, and so was Andy."

NEAL AND PREY—*Escaped prisoner Ralph Neal (Arthur Batanides) makes his point with Barney in "Barney's Bloodhound."*

"Bloodhound" writer Bill Idelson gives his sense of Mayberry: "Andy was a big fan of the radio series *Vic & Sade* in which I played the part of Rush for twelve years. When I was on the set, Andy would occasionally lean over and say confidentially, 'You know what we're doing here, don'tcha Bill? *Vic & Sade*.' And actually, *The Andy Griffith Show* was highly reminiscent of the radio show. The low-key, off-the-cuff manner was much the same. The tolerant, amused perspective on the small-town folk mirrored *Vic & Sade* closely.

"I think the charm of *The Andy Griffith Show* was the fairy tale of a small town and its sheriff. Andy dispensed justice with mercy and sometimes love, recognizing the weakness and common humanity in us all."

MUGGING IN MAYBERRY—
Barney looks flushed as Fred Plummer (Allan Melvin) threatens him in "Barney's Uniform."

Allan Melvin, who played eight characters in six different seasons, talks about his time in Mayberry: "I didn't really play that many heavies in my career, but I was always a heavy on *Andy*. It seemed like I was on it more than I was. I always enjoyed doing that show. We had a lot of fun doing it. They were a great bunch. Andy and I hit it off right away. And between Andy and Aaron, I never for a moment felt like the 'new kid on the block.'"

THE DARLING BABY—*The Darling family returns to town looking to betroth baby Andelina to a Mayberry boy. If Opie's smart, he'll make himself disappear before it's too late. Meanwhile, the Darlings need to be careful not to play "Will You Love Me When I'm Old and Ugly?" because "that one makes the baby cry."*

Dillards bass player and raconteur Mitch Jayne: "Anything that lasts forty years in this fast-forward time of altering values is worth a celebration. We live in an age of replaceable parts. The things that we saw happen in Mayberry, however—funny and touching and endearing—were those irreplaceable moments in time that touch our hearts. It is to our credit that we haven't really tried to replace them, because Mayberry was, and is, somehow the best in all of us."

One of the touching moments in "The Darling Baby" is the Darlings singing "There Is a Time," a song written by Mitch Jayne and Rodney Dillard. Rodney comments: "The song speaks for itself. Mitch did a wonderful job and I helped. There are some things that you do that you don't realize are going to last forever."

"COUNT ISTVAN TELEKY EXISTS!"—*If only the Count had left fingerprints, Barney would be set. As it is, Barney still has all of the proof he needs that everything about the Count adds up. Goober and Floyd appear to be down for the Count, too, in "Three Wishes for Opie."* COURTESY OF CBS PHOTO ARCHIVE.

George Lindsey praises Don Knotts: "He's the best there is—the greatest character actor I think there has ever been in television and in motion pictures. Period."

Goober and Gilly are in the clutches of an argument:

GOOBER: Just keep your shirt on, Gilly. The way you treat this car, you're lucky it runs at all. Now, I've told you and I've told you.

GILLY: Well, don't tell me. Just fix it.

GOOBER: Gilly, you don't run a car fast all the time. You drive her slow ever now and then.

GILLY: Don't tell me how to drive, Goober.

GOOBER: Somebody ort to.

GILLY: Oh yeah?

GOOBER: Yeah.

GILLY: Well, don't you.

WALKER WANTS HIS CAR TO RUN BETTER—*Gilly Walker (Larry Hovis) sure likes to drive fast. As Goober says, "Speed, speed, speed. That's all he understands." Gilly won't be satisfied until "Goober Takes a Car Apart."*

Larry Hovis has no argument with Mayberry here: "I did two episodes. The first one was really fun for me. I was relatively new to L.A. I had been doing *Gomer Pyle*. I was offered this piece. I had a great time on the show.

"I remember everything and everyone very fondly. It was one of the quietest, most low-key sets I'd ever been on. They were a first-class organization all around–great people. George Lindsey and I kind of became friends out of that first episode, too. We really enjoyed working together. Over the years, I would see Ronny Howard because there would be these silly celebrity softball games. When Ronny was a kid, he loved baseball. I'd see him and we'd hang out and stuff like that.

"I just loved Howard McNear. He was ill by then. He had had his stroke. His wife would be there. She was so sweet. He was wonderful and I was just like walking on eggshells because I really revered him. He was a terribly unusual comic actor, one of the best ever. But he was so giving and so sweet to work with. [It is] one of those things for me that just gives me chills every time I think about it.

"Plugging into that show, you just became laid-back. You'd meet with Aaron Ruben and he's just a very quiet, nice, unassuming man, and very funny. A wonderful writer and a wonderful producer with writers. That's one of the reasons that I went to Hollywood. My wife and I would sit and watch *The Andy Griffith Show*. I loved it. I was an actor and a comic and a writer.

"If you ask anybody in Hollywood that did comedy during the '60s and '70s they're gonna talk about Aaron Ruben as being one of the really fine producer-writers. He understood script. He understood comedy. He understood character. He was uncompromising in getting it right.

"Andy himself is such a master in terms of acting and making it look easy. Very good actor, consummate professional. When everybody else is tired, Andy is still willing to work. He was really something. And he would take you aside and say, 'Just take it easy.' The part that was fun was when Andy and Don Knotts would sit around between takes and play guitar and sing hymns. It was like a family. Everyone was wonderful. This is one show you always give back to."

A DIFFERENT KIND OF BODY WORK—*Andy has points he wants to plug as he explains to Goober that he is about to tire of the garage sale going on in the Courthouse. When the shock wears off, Goober knows he had better get cranking if he doesn't want to get flattened.*

George Lindsey speaks about Andy Griffith: "Andy was the keeper of the flame. He would not let you be mediocre. In a word: genius."

Andy blows a gasket when he sees that Gilly's car is still in the Courthouse:

ANDY: Floyd, what are you doing up on that thing?

FLOYD: Well, I tell you, Andy. I just might buy this car. Goober thinks I might get it pretty cheaply. What do you think?

ANDY: Floyd, this isn't a used car lot. It's the Courthouse!

FLOYD: I know that. I realize that, Andy. But as long as the car was here.

GOOBER: Yeah, I could set it up in your front yard. You could watch me, Floyd.

FLOYD: Oh, I'd like that. You'd like that too, Andy. Oh, it's a beautiful thing to watch, just beautiful.

ANDY: Now Goober, I'm gonna get out of here, 'cause if I don't I'm liable to start hollering and when I get done hollering. I'm liable to take one of these guns out of this rack here and shoot you. Do you understand that?

GOOBER: Yo!

ANDY: Now, I'm going home. When I come back here in the morning, I want all traces of that car to be gone. You understand that?

GOOBER: Yes sir. I understand that. By tomorrow morning, you won't even know there's a car in here. I promise.

ANDY: You better keep that promise.

A story from George Lindsey about Howard McNear shows that life can indeed imitate art: "I was over at his house a lot. I believe I sold him a used car, a red Ford. We all know how good he was. He and I hit it off. He liked me and I liked him, not as actors but as buddies. I would go get him and go out with Helen and him to eat. It was a good feeling knowing him and working with him."

Hal Smith's wild ride: "It wasn't easy. I'd ridden horses for a long, long time. The shoulders on that cow came right to a point. I sat back as far as I could get and she'd take three steps and stop and I'd go brrrt...right up that backbone. That almost ruined me. It was just like riding a xylophone, and if you've ever ridden a xylophone, you know what I'm talking about."

BACK IN THE CORRAL—*Barney and Andy wrestle with Otis as "Old Paint" watches in "The Rehabilitation of Otis."*

HERD, THE NOOSE?—*Otis doesn't seem to mind that somebody apparently steered him wrong when buying a new horse. And would this be his new pony, too? This photograph was taken on November 24, 1964, during the filming of "The Rehabilitation of Otis."* COURTESY OF STEVE COX COLLECTION.

SPOKESMEN FOR MAYBERRY—*It looks as if Goober's mind might be on Lydia Crosswaith or maybe Maureen O'Sullivan ("she sure can swim"). Either way, Andy will have his work cut out for him in "Goober and the Art of Love."*

Fred Freeman, who, with Larry Cohen, wrote nine episodes, including "Goober and the Art of Love," talks about writing for the show: "It was one of the more satisfying shows. I did a lot of shows in the '60s–*Gilligan's Island*, *Dick Van Dyke*, *Bewitched*, etc. The reason it was satisfying was that we worked so hard. Bob Ross and Aaron Ruben were tough taskmasters, but fair. Getting stories was difficult. The emphasis was much more on character than on jokes.

"We'd sit in on the sessions and we'd all grab for what we thought were the best stories. Bob Ross would sometimes make us crazy. Just a stickler on points that we didn't think were important. But it was their show and we listened. If you listened, you learned.

"First comes the script, and then the actors take it. I always thought Andy was very smart and had terrific instincts. We came in after the show had been on for a while, so the stories get a little harder, but also the actors know their characters as good or better than the writers.

"Those things start at the top with Aaron Ruben and Andy. They were decent and reasonable and knew what they wanted. It's always a pleasure to work with anyone who knows what they want. It was just a great learning experience—that character is more important than the jokes. The jokes come naturally when you know the characters.

"The one that was fun to us was 'Goober and the Art of Love.' That was fun to watch it come out. I always remember one of the nicer moments was after we did 'Goober and the Art of Love,' and Jim Fritzell called and said how good he thought the show was.

"There are very rare occurrences in television history when the writing, casting, etc., come together–shows like *Van Dyke* or *Sgt. Bilko* or *Honeymooners*. They all came together. It was like one of those great chemistries. The *Griffith* show was one of the more satisfying experiences. It was tough. It took a long time to get a story and then to write it. And the rewrites were sometimes massive.

"But I always remember the one show that Larry Cohen and I did that, when we finished, we were embarrassed to hand it in because we thought it was so dull, and it was the one where we had no rewrite. It was called 'Aunt Bee on TV.' I thought it needed punching up."

"BLOODHOUND OF THE LAW, SNIFFING OUT CRIME"—*This was Barney's choice for a photo to use for his campaign poster when "Barney Runs for Sheriff."* COURTESY OF PHIL BOWLING COLLECTION.

Don Knotts talks about friend and "Barney Runs for Sheriff" director Alan Rafkin: "Alan directed *The Ghost and Mr. Chicken* and a couple after that. Alan was a wonderful director and very fast, he could move that camera around very fast. He was also a funny guy. Alan could make you laugh at the drop of a hat."

GEE, WHAT COULD POSSIBLY GO WRONG HERE?—*Multiple choice: A. The gun slides down the leg of Barney's pants; 2. Barney rips the seat of his pants trying to remove the gun; or C. Barney shoots the gun off through the seat of his pants. If you answered "all of the above," you win a trip to the "artistic weavers" in "If I Had a Quarter-Million."*

SPECIAL ORDER—*The steak dinner may not be all that gets pounded if Andy doesn't stop being so nice to "Guest in the House" Gloria.*

MAN IN THE MIDDLE—*We don't know about this, Ange. Helen still looks a little wary of Gloria (Jan Shutan).* COURTESY OF GILMORE-SCHWENKE ARCHIVES.

FRANK THE BOYFRIEND:
George Spence

One of the best examples of how even a momentary visit to Mayberry can inspire great depth is the eloquent storytelling of George Spence. His two lines spoken in Mayberry are, "Hi, Gloria" and "Bye." He gets to say more here: "I first met Andy Griffith in 1948 when I joined the cast of *The Lost Colony.* Andy, then a student at UNC, had joined the cast in 1947, the year in which a fire destroyed the entire stage area of the theater. At the time, I was a student at Wake Forest College and auditioned for *The Lost Colony* as a summer job, never realizing that I would become so enthralled with acting and the theater. Being a neophyte, I looked upon Andy and the rest of the Carolina Playmakers involved as 'professionals.'

"That first year for me introduced me to the theater. I was cast as Captain Amadas, a nonspeaking role, and a colonist, while Andy was playing the second soldier, a speaking role. If my memory serves me correctly, we were both in the show for five seasons. He went on to play the role of Sir Walter Raleigh, while I went on to play the role of Simon Fernando, the villain of the show. As these characters, we shared only one scene together.

"Andy was, and continues to be, a good friend whom I greatly respect, one who has always been cordial to me and one who was willing to open doors for me by paving the way for my first audition in Hollywood—on *The Andy Griffith Show.* Shortly after going to Hollywood in 1964, I received a call from Andy asking me if I wanted to come to the studio to meet his producer and casting director. Of course, I jumped at the opportunity, and a few weeks later I was featured with a young lady named Jan Shutan in 'Guest in the House.'

"Although only in two scenes, one of which is usually cut to make room for commercials, I was able to acquire my Screen Actors Guild card and the opportunity to move forward. Andy not only offered me this opportunity, he offered it to several other *Lost Colony* cast members as well. To me, that says a great deal about the man.

"My role in 'Guest in the House' was that of Frank, a young man who had broken up with his girlfriend. The young lady, Gloria, had gone to Mayberry to be consoled by Aunt Bee, her late mother's best friend. While there, she becomes infatuated with Andy, which makes Helen jealous. Realizing this, Andy calls Frank to come to Mayberry to reconcile with Gloria. So, in my first scene I am to walk into the room and speak Gloria's name. She sees me, rushes into my arms, and we kiss.

"I was casually introduced to Jan Shutan, an extremely attractive young lady, in the morning prior to her first scenes. Knowing that we had this kissing scene coming up and that I was doing my first stint in front of a camera on a major show, I was a bit nervous, to say the least. But, on the other hand, being a single male, I was attracted to the thought of having to kiss this beautiful lady. I thought to myself, 'I know I will have to kiss her at least five times as we rehearse the scene, due to my inexperience at performing before a camera.'

"When the time came, the director, a gentleman named Coby Ruskin, said that we would not rehearse the scene, 'Oh, well,' I thought, 'there goes five kisses down the tube. But I know I'll mess up the actual kiss and we'll have to do it at least ten times or more.' With the word 'action,' I walked through the door, uttered, 'Hi, Gloria,' and she raced into my arms and we kissed. 'Cut. That's a print,' said the director, as Andy, standing nearby, roared with laughter. As we walked back to the prop room, which they used as an after-shoot lounge, Andy said to me, 'That's the hardest type of scene to do on camera, a kissing scene, and you got it right the first time.' I turned to him and said, 'I've been kissing girls all of my life, Andy!'

"The other amusing thing that happened to me on that show involved a Cadillac. Although I was thirty-five years old at the time, I was not used to being associated with a rich man's car, a Cadillac. I was more used to a Ford or Chevy. Somewhat unsophisticated, I guess. Anyway, the scene called for Miss Shutan and me to be seated in the car, exchange some dialogue with Andy and Helen, start the white Cadillac convertible, and drive off into the sunset.

"I looked at the director prior to getting into the car and noticed that he had the gout in one foot. He was seated right next to the left rear wheel and had his foot extended dangerously close to the rear tire. I thought to myself that if I hit his foot I'd never work again in Hollywood. Thinking of the foot, I got into the car, we exchanged dialogue, and I went to start the car, but couldn't find the ignition. The director yelled 'Cut!' The second time, same procedure! I started the car and, thinking of the foot, ran the car into the right curb. The director yelled 'Cut!' Third take. Same procedure. I started the car and drove ahead ten yards. The director yelled 'Cut!' Success…I hadn't run over his foot! It took three takes to drive ten yards. The kiss was much easier and much more pleasant.

"As evidenced by the continuous reruns through the years, the ever-increasing fan support, and the love exhibited for the characters of Mayberry, *The Andy Griffith Show* has got to be the most memorable show ever produced on television. The small-town atmosphere, devoid of big-city crime and inhabited by people who cared for one another, offered the TV viewers a utopia to which they could retreat from the worries of the world at that time.

"As long as people wish to remember when there was no need to lock their doors at night, when porch-sitting at night was a satisfying means of passing time; when friends could exchange pleasantries at the local barbershop or Snappy Lunch, when hometown humor would bring a smile to every face, there will always be a Mayberry."

Author Richard Kelly offers this comment: "After these many years, Mayberry remains inviolate, a small town community that has enticed millions of visitors to its quaint neighborhood, where their dreams, laughter, and observations, like gentle ghosts, leave no trace of their having been there. The first and most important of all the dreamers, however, are men like Harvey Bullock and Everett Greenbaum. In the beginning was the word, and it was the wondrous words of the writers that breathed life into all the characters and created their comfortable world. The writers—these are the ghosts that haunt Mayberry to this day. They live in every syllable of every character and their elusive spirits can be found lurking anywhere from the pickle jars to the insufferable music of Leonard Blush."

WRITER'S CONFERENCE—*Writer Harvey Bullock and Andy Griffith examine a script on the* Griffith *set during the filming of "Guest in the House" in January 1965.*

OPIE'S NEWSPAPER—*Andy and Barney are not pleased when Opie and Howie Pruitt start publishing a newspaper filled with overheard gossip by adults.*

Dennis Rush (Howie Pruitt) files this report: "My least favorite episode was 'Barney Fife, Realtor.' This episode really confused me. I had been one of Opie's pals for a number of episodes. I had had a number of adventures with Andy, Opie, and all of the good folk of Mayberry. The trouble was that my character had been Howie Pruitt. For no explainable reason, my new name was Howie Williams. Had I been kidnapped? Was I recently adopted? No one really seemed bothered, so on with the show. Some of the dialogue was awkward. Andy and Aunt Bee came to visit the Williams's house to see about buying it. My father introduced me to Andy like we had never met. This really seemed strange and just one of those quirks that puts me in the Mayberry

trivia of mistakes that we all love to catch.

"My last episode was 'Opie's Newspaper.' We had fun catching all of the gossip in Mayberry and producing our version of 'Mayberry After Midnight.' I was a few years older than Ron, and I think the difference began to show. He needed some new pals, so it was time for me to move on. I hated leaving Mayberry, but I loved every minute I had there.

"Five years later, I was in the Marines and was stationed temporarily in North Carolina. Yes, I did go looking for Mayberry. Mt. Pilot was as close as I could get. We all know Mayberry didn't really exist, but it's funny how all of us still want to believe it did."

"HELLO, DOLL!"—*When Daphne and Skippy come flying through town in their jalopy, Andy and Barney try hard not to make "The Arrest of the Fun Girls," but to no avail. As if it hadn't been enough of a circus the last time by having to deal with the fun girls together with Gomer and Goober, this time Otis stumbles onto the scene.*

"Opie Flunks Arithmetic" was the last episode for Don Knotts as a regular cast member. He reflects on his time as part of the cast: "That experience was the greatest for me in the business. It was almost like that's what I was here for. It was five years that was just so good. It's hard to describe what it's like for an actor to be that involved in a project that creative and that much fun. It was just really fun to do. I couldn't wait to go to work in the morning. It was just great. Not only the work but the camaraderie we had as a company and the fun we had off camera. It was a joy. Andy was responsible for a lot of that."

SEATED, BUT OUTSTANDING—*Aaron Ruben and Don Knotts always sit well with Andy Griffith. After the fifth season, Andy and Mayberry would continue without the daily creative input of these two talented friends.* COURTESY OF AARON RUBEN.

END OF SEASON GRIN—*"Opie Flunks Arithmetic" aired during the week of this TV Guide in 1965. TV GUIDE FURNISHED BY JOEL RASMUSSEN COLLECTION. REPRINTED WITH PERMISSION FROM TV GUIDE MAGAZINE GROUP, INC., PUBLISHER OF TV GUIDE MAGAZINE; COPYRIGHT © VOLUME 13, ISSUE 17, 1965, TV GUIDE INC. TV GUIDE IS A TRADEMARK OF TV GUIDE MAGAZINE GROUP, INC.*

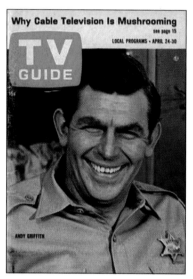

TRYING TO PATCH A *HOLE?*—*Many folks have speculated that it was intended that Jerry Miller (Jerry Van Dyke) would become the new permanent deputy after Barney moved to Raleigh. In the real world, that may not have been the case. According to Richard O. Linke, associate producer of the show and personal manager at the time for both Andy Griffith and Jerry Van Dyke, "Jerry was never supposed to be a replacement. We used him in that episode for his talent, but he was never considered for that job." This photograph was taken on March 22, 1965, during the filming of "Banjo-Playing Deputy."* COURTESY OF RICHARD HELLMERS COLLECTION.

Aaron Ruben reflects on working with Andy Griffith: "Andy Griffith was the ideal star to work with—thoroughly professional, never contentious, and never temperamental. A brilliant actor, he knew his craft and his own capabilities better than anyone. It was Andy who decided he could not be the funny character he played in *No Time for Sergeants*. It was Andy who made Barney and Floyd and Gomer, etc., that much funnier. And it was Andy's totally unselfish attitude that enriched the show. Often he would say, 'Give that line to Don. He'll be funnier.'

"Actors would tell me how much they enjoyed doing the show and would I please have them come back. The reason being that the star establishes the atmosphere of the set. The *Griffith Show* stage was always calm and warm and friendly. And often while waiting for a scene to be set up, Andy and Don would harmonize on some of their favorite hymns, or Andy would play the guitar and be accompanied by Lee Greenway (our makeup man) on the banjo. As was the case with Sheldon, there was never any argument over scripts. Differences were reasoned out, and Andy's input was invaluable. After all, I think there was hardly a writer on the show who was from the South.

"That was another of Andy's admirable qualities, his respectful and appreciative attitude towards the writers. He gave me five wonderful years and was a joy to work with. He was and remains to this day my dear friend."

And Griffith says it all: "Don Knotts is the finest comic actor I've ever known. Doing that show with Don was like getting up to go home. It was the best five years of my life."

BIG BARN—*This is likely the most reproduced color image of Barney Fife in history. But there's a reason that it is, so here it is one more time. Whatever the future holds for this Mayberry favorite, he'll always look nervous about it.*

WHAT IT IS, IS FOOTBALL—*During the summer break between filming seasons in the 1960s, Andy Griffith and Ronny Howard participated in the Ottawa Exhibition in Canada. They're seen here playing ball with members of the Ottawa Rough Riders football team.* COURTESY OF JOHN O'QUINN.

DEEP IN THOUGHT—*Maybe Goober, Floyd, and Andy are contemplating the transition from a world where everything is black and white to one…*

…ALIVE WITH COMIC COLOR—*In reality, the three are discussing Opie's chances of winning the contest for the new job at Mr. Doakes' grocery store. This photograph was taken during the filming of "Opie's Job" on July 7, 1965.*

COLORFUL TIMES
Season Six

$$1965\text{-}1966$$

There were major changes in *The Andy Griffith Show* at the opening of its sixth season. Two are easily seen: the series is now in color and Barney Fife has left Mayberry for the "concrete jungle" of Raleigh.

Behind the scenes, after producer Aaron Ruben left to work full time as executive producer of *Gomer Pyle, U.S.M.C.*, Bob Ross stepped in as producer, a position he would continue to hold through the end of the series. He would go on to create and produce *Mayberry R.F.D.*

The new season introduces two new significant Mayberry characters—new deputy Warren Ferguson and county clerk Howard Sprague. And it sees the last of two of its favorite friends, Ernest T. Bass and Malcolm Merriweather.

The season also travels afar as Andy, Opie, and Aunt Bee make a three-episode excursion to the bright lights of Hollywood. And one favorite son of Mayberry also returns. Barney Fife comes home for a

visit of his own. It is a bittersweet occasion as he discovers that his longtime sweetheart Thelma Lou has moved away and married, though she, too, returns for a visit.

For his efforts, Don Knotts won his fourth Emmy for outstanding performance by an actor in a supporting role in a comedy for "The Return of Barney Fife." For the season, *The Andy Griffith Show* was the sixth highest ranked series in TV's prime time ratings.

George Lindsey shares thoughts about his fellow cast members: "They all were a joy to work with, mainly because they came to work. They all knew their words and they were all excited about working. Sometimes we would come to the set when Howard McNear was working because he was so good. I think everybody appreciated everyone else's talent."

PRIME CUT—*Andy is a happy customer at Floyd's shop...but maybe a little of that happiness comes from his impression that Opie is doing so well at his new grocery job.* COURTESY OF JOEL RASMUSSEN COLLECTION.

GO FIGURE—*After he fires Ernest T. from his beloved job manning the school crossing, Andy warns Ernest T. not to throw any more rocks, which of course is what got Ernest T. fired in the first place. Ernest T. nods to Andy's request.*

BRICK...HOUSE...CRASH!—*Unfortunately, when Andy warned Ernest T. about throwing rocks, he "didn't say nothing about no brick."*

BENCHED—*With Ernest T. more or less grounded after losing his crosswalk job, Andy apparently knows that he needs to guard this wall made of potential Ernest T. ammo. Goober and Floyd seem to know to keep an eye on Ernest T., too. As for Ernest T., he's watching Malcolm Merriweather do his old job.*

Howard Morris talks about his Mayberry connections: "*The Andy Griffith Show* to me, in my head, is on a par with *Your Show of Shows*, which was an incredible experience—where I found my legs as a performer of fair importance. I blossomed because of working with people like Sid Caesar and Imogene Coca and all the people along the way, and Andy and Don and all the folks of Mayberry. In my head it is tied in directly with that experience."

MALCOLM AT THE CROSSROADS—*"There comes a time when a man has to fight. And if remaining in Mayberry means fighting Mr. Bass, that is it."*

FABLED POLITICIAN RETURNS HOME—*Retiring Congressman John Canfield (Charles Ruggles) visits with Opie while waiting for his date with "Aunt Bee, the Swinger."*

WARREN GETS THE CALL—*Andy hires Floyd's nephew Warren Ferguson as Mayberry's new deputy, "know what I mean, huh-huh-huh?" (Please don't get him or us started!)*

BAZAAR SITUATION—*With hands full, Aunt Bee gives eager deputy Warren an earful about his being a stickler on bingo regulations for "The Bazaar."*

Ruta Lee enjoyed her two episodes on the show: "Lee Greenway (the makeup man) and Andy were practically a comedy team in themselves. Coming into makeup was more fun than going to a nightclub performance. They would carry on. Andy would do the devout preacher—doing the revival preacher man doing his thing, saying, 'O.K., now folks, we've saved your soul (have you got the Cadillac warmed up, is it ready to roll?).' Andy and Lee would do this number and it was just hysterical.

"It was fun to be able to be a part of this wonderful silliness that was so sweet and loving. None of it was vulgar. And when they had me, who laughed, I was always a tremendous audience.

"I'm so grateful to the Almighty that He gave us a gift like Andy Griffith, who came to us by way of Broadway and by way of film before he did the series. How wonderful a blessing God gave us that we have not just this man, Andy Griffith, and his talent, but this compilation of actors and performers that were part of this wonderful *Andy Griffith Show* that will be with us forever. I think that everybody who worked on that show will agree that it was a tiny touch of the angels around our shoulders and tickling our noses to make us laugh and tickling our funny bones and tickling our hearts, and that's God's blessing on all of us."

George Lindsey shares memories of Lee Greenway: "Lee was more of a mentor to me. He would tell you little things to do that would help get you noticed. But he loved pranks, too. If a new actor came on, Lee would make him up and ask him to slip his left shoe off. The guy would never ask why he had to take his shoe off. We would all be watching from behind the curtain and falling down laughing."

A CLOSE MATCH—*Helen can never stay mad at Andy for too long. They always make up.*

INSPECTOR, GADGET—*Andy shows Goober the walkie-talkie that allowed Spot to seem so smart (he really is, you know). This photograph was taken during the filming of "A Man's Best Friend" on September 21, 1965.*

Art Baer, who wrote seven episodes (including "A Man's Best Friend") with Ben Joelson, describes the procedure they followed for their writing on the show:
"My late partner, Ben Joelson, and I were living in New York City when we were writing the show and never visited the set. We would go to Los Angeles for story meetings with Sheldon Leonard, Aaron Ruben, and Bob Ross; do a detailed outline; and then go back home, write the first draft, and mail it in. Usually, Bob would call with whatever changes they wanted us to make and we'd do a second draft, which, except for some tinkering, was pretty much the final draft.

"Fortunately, Andy would sometimes sit in on the meetings, giving us the opportunity to meet him. He was a very positive voice in these sessions—encouraging, insightful, and creative."

Betty Lynn, whose twenty-sixth and final appearance as Thelma Lou on the show was in "The Return of Barney Fife," talks about her time in Mayberry:
"It's been an amazing thing that people still love the show. We all love it. I love to watch it. I laugh just as hard as I did the first time. I'm so grateful that I could be a part of it. People seem to appreciate it forever. I hope they always will. I feel a great love for it."

FINE ART WORK—*Writer Art Baer and Andy Griffith participate in a meeting to discuss script ideas for upcoming episodes.* COURTESY OF ART BAER.

PERFECT COUPLES—*It may take a few more years than planned, but it's certain that Mayberry's legendary couples will indeed be together and live happily ever after.*

Don Knotts shares a thought about a dear friend: "Betty Lynn's wonderful to work with. You couldn't have a nicer gal to work with. She's just great and a fine actress. She could do anything they gave her to do."

A LIVING LEGEND—*Warren can't believe he's getting the chance to work with his hero, Barney Fife. The fittings may be loose on the fuel pump for Barney's Edsel that Goober's holding, but Barney himself will always be a tight fit for Mayberry. This photograph was taken during the filming of "The Legend of Barney Fife" on November 29, 1965.*

When asked about his own teen years, Jack Dodson, once stated: "I *was* Howard Sprague." And when asked by the producers if he could play a county clerk who had allergies and lived with his mother, Jack responded, "Yes! I've got the sniffles right now."

Jack Dodson described his approach to Howard Sprague: "I didn't seek to make Howard be a particular way. I conformed myself to the character that was created for me, but at the same time, the producers and Andy and I all worked to create Howard together. He was kind of a sitcom character with definite boundaries. The writers elaborated things I had done well, and there was very much of an exchange of ideas and suggestions. The character just kind of grew out of that exchange."

(Richard) Keith Thibodeaux, whose last episode as Johnny Paul Jason was "Look Paul, I'm Dancing," reflects well on Mayberry: "It takes us back to a time when things were slower and things were a little bit more real. Nowadays, we live in such a fast-paced society. Everybody wants information at the drop of a hat, but *The Andy Griffith Show* was like a long, southern summer out at the lake—that kind of feeling you never want to leave."

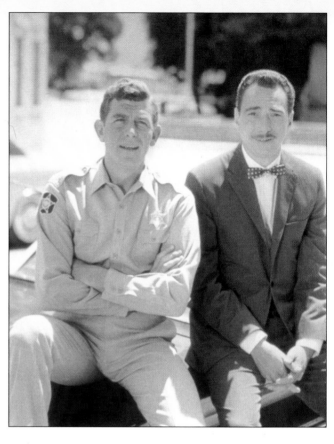

MAYBERRY SUITS HOWARD SPRAGUE—*Howard Sprague must have been keeping his nose pretty close to the grindstone for all those years when he's never seen, but all of the sudden he becomes "one of the fellas," working shoulder to shoulder with Andy.*

THE TWAIN SHALL MEET—*There's no telling how often Floyd and Andy might have sat here over the years and talked about whether Calvin Coolidge might have said one thing or another. You might say, "Everybody complains about the* whether, *but nobody does anything about it." You know who said that?*

George Lindsey describes his admiration for Howard McNear: "We would show up early to watch Howard McNear do a scene. He was phenomenal. I loved doing scenes with him. You knew he was going to steal it, but it didn't matter because he was so good. He took a hesitation in a sentence and made it into a whole play. He was a good guy to work with. He never was mad, he never was angry, and he never was upset. He really enjoyed being Floyd."

TV GUIDE

A TRUE 'BATMAN' ESCAPE: THE ACTOR WHO CAME BACK

see page 12

LOCAL PROGRAMS • JUNE 4-10
15¢

Andy Griffith

John Oszustowicz shares his thoughts: "To me, *The Andy Griffith Show* means:

* Being warm, safe, and happy with my family on a cold winter Monday night watching Mayberry come to life on a fifteen-inch black-and-white TV
* Being able to solve most of life's problems by wondering, 'What would Andy do?'
* Sitting on the front porch counting cars
* Being greeted by strolling townsfolk
* Searching for the goodness in people
* Knowing that the best of us are as loyal as Goober, as compassionate as Aunt Bee, as human as Barney, as incorruptible as Floyd, and as wise as Andy
* Truly believing that Mayberry was not a fictional town on television, but a dream of civility, friendship, and simple living that we can wish on our children"

THINGS ARE LOOKING UP—*An all-around special group gathers for Mayberry's seventh season.*

CONTINUING ADVENTURES
Season Seven

1966-1967

Though *The Andy Griffith Show* reached its highest Nielsen ratings to date this season, it is also a season of several important lasts. Most notable is the final work of the greatly beloved Howard McNear as Floyd the Barber and of Hal Smith as Otis Campbell. Like Barney Fife, no one could replace Floyd and there certainly would be no doubles for Otis.

The Darlings also roll into town on their truck one last time this season. A sign of changing times is that Charlene, not Briscoe, is behind the wheel, when we last see the Darlings driving out of Mayberry. More power to 'em.

Meanwhile, Opie finds a new best friend in Arnold Bailey, played by Sheldon Golomb (Collins). Andy pays a visit to Barney Fife, and (bread and butter) Barney makes a visit to Mayberry.

Don Knotts earned his fifth Emmy for his work in "Barney Comes to Mayberry." Also winning an Emmy for this season's work was Frances Bavier, who received the award for outstanding performance by an actress in a supporting role in a comedy. For the year, the show ranked third in the ratings.

POP, POP; FIZZ, FIZZ—*What a relief it is that Opie and Helen's niece, Cynthia (Mary Ann Durkin), are getting along so well. It would sure be a black eye for Mayberry if they didn't. This photograph was taken during the filming of "Opie's Girlfriend" on June 20, 1966.*

MAYBE WE SPOKE TOO SOON—*Things are more rocky for Cynthia and Opie than they appeared at first glance. Lee Philips, director of the entire seventh season, is refereeing the bout and seems well-prepared for the glare of Andy's son's shiner.* COURTESY OF CBS PHOTO ARCHIVE.

LODGING A COMPLAINT— *Not willing to gamble with Howard's well-being, Keeper of the Door Goober bars the genteel county clerk from the Regal Order of the Golden Door to Good Fellowship (a.k.a. "The Lodge").*

"HIT ONE FOR THE OLD GOOBER!"—*"The Ball Game" is on the line for the Mayberry Giants against the Mt. Pilot Comets when Opie comes to bat.*

A FACE IN THE CROWD—*This familiar face around Mayberry is known by the names Judd Fletcher, Jud, Burt, Old Man Crowley, Old Geezer, Old Man, and Sam Benson, but in reality "he's Burt Mustin." He eases his way around fourteen episodes in six of the first seven seasons (missing the fourth) and even resurfaces as Harvey Benson in the third season of* Mayberry R.F.D.

Rance Howard talks about his favorite episodes and the whole "Ball Game":
"Most of them are terrific and to pick episodes is very difficult. I would have to say episodes like 'Opie the Birdman,' 'Mr. McBeevee,' and 'The New Housekeeper' were terrific, very memorable. Then there's Aunt Bee's pickles. And I like the one that I created, 'The Ball Game.' I thought it was a pretty powerful episode.

"Andy is a champion of the underdog. He knew that I was a writer and an actor. I was trying to write and submit story lines. I submitted one that they actually bought. 'The Ball Game' was based on a true incident. I had told Andy the story. He said. 'That's really good. You ought to go in and pitch that to Bob Ross.' So I pitched the story to Bob Ross, and Bob didn't just take to it immediately. He was pretty cool. So time went on and I ran into Andy. He said, 'Did you pitch that story to Bob?' I said, 'Yeah. I did' And Andy asked, 'What happened?' I told him the story, and he kind of nodded his head and said, 'I'm gonna talk to Bob.'

"A short time later I got a message to come in and talk to Bob again. That's when he said, 'O.K., I'm gonna give you an assignment to write this but with the understanding that after you write it, we may have to bring another writer in.' So I did write it and I've got to tell you it was a good script, but Bob was an old Hollywood writer. He had a tendency to be a little 'clique-ish.' I got word right away that Sid Morse would do a rewrite. So Sid did a rewrite. I know him. He is a good writer. I probably could have garnered a screenwriting credit, but I had told Bob I wouldn't do that. So they gave me story credit and Sid screen credit. Through that, I was able to join the Writers' Guild."

YOU MAKE THE CALL—*When the dust settles after umpire Andy calls Opie "out" at home plate, Andy finds out that Opie isn't the only one who won't be safe at home for a while. This photograph was taken on June 26, 1966, during the filming of "The Ball Game."* COURTESY OF CBS PHOTO ARCHIVE.

Ron Howard talks about his favorite episode: "'The Ball Game' was the closest thing to real autobiography that I experienced on *The Andy Griffith Show* because I didn't live in a small town like Opie did—like Mayberry. I didn't have the run of the town. I was growing up in a city. It was a much different way of life. Life around Mayberry was kind of idyllic. There were certain moments and scenes that I could relate to, but it was pretty much another world, kind of a better world, but another world. With 'The Ball Game' episode, it was drawn from this experience that I had had with my dad, and I was proud of him that he wrote it up and sold the show and that they were making the episode. Plus, I got to play baseball for a day when we were filming, so all those things converged to make it a really happy memory for me."

ALL KEYED UP—*The looks on the faces of the Darling boys (left to right: Dean, Rodney, Doug, and Mitch) speak volumes as they, along with Briscoe and Charlene, enjoy a final visit with Aunt Bee.*

Though they aren't known for saying much in Mayberry (in fact, they speak just those very few amenities when thanking Aunt Bee for the nice meal in the jail during their first visit), that doesn't mean the boys weren't thinking. Mitch Jayne speaks now for the Darling boys: "The informality of *The Andy Griffith Show* set was its charm, and at the same time, its illusion, because, while a visitor felt the friendly, laid-back 'personality' of the place (largely due to Andy), it was a set where everything got done efficiently.

"Like the actors themselves, the crew knew what was expected of them and didn't waste anyone else's time. I got the feeling from watching these experienced people, that Andy Griffith's professionalism was the key to everything. Since he never complained, never carped or made excuses, neither did anyone else. There is something really inspiring about watching someone who is good-humoredly doing the very best he can at work he's good at. I always had the impression that people who worked with Andy could do no less. It was a happy set, because we were all happy in our own ways, to be part of anything that good."

Rance Howard talks about good friend and longtime neighbor Denver Pyle: "He was so good in that character and his family was so wonderful that they could have become a series themselves. I'm surprised that, between Andy and Danny Thomas and Aaron Ruben, they didn't do a spin-off called 'The Darlings.'"

Rodney Dillard speaks about Denver Pyle and all of Mayberry: "Denver gave me a lot of insight into how television and acting worked. He was a wonderful person and a friend. Denver was always an idea man. He was a very good man. I liked him a lot and I miss him.

"I think we all carry a little piece of Mayberry in our hearts, and I think this country needs a Mayberry philosophy, an attitude. It was not a mean-spirited show, one that got laughs on being mean-spirited, which is in contrast to what

happens today, when so much is mean-spirited and there is no connection with people. *The Andy Griffith Show* reflected traditional family values–and values that I think are beginning to fade in these years. I think we need something like that to hold on to."

And adds big brother Doug Dillard: "Mayberry is my home away from home. It seems like the town that I grew up in. That's where I'm coming from."

While speaking of the Darlings, it is probably a good time for a few more words from music director Earle Hagen: "I know from my standpoint, I never worked on a show that I enjoyed more or had a better time. It was eight years of good product, good relationships, and a chance to cover a broad spectrum of comedy

as well as dramatic music. Incidentally, the dubbing and presence of music is as good on the *Griffith* show as it ever got in TV. Jimmy Stewart (not the actor but the sound mixer) handled dialogue and music; when one didn't predominate, the other did. Andy Griffith is the total professional and fun to work with as well as be around. Andy Griffith, one of the good guys."

Hal Smith, whose last episode was this season's "Otis the Deputy," once said about his years on the show: "It was such a fun show to do. Everybody liked everybody else on that show and we had a great crew. The writers we had were so fantastic that anything they wrote was funny. The *Griffith* show was just a thing you could find in any little town anywhere."

"THE THINKER"—Helen and the rest of Mayberry are less than pleased when "Goober Makes History" with the brains that he thinks he has grown on his face. Or as Goober puts it: "It seems like the me that is really me and was being held back by the I that I am is coming out all over my face." Whatever happens, don't let him see a microphone, or he might have the whole world suffering with his "zingers" and brilliant doctrines.

LOOKING SMALL, BUT THINKING BIG—*After his cowboy days as quiet Leon, Clint Howard visits Andy Griffith and brother Ronny on the set. But bear in mind, gentle Clint soon has giant things ahead for himself with his own TV show in the Florida Everglades. This photograph was taken on August 1, 1966, during the filming of "Goober Makes History."*

Rance Howard talks about his experience with the show: "I am very grateful to have been associated with the show to the extent which I was, to have known Andy and Don, to have been a part of such a powerful piece of entertainment, and above all that our son Ron was fortunate enough to sort of 'get in with that group.' I think that it was a very formative experience and life for Ron. I think he just learned immensely—beyond trying to numerate what he took from that show in knowledge.

"My goodness, it provided an education in show business, in acting, in writing, in directing. I'm thankful for Ron that he left *The Andy Griffith Show* with that in his head. I'm very grateful for Ron that he had that experience. It has been such an important part of my life. Sheldon Leonard, Aaron Ruben—listening to those guys and being able to talk with them. It's been just invaluable to me having been kind of in the atmosphere of guys like Andy and Don and Frances. And Sheldon and Aaron—both of those guys contributed highly to the show, but not beyond what Andy did. Andy was the guardian. Andy was the guy, he was the center, he was the focus, and he was the guy who kept everyone honest.

"Andy is a very instinctive actor–an instinctive person. He listens to his instincts and abides by them. He knew those people and he knew the country, the small towns, and that's the story that was told. I feel that it provided kind of a guideline for America. Mayberry was a place that everyone would like to go to, and I think they held the show in very high esteem. And people still do. I think that speaks so well for the show."

FANNING OUT—*Something tells us that this particular Mikado might make a very fine small-town sheriff someday.* COURTESY OF RICHARD O. LINKE.

Floyd has ideas of about what the kids should do for "The Senior Play":

FLOYD: Music! Oh, I like that. Say, you know what they ought to do?

ANDY: What?

FLOYD: Talk Helen into doing *The Mikado.* Oh, it's beautiful.

GOOBER: *The Mikado?* What's that?

FLOYD: That's the play we did when I was in high school. And I was in it.

GOOBER: I didn't know you was an actor, Floyd.

Floyd beams.

GOOBER: And you was in the dramatic club?

FLOYD: The backbone.

GOOBER: *The Mikado,* huh?

FLOYD: Oh, it's a wonderful play. Lots of ginger.

GOOBER: What's it about?

FLOYD: Well, it all took place in this little town called Titipu.

GOOBER: Come on, Floyd, be serious.

FLOYD: Well, I *am* being serious. This is in Japan and the Lord High Executioner was Ko-Ko. And there was these two other fellows. There was Pooh-Bah and Pish-Tush.

GOOBER: Look Floyd, if you don't want to tell it.

FLOYD: Well, I *am* telling you.

GOOBER: Hah!

FLOYD: Do you want to hear this or not?

GOOBER: Go ahead.

FLOYD: Well, all right. Now there was another fellow too, and he was a sort of a wandering guitar player. He was in love with Yum-Yum and his name was Nanki-Poo.

GOOBER: Nanki-Poo!

FLOYD (to Andy): Why don't you talk her into doing it?

ANDY: Well, I would, but they already started something else.

FLOYD: Yeah, but the songs are so beautiful. Oh, they'd be…listen:

FLOYD (singing): A wandering minstrel I, a thing of shreds and patches, of ballad's song and snatches, and a dreamy lullaby.

(He continues singing).

ANDY: Listen, Floyd, I got to go!

FLOYD: I haven't finished.

ANDY: Oh, I loved it up to that.

Andy leaves. Goober sits down next to Floyd, eager to hear the song.

GOOBER: More, Floyd, more.

TUCKERED OUT?—*Through "a triumph of science over animal cunning," novice fisherman Howard Sprague lands elusive silver carp Old Sam at Tucker's Lake, but the finned legend will no doubt live to rule these very waters once again as the "Big Fish in a Small Town."*

According to George Lindsey's description of Jack Dodson, maybe Howard Sprague came by his "triumph of science" naturally: "I thought Jack was an actor like an engineer. He took his dialogue apart and stacked it up like you were building a house. He was a technician. He was a good guy."

SEEN YOUR BARBER LATELY?— *Perhaps Floyd thinks camouflage will help him catch Old Sam by surprise. Howard McNear is obviously enjoying this silly moment. Trying to wiggle out of any role as an instigator, George Lindsey, famous for such get-ups, finally admits, "Well, O.K., maybe it was me. Who else would have done that?" This photograph was taken during the filming of "Big Fish in a Small Town" on August 8, 1966.* COURTESY OF CBS PHOTO ARCHIVE.

GOOB EATS—*Little does Andy suspect that "Dinner at Eight" is going to mean three different meals in one night. Correction: make that "separate" meals, because there's very little difference in Andy's dinners, all of which even have the same secret ingredient.*

DOLLY, DOLLY—*Opie seems almost to be stuck like glue (sorry, poor choice of words) to Dolly, the loyal old horse who loves to pull Walt Simpson's milk wagon. Not to worry, it won't be "Goodbye Dolly" with everybody in Mayberry pulling (and pushing) for her.*

"BEEP-BEEP! OUTTA THE WAY, SUNDAY DRIVER"—*Ronny and Clint Howard are intent in their playing with this toy race track. Of course, with just the one car on the track, you have to use your imagination about how the race is going. Even so, clearly these two have been raised to enjoy sharing.*

TV SET—*Andy Griffith and Aneta Corsaut represented Mayberry on the cover of* TV Guide *in 1967. Aneta described the seventh season's "Helen, the Authoress" as her favorite of the episodes that she was in: "Generally, I liked the ones best where Andy and I got to fuss with each other. We got to scratch at each other, which was fun."* TV GUIDE FURNISHED BY JOEL RASMUSSEN COLLECTION. REPRINTED WITH PERMISSION FROM TV GUIDE MAGAZINE GROUP, INC., PUBLISHER OF *TV GUIDE MAGAZINE*; COPYRIGHT © VOLUME 15, ISSUE 20, 1967, TV GUIDE INC. *TV GUIDE* IS A TRADEMARK OF TV GUIDE MAGAZINE GROUP, INC.

Production Manager Frank E. Myers discussed his seven seasons working on the show: "It was the highlight of my career. They were my happiest years because of the high caliber of both creative and performing artists under the Thomas and Leonard banner. And working with Sheldon Leonard, Aaron Ruben, Dick Linke, and the rest of the guys was just great. And all the great writers, the root of any series success. Wonderful people. Those were happy days!"

BEE YOUNGER—*Frances Bavier around 1930.*

Don Knotts: "We had a wonderful cast. There was not a weak actor in it, and Frances came across as an old pro. She was just great, and she just made Aunt Bee a lovable character."

PEARLS OF WISDOM—*Beginning to look more like Mayberry's Bee, Frances Bavier is seen here around the early 1940s.* COURTESY OF GILMORE-SCHWENKE ARCHIVES.

STILL CLOSER—*Frances Bavier in approximately the early 1950s.*

GLAMOROUS POSE—*Not quite Aunt Bee, but close.*
COURTESY OF PHIL BOWLING COLLECTION.

Rance Howard remembers Frances Bavier: "Frances always had a pleasant good morning and a pleasant good night and she loved theater and she loved acting. I think in the business she was probably underestimated. Probably given other circumstances, Frances could have been a huge film star, but she didn't go that way. I think she did very well. Just a fine, fine artist."

BEE-'67...BINGO!—*Our Aunt Bee! Frances Bavier won an Emmy for her portrayal of Aunt Bee during the show's seventh season.*

Jim Nabors: "I'm sorry Frances is not around. She was very dear to me. She was a great help to me, and we became good personal friends. I heard from her right before she died. She wrote me a little note. She had a way with words. It was a cute card, quite personal. I'll never forget it. It was the last time I heard from her. She said, 'My dearest Jim, I was just wondering where you are and how you are. What you are is quite wonderful.'"

George Lindsey has fond memories of Frances Bavier and Hope Summers: "Frances and I got along well, Frances liked me. I would always be in her trailer talking to her. Hope was almost like my surrogate mother on the set. If I had any problems, I could talk to Hope, and Hope would rub the back of my neck where the tension was. She was like a mom to me on the set. I never saw her show any negative emotions about anything. Hope was my Aunt Bee."

Neal Brower shares his feelings: "Andy, Barney, Opie, and the other citizens of Mayberry are more than television characters. Over the past forty years, they have become my friends. I've often wondered why I wasn't a *Star Trek* fan or a diehard watcher of *The Honeymooners*. For some reason I never connected with those shows. *The Andy Griffith Show* was different. Its characters, setting, story lines, and humor touched something deep within me…and I knew I had found 'my' show."

BEE FRIEND, A NEIGHBOR—*And let's not forget Clara Edwards (Hope Summers).*

FATHER AND SON TEAM—*As the eighth year of the adventures of Mayberry starts, the strong backbone is still the relationship between Andy and Opie.*

OVER THE RAINBOW
Season Eight

$$1967\text{-}1968$$

The *Andy Griffith Show* introduces the world to several solid citizens during its final season. First Emmett Clark (joined soon by wife Martha) opens his Fix-It Shop where Floyd's Barbershop had held forth. Next, Millie Hutchins starts working behind the counter at Boysinger's Bakery. We also meet farmer Sam Jones and son Mike. This foursome would be among the main cast for the spin-off *Mayberry R.F.D.* the following season.

There are a couple of more episodes set away from Mayberry as Aunt Bee and her friends tour Mexico, and for a short time Howard Sprague checks out the good life on a Caribbean island.

Barney pays one last visit to Mayberry in "Barney Hosts a Summit Meeting," which ended up being the single highest-rated episode of *The Andy Griffith Show*. That achievement contributed to another fitting milestone for *The Andy Griffith Show*: the series completed its final season as the top-rated show in prime time. The Nielsen ratings had, at last, caught up with where millions of our hearts had already been for eight years.

Ron Howard reflects on eight golden years: "I say, above all, that I am grateful to Andy. Not only did he play the central role—not only as an actor but as a creative influence on the show that laid the foundation for my career—but I also think that the tone that he helped establish on the show, the working style, is something that I've adopted and benefited from throughout my life and my career. It's a balance between real dedication and joy in working in this kind of creative field. So there was a lot of laughter on the set, and at the same time, hand in hand with that laughter, was very good work being done on a consistent basis. Anything less than 100 percent effort would just never fly—not because he would start yelling, but because simply that wasn't the way we worked on the show. It was never lazy, never that feeling of a tired, old show and nobody's really paying that much attention, but just cashing the checks.

"There was a feeling of, 'Hey, here's what we're doing, and therefore it's important. People are gonna watch it. It represents us and let's do it right.' I felt like Andy was really a great role model as well as being the key factor in creating a show that has endured."

MR. FIX-IT—*A master toaster of Mayberry, Emmett Clark.*

Ken Berry remembers a friend and fellow dancer: "Paul Hartman and his wife, Grace, were a famous dance team. I asked him if he had any old film and he did and we went out to his house one night, and, doggone it, something went wrong with the projector and it was feeding the film to the floor in the dark. I saw part of it and they were brilliant, just wonderful. It was a thrill to work with him."

And Paul Hartman's grandson, Bill Hartman, shares some of his memories of his grandfather's work in Mayberry: "I did visit the set on a couple of occasions. It was a very relaxed atmosphere. My grandfather explained to me the process of putting together a show in that short a time. My grandfather was pretty good at learning his lines after working in theater for so long.

"As a person, he really wasn't a handy person, but it was amazing the number of things that were actually sent to him by fans to be repaired.

They'd send him box radios, toasters. He worked out a deal with an engineer on the set that if he could repair it, then they'd actually send it back to the person. People really got into him and into the roles. He was a lot like the character. He was a very relaxed person and he did like entertaining people from the cast. He really knew how to cook and throw a party. He and George Lindsey were good friends. He was at a party at my grandfather's and it struck me that George was a natural comedian."

And about the fact that folks still enjoy Mayberry so much, Bill says: "It really validates all the years he was in show business. He really did make a lasting impression. I think he would like to be remembered as an entertainer, as a person that made people laugh."

HAVING A BALL—*Howard poses for a photo with fellow teammates Andy and Goober and team sponsor Emmett on the occasion of his bowling the first perfect game in county history.*

Ken Berry talks about Mayberry's surprising bowler: "Jack Dodson got to be a dear friend of mine. We had such a great time with Andy and Lee Greenway. That character that he did was terrific."

NEW KID ON THE BLOCK—*Arnold Bailey becomes Opie's best friend during his early teens.*

As is fitting for the one who played silver-tongued Arnold Bailey, Sheldon Golomb (Collins) articulates his Mayberry experience well: "It wasn't until 1999, when I happened to be watching 'Opie Finds a Baby,' that I realized it was Jack Nicholson who was the baby's father. Of course, he was a virtual unknown then.

"Playing basketball with Ronny is one of my fondest memories. Perhaps that's because I love basketball. They built a basketball court on the set for us to use when we weren't working or schooling. I always prided myself on being a very good basketball player, so I was surprised to find that Opie was better. (Of course, he was older, too.)

"It's amazing how some of the not-so-pleasant memories linger. I remember there was an episode where I was talking with Opie. I was supposed to throw a pair of sneakers into a locker, close the locker, and say my line. For about fifteen or maybe more times, I couldn't get it right. Either the locker wouldn't close or the shoelaces would stick out or I'd fumble my line. Everything that could go wrong, did. We broke for lunch, came back, and the same things started happening. I think I eventually got it right.

"My general memory of doing *The Andy Griffith Show* was how smoothly everything flowed. It was a very relaxed, but efficient, situation where I always felt very comfortable.

After forty years, it's amazing to me to see how strong and alive the show still is. Who would have known just how special it was going to become, and I feel privileged to have been part of it."

Ron Howard talks about Sheldon Golomb (Collins): "He's a great guy, a very smart guy, and we really had fun. He's a funny guy and at that age I could tell who was a good actor and who wasn't. He was a good actor and fit right in. I loved that Opie had a pal, and Sheldon was a really fun kid to goof around with and do scenes with."

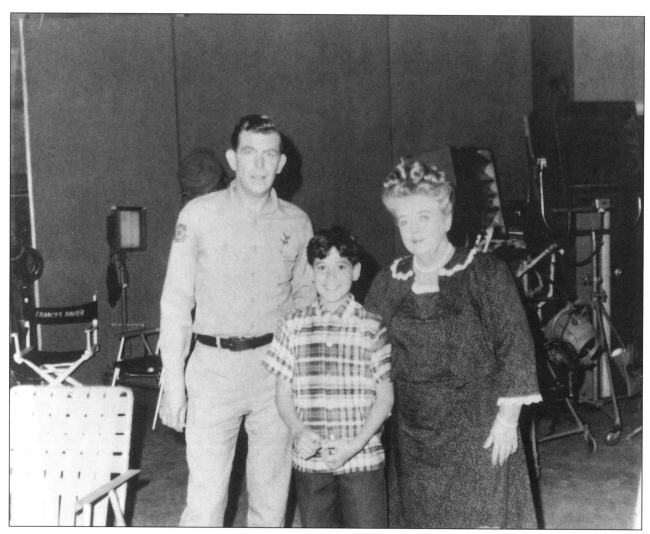

BACKSTAGE VISIT—*Sheldon Golomb (Collins) poses with Andy Griffith and Frances Bavier during a break in filming.* COURTESY OF SHELDON GOLOMB.

OPIE TAKES THE CAKE—*Kid Taylor doesn't realize it, but he's interrupting an important proposal for "Howard and Millie."*

Arlene Golonka discusses her Mayberry experience: "I owe all my wonderful times on *Mayberry* to Bob Ross. He is the one who auditioned me and hired me. He was just a kind, good, lovely man.

"I loved Jack Dodson. The episode when I asked him to shave his mustache and then looked into his eyes and they looked like a disappointed puppy's eyes—I'll never forget that expression when he looked at me. I kept breaking up during that scene because every time he looked at me, I'd laugh. They got really mad at my breaking up. They kept reshooting the scene. They were not very pleased, but I had a wonderful time working with Jack. He just made me laugh all the time."

CURIOUS CHURN OF EVENTS— *"Aunt Bee's Cousin" Bradford (Jack Albertson) is full of strawberry ice cream and grand ideas, most of which seem to melt away rather quickly.*

Mary Dodson, widow of Jack Dodson, reflects on his Mayberry experience: "How Jack enjoyed working with that great family of good friends. Jack had some wonderful tales, but most of them were of personal experiences off of the set. I remember so vividly the many evenings spent at Paul Hartman's apartment overlooking the Pacific with riotous storytelling by Jack, Paul, and Eddie Foy Jr. Occasionally, Jack was able to get Andy and Lee Greenway to join us. Great memories. Aneta Corsaut's remark is so insightful that it bears repeating: 'Jack likes to play the crankiest man in the world, and he tells outrageous lies. He was one of my favorites.'"

Jack Dodson's favorite episode was "Howard's New Life" and it continues to be his family's consensus favorite as well.

Andy Griffith recalls: "I met Jack Dodson after a performance of the Eugene O'Neill play *Hughie.* Pretty soon after that there came a small part of an insurance adjuster who was a little hesitant to pay off. While we were shooting that little scene I called Jack aside and asked him if he would like to be a regular. He did, and added a great deal to the show and became one of my best friends for the rest of his life."

SOMEWHERE OVER THE RAINBOW—*Looking to break out of what he believes is the hum-drum of his daily life, Howard Sprague follows his rainbow to the Caribbean island where native boy Sebastian (Mark Brown) gives the first hint that "Howard's New Life" is not all that he dreamed it would be. As Howard himself explains, "I guess I just followed my rainbow to the wrong end. My pot of gold is right here in Mayberry."*

Ron Howard summarizes his feelings about the show:
"I think it's one of the most unique shows in the history of television. It has a style that is so uniquely its own. Each one is almost like a movie and yet it's not an anthology. *The Andy Griffith Show* somehow created a remarkably original tone and sense of itself that has never really been repeated. There's truth and humor and heart and whimsy—all kind of wrapped up in every episode—and rich character studies that are still delightfully entertaining and make you laugh. It's just a kind of an impossible recipe to repeat. And so as an adult and a filmmaker and storyteller myself, I have nothing but respect for it."

EXECUTIVE DECISION—*Goober and Opie are huddling to figure out a method to correct the declining balance sheet at the filling station after Goober buys out Wally. And, by George, soon there'll be decisive action and service with a smile on their faces. This photograph was taken on June 26, 1967, during the filming of "Goober the Executive."*

NOTHING LOST IN THE TRANSLATION— *Aunt Bee uses a universal language (that is, potato salad) to help Russia's Mr. Vasilievich (Ben Astar), U.S. Ambassador Clifford (Michael Higgins), and the interpreter, Mr. Ruskin (Alan Oppenheimer), make headway when "Barney Hosts a Summit Meeting." But leave it to the Russian diplomat to rummage around and find a jar of pickles in the refrigerator. Talk about a recipe for disaster! Fortunately, they are good old store pickles, and an international incident is averted.*

Andy Griffith and Richard O. Linke. COURTESY OF RICHARD O. LINKE.

Richard Linke comments:
"Somebody asked me if I thought the show could be successful nowadays. I definitely think it could be and would be because of all the stuff that's going on in television that's not too good—all the violence and all the things we don't want to see. If something like *The Andy Griffith Show* came along, I think it would be so refreshing, that it would grab the audience."

ROOM FOR ONE MORE?—*Nope, just one person aboard today because it's Aunt Bee's time to flap her wings and buzz off solo into the wild blue yonder. But maybe next time? This photograph was taken during the filming of "Aunt Bee's Big Moment" on January 4, 1968.*

Two-time Mayberry visitor (including for "Emmett's Anniversary" in the eighth season) Ronnie Schell comments: "I was just thrilled to be there, to be a part of *The Andy Griffith Show*. I was always a huge fan of the show even before I got *Gomer*. So to take time off doing *Gomer* and to play on the father of all shows was quite a thrill—to get to work with Frances Bavier and Paul Hartman. And it was quite another thrill meeting Howard McNear. He couldn't have been nicer and funnier."

He adds: "It's a sentimental feeling I get on the fortieth anniversary. It's a time of the *Gomer Pyles*, the *Andy Griffiths*, the *Dick Van Dykes*—the golden age of comedy that we'll never see again because of the more loose moral line that's going on today. It was a more innocent time and perhaps a happier time. I was just glad to be a part of the golden age of television comedy."

SAM BY A NOSE—*It's a hard-fought race with Emmett versus "Sam for Town Council," but in the end, Emmett acknowledges that "the people have spoken" and graciously congratulates Sam on his victory.*

Ken Berry tells how he won the role of Sam Jones: "I think they had interviewed a lot of people, and finally, I got called in. The reading went very well. I got the part. My feelings about it were that nobody could replace Andy, but I think we had a whole season. I really wanted this. So that was my feeling. I didn't think we would last past a season, but I didn't count on the strength of the other people. The network didn't want to change it that much. They wanted to stay with *The Andy Griffith Show* people.

LOOKING FOR A HIT—*Under Andy's watchful eye, Sam and Mike Jones are hoping for a winning season when their turn at bat comes around.*

Showing a good feel for Mayberry, Ken Berry says: "Mayberry was just a wonderful place to visit. I watched *The Andy Griffith Show* every week. It was a nice, gentle place to visit. You wished you could live there. It was all character-driven comedy and done by people who knew that kind of comedy."

THAT'S ITALIAN!—*It's hard to read Andy's mind, but maybe he's thinking that the Vincentes, the Italian family planning to stay with Sam Jones, probably cook a lot of spaghetti with a certain secret ingredient and that maybe that's a sign he should start thinking about leaving Mayberry and taking a job with the North Carolina Bureau of Investigation in Charlotte. With Sam and Andy here are Sophia Vincente (Letitia Roman), Papa Vincente (Bruno della Santina), Mario Vincente (Gabrielle Tinti).* COURTESY OF GILMORE-SCHWENKE COLLECTION.

NAME THAT TUNE—*Goober and Clara prepare to sing "O' Sole Mio" (thought by some to be the Italian national anthem) to welcome the Vincente family to Mayberry. This photograph was taken during the filming of* Mayberry R.F.D. *on December 4, 1967. (When the episode aired on April 1, 1968, it was no April Fool's joke that it was the final original broadcast of an* Andy Griffith Show *episode.)* COURTESY CBS PHOTO ARCHIVE.

WHAT A GREAT RUN—*This TV Guide is from 1968.* TV GUIDE FURNISHED BY JOEL RASMUSSEN COLLECTION. REPRINTED WITH PERMISSION FROM TV GUIDE MAGAZINE GROUP, INC., PUBLISHER OF *TV GUIDE* MAGAZINE; COPYRIGHT © VOLUME 16, ISSUE 28, 1968, TV GUIDE INC. *TV GUIDE* IS A TRADEMARK OF TV GUIDE MAGAZINE GROUP, INC.

Jack Dodson once commented: "*Mayberry R.F.D* was a great deal of fun, too, but the *Griffith* show was truly special. It speaks to a lot of things that are common to growing up in the '30s, '40s, and early '50s."

Author Dale Robinson expresses his gratitude for Mayberry: "Thank you to *The Andy Griffith Show* for: Front porch singing, kerosene cucumbers, Morelli's, 'Good ol' 14-A,' Miracle Salve, adventure sleeping, Checkpoint Chickie, lake loons, Mayberry Minutemen, Chief Noogatuck, fingerprint sets, 'Old Aunt Maria,' 'Salty Dog,' Old Sam, and too many spaghetti dinners! Most of all, thank you for being there for forty years."

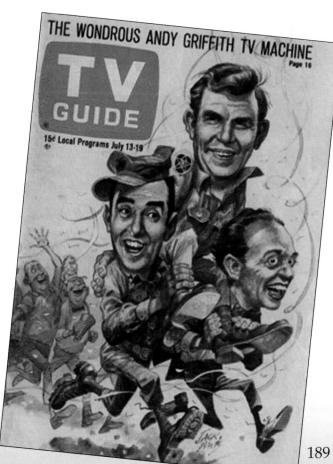

189

GUNNING FOR THE FUNNY BONE—*Gomer shoulders a lecture by Sgt. Carter.*

MORE MAYBERRY
Other Legacies:
Gomer Pyle, U.S.M.C., Mayberry R.F.D., and Return to Mayberry

The legacy of *The Andy Griffith Show* is evergreen in and by itself, but before the 1960s were history, the memorable characters from Mayberry spun themselves into two other successful television shows.

Gomer Pyle, U.S.M.C. debuted September 25, 1964, as Mayberry's friendly filling station attendant joined the Marines. Starring Jim Nabors in the title role and Frank Sutton as the cynical and tough Sgt. Vince Carter, the comedy series ran for 150 episodes during five strong seasons and was ranked twice at both number two and number three for the year in the Nielsen ratings, and was always in the Top Ten.

Sgt. Carter is forever the foil to Gomer's naive and innocent ways, but both find friendship with their girlfriends Bunny Olsen (Barbara Stuart) and Lou Ann Poovie (Elizabeth MacRae). Other Marine comrades at Camp Henderson include Sgt. Charlie Hacker (Allan Melvin), Col. Edward Gray (Forrest Compton), Cpl. Chuck Boyle (Roy Stuart), Pvt. (and later Cpl.) Gilbert "Duke" Slater (Ronnie Schell), Pvt. Frankie Lombardi (Ted Bessell), Pvt. Lester Hummel (William Christopher), Larry (Larry Hovis), and Cpl. Nick Cuccinello (Tommy Leonetti).

Mayberry R.F.D. succeeded *The Andy Griffith Show* in 1968 as it took over the same night and time slot of its predecessor. The town stays the same, but Andy and Opie are gone as farmer Sam Jones (Ken Berry) and his son Mike (Buddy Foster) fill the father-son relationship.

Also along were regulars Goober Pyle, Howard Sprague, Emmett Clark, the Fix-It Man, and Millie Swanson (Arlene Golonka). Aunt Bee stays with the Jones household for two seasons as housekeeper, until Alice (Alice Ghostley) takes over the domestic chores.

For its three seasons and seventy-eight episodes, *Mayberry R.F.D.* ranked in the Top Ten its first two years and the Top Twenty its last year.

The Andy Griffith Show cast made one memorable last hurrah when they gathered for the TV reunion movie, *Return to Mayberry*, which premiered on April 13, 1986, on NBC.

The two-hour show took a good look at Mayberry fifteen years after fans last saw new stories about life in the town. Andy and Helen Taylor return just in time to see Barney Fife in the race of his life for sheriff. Gomer and Goober are running the garage together. Opie is now editing the town paper, married (to Eunice), and expecting the birth of his first child. Howard has his fingers on the pulse of the town, Otis has reformed and is peddling ice cream, the Darlings are still making music, and Ernest T. Bass is still making mischief and throwing rocks. And Thelma Lou and Barney are rekindling old flames.

Guided by longtime *Andy Griffith Show* director Bob Sweeney and written by Mayberry veterans Everett Greenbaum and Harvey Bullock, *Return to Mayberry* was the highest-rated TV movie of the 1985–86 season.

GOMER PYLE

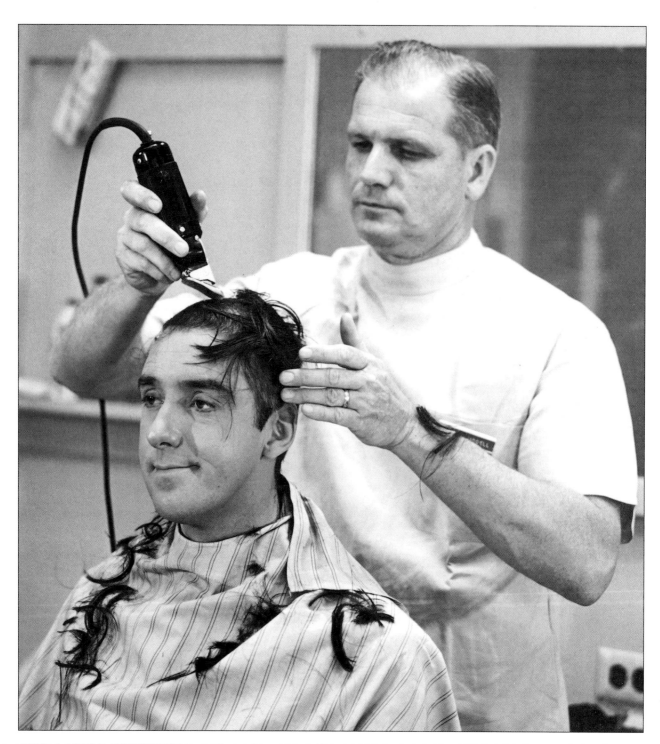

"JUST A LITTLE OFF THE TOP, PLEASE"—*Gomer gets his hair razed by a genuine, regulation Marine Corps barber.*

GOMER AND THE OBSTACLE COURSE—*Aaron Ruben instructs Jim Nabors during filming of the second episode of the series as Frank Sutton inspects the situation.* COURTESY OF AARON RUBEN.

Jim Nabors praises Aaron Ruben: "Aaron was our in-house genius, I think. He was so gifted. He created *Gomer*. Aaron was the molder of the whole thing. I think his work deserved a jillion awards. He was marvelous."

And actor Clint Howard admires the special genius of Jim Nabors: "Gomer is the absolute silliest, dumbest human being—makes Forrest Gump look like a brain surgeon, and yet, you know, I bought it. That's not easy to do, and Jim did it very well."

***Gomer Pyle* series creator Aaron Ruben describes how Gomer became a Marine:** "From his first appearance on the *Griffith* show, Jim Nabors was a hit. His naiveté and country charm endeared him to our audience. And it wasn't long before Andy urged me to come up with an idea for Jim to have a show of his own. Because of that complete innocence and gentle manner, there seemed to be only one place for a character like that—the U.S. Marine Corps. And Gomer had to adjust to the roughest, toughest war machine ever. And he did…in his way. And we took advantage of Jim's splendid singing voice as often as the show permitted. Gomer has been variously identified as something of a goof. Nothing could be further from the truth. He was not written as a goof, and he never performed as a goof. He simply was something of an oddball in that highly structured institution—the U.S.M.C."

MISS BUNNY?—*Gomer, Duke, and Sgt. Carter appear to be afraid that they might be missing a beautiful show behind them.*

HAT, A BOY—*Andy comes to get Opie and they come to the understanding that Mayberry, not the Marines, is the best place for Opie to be for the next couple of years.*

Elizabeth MacRae tells how *Andy Griffith Show* director Lee Philips helped her land the role of Lou Ann Poovie:
"When I was out in California in 1966, I was going in to read for Aaron Ruben for another part in *Gomer Pyle*, not Lou Ann Poovie. And the door was open, and Lee Philips happened to be walking down the hall and looked in Aaron's office and said, 'Well, there's Elizabeth MacRae, my favorite Southern belle.' We started talking and Aaron said, 'Are you from the South?'

"And I said, 'Yes, I'm from North Carolina.'

"And he said, 'Can you talk with a southern accent?'

"'Well, sure. That's who I am.'

"'Can you sing?'

"I said, 'Oh, no, I'm afraid I'm tone deaf.'

"He said, 'Perfect. You've got the part. We want you for another episode.'

"It turned out to be a wonderful role that ran on for three seasons. So it was Lee really that was the catalyst for all that. That was the atmosphere at Desilu. Everybody was neighbors."

She adds: "Aaron brought me on the show and I was supposed to do just the one episode. Lou Ann, because of Gomer, decides that she's homesick for the South and she goes back to her old hometown of Turtle Creek, North Carolina, to marry her longtime beau Monroe Efurd. After the episode was finished and came out, they liked the chemistry between Gomer Pyle and Lou Ann Poovie and they thought, 'Well, how can we fix this, because she's gone home to marry somebody else?'"

COMPANY BEE—*Sgt. Carter comes clean during "A Visit from Aunt Bee" in 1967. (Psst, Aunt Bee, you missed that mark on the floor by Sgt. Carter's feet, though Carter himself obviously didn't miss it.)*

Elizabeth MacRae reminisces about her time working on *Gomer Pyle*: "It was a wonderful experience. It was really a sense of family. Andy Griffith and Jim Nabors were so close. When I first came on the set of *Gomer Pyle*, the very first show I did, Andy came over and was very much a part of the filming. He wasn't in it, but he was there helping Jim Nabors coach me to sing because my character, Lou Ann Poovie, was totally tone deaf. So Andy and Jim were standing behind the camera mouthing the words trying to help me. Andy himself is lovely and Don Knotts is wonderful. Don and I worked together on *The Incredible Mr. Limpet*."

Aaron Ruben salutes Frank Sutton: "Frank Sutton was the perfect sergeant for Gomer. The long-suffering sergeant had to endure the love and devotion and dedication that Gomer relentlessly plied him with. Frank was one of the most professional actors I ever worked with. He would not leave the conference table until he was sure and satisfied with his lines and his participation. He had a built-in sense of comedy and timing. He was the consummate actor and a joy to work with."

Jim Nabors shares that admiration of Frank Sutton: "My main memory of Frank is his incredible professionalism and his great talent as an actor."

SHAZAM!—*Gomer meets his match with Lou Ann Poovie.*

CREW CUTS IT—*Production manager Frank E. Myers (who also worked on* The Andy Griffith Show*) visits with his sons on the* Gomer *set. At left in this 1965 photograph is Charles (Chuck) Myers, an assistant director for* Gomer, *and at right is Tom Myers, who was extra on the set while attending college.*

Ronnie Schell shares his thoughts about working on *Gomer Pyle*: "Working on the *Gomer Pyle* show was sensational. I got along very well with Jim. Working with such great talents as Frank Sutton, the late Ted Bessell, and Elizabeth MacRae was a real pleasure. And Barbara Stuart was super. Jim Nabors was like a brother to me.

"It was my first television series as a regular. Many of the top shows in television were filmed on that lot, *Dick Van Dyke*, *Make Room for Daddy*, *I Spy*, and *That Girl*. It was just a fun, fun, fun time. I'd gladly go back and live the memories anytime."

Barbara Stuart recalls the pleasant experience of working with Jim Nabors and Frank Sutton on *Gomer Pyle, U.S.M.C.*: "Jim and I just had a great time. We laughed all the time. We used to laugh about Frank, who was a very serious actor. Jim and I used to get so tickled because Frank would be over somewhere working like crazy making sure the lines and comedy were just right because he was such a serious and absolutely *wonderful* actor."

She adds: "I just loved doing the show. I think at the time we didn't appreciate it. I don't think you ever really do until it's over and you see what an impact you've made. We just really had fun. And of course I loved it because there were all those men. Miss Bunny loved being around all those men!"

MORALE BOOSTER—*Miss Bunny Olsen (Barbara Stuart) makes a congenial buffer between Gomer and Sgt. Carter.* Courtesy of Barbara Stuart.

Elizabeth MacRae talks about *The Andy Griffith Show* and *Gomer Pyle, U.S.M.C.*: "I think the reason that both shows have had such a long life is because of the whole format of the show. It was all about goodness. It was essentially about discovering the goodness in people.

"There were wonderful stories and great actors. They don't come any better than the actors on *Andy* or *Gomer*. Not just professionally good, but I think it translates onto film as a chemistry. It becomes almost like regional theater with your characters and your scripts.

"I think the values that were displayed on those shows are timeless. In a way, we were all role models for people growing up to learn good values—goodness and love and respect and all those things—and the same translated over to *Gomer*. He handled difficult situations coming at him with goodness and truth and trust and love and honesty. Of course, you had the wonderful foil in Sgt. Carter, too. When the show ended, it was like losing my family."

Author Terry Collins writes: "For a lifelong fan of *The Andy Griffith Show*, I was lucky as a kid. First, I was born and raised in Mount Airy, North Carolina. I still make it my home today. Second, I've always had daily access to the series via the afternoon reruns that have been airing on WFMY-TV out of Greensboro since I was old enough to turn on the television set.

"You must realize, this goes back decades ago, long before the days of cable television and the VCR. If I needed a daily fix, Andy was always there to offer counsel. However, I have a confession to make. While at this young and impressionable age…I preferred the antics of *Gomer Pyle, U.S.M.C.* (also shown on WFMY) to the more stately *Andy Griffith Show*. What can I say? I was only six years old!"

JUST OUR TYPE, BEE POSITIVE—*WFMY-TV in Greensboro proved that Mayberry is truly in its blood when Frances Bavier (being interviewed here by Judy Walker) visited the station for its annual holiday blood drive in the early 1970s. The CBS affiliate has broadcast* The Andy Griffith Show *from the very start and considers it a point of honor that the station has continued to air the epilogues (treasured by fans) that other stations often no longer air.* COURTESY OF WFMY-TV.

MAYBERRY R.F.D.

A BIG CHAIR FOR MAYBERRY—*Even though Andy, Opie, and Helen become scarcely seen in Mayberry, many favorites still provide lots of laughs and tender moments in* Mayberry R.F.D.

WHERE ARE THE FUN GIRLS WHEN YOU NEED THEM?—*It's a pretty low-key bachelor party when "Andy and Helen Get Married," the first episode of Mayberry R.F.D. Though not seen here, the life of the party, Mr. Schwamp, is indeed included in the occasion.* COURTESY OF PHIL BOWLING COLLECTION.

"LET'S LET ANDY MAKE THE SCENE" (below)—*And quite a scene it is when preparations begin for Andy and Helen's wedding.* COURTESY OF PHIL BOWLING COLLECTION.

IT'S SHOES AND RICE TIME—*There was no question who the best man would be for this wedding.* COURTESY OF PHIL BOWLING COLLECTION.

OFFICIAL WEDDING PARTY—*Andy, Helen, and Barney do their best to look relaxed, but there's only one way to describe all present: tense.*

THAT'S MORE LIKE IT—*There's the expression we were looking for from the best man.*

NOT ONLY A BUDDY, BUT CLOSE KIN—*Sam and Mike Jones continue Mayberry's tradition of strong bonds between father and son.*

CUTTING IN—*Sam and Goober are both interested in dancing with Millie at the "The Harvest Ball," but in the end, everybody realizes that Sam and Millie are a good match.* COURTESY OF BART BOATWRIGHT COLLECTION.

Perry Grant, who wrote thirty-one episodes of *Mayberry R.F.D.* **with partner Dick Bensfield, talks about the episode "Mike's Losing Streak":** "One of my favorite episodes we wrote was when Mike kept losing things, leaving his jacket at the park, etc. Still, Sam gave him a watch for his birthday, which he immediately lost. The whole town of Mayberry was looking forward to a big baseball game with Mt. Pilot, but Sam said Mike couldn't go unless he found the watch. He couldn't find it. The whole town was against Sam. So Sam bought another watch and 'hid' it at the park for Mike to find. Mike couldn't find it for looking. Of course, Sam eventually gave in and they went to the ball game…with the watch. Mayberry was a pleasure to write."

Arlene Golonka talks about two Mayberry favorites: "Paul Hartman was a wonderful man and a great dancer, and he was so good to me–always there for me when I had a question. At cast parties, I had the honor of dancing with him and he said he loved dancing with me, and I was thrilled because he was a professional dancer.

"Oh, and George Lindsey was another incredible, talented man. So funny in real life. He's so much more than just being Goober. He always broke me up in real life too. His son wound up in my acting class and he's another wonderful talent."

SWEET LOOKS—*All seem happy with what they see in Mayberry this day.*

Ken Berry compliments a fellow Mayberry star: "Arlene Golonka is as sweet as she looks and a lot of fun. I had seen her on Broadway. That working experience was terrific."

ANXIOUS MOMENT—*A characteristically calm Rev. Tucker holds Andy Taylor, Jr., while parents Helen and Andy seem concerned about something they see. Could their concern have something to do with the baby's four godfathers (that would be Howard, Sam, Emmett, and Goober) not being able to decide which one of them should be the official spokesperson for the group? You betcha.*

HAPPY FAMILY—*Proud parents Helen and Andy pose with Andrew Samuel Taylor, Jr. Some might quibble with the fact that Andy Taylor, Sr.'s middle name used to be Jackson back years ago when he and Barney were looking through their old high school yearbook. But you'll find no argument here, because Mayberry has a higher power whose middle name just happens to be Samuel.*

UH-OH, HERE WE GO AGAIN (below)—*With Howard Sprague and others offering a chorus of support, Aunt Bee makes her second recorded stand against a bulldozer—this time to save Grover's Woods in "The Mayberry Road."*

REVOLUTIONARY PERFORMERS—*Jack Dodson and George Lindsey relax on location while filming "The New Housekeeper" in the third season for* Mayberry R.F.D. *(Howard and Goober are leaders of the honor guard trumpeting the dedication of a new flag pole.)* COURTESY OF MARY DODSON.

Ken Berry gives credit: "Bob Ross was one of the few people who could write for that show. Andy had a strong hand in it. In order to get that special quality to write a script for *The Andy Griffith Show* or *Mayberry R.F.D.*, you had to have Bob Ross or the writers that did so well on the *Griffith* show. You had to have your fingers on the pulse."

ON FIRE—*The cast for the third season of* Mayberry R.F.D. *is red-hot and ready to roll.*

Author David Fernandes comments: "For forty wonderful years, *The Andy Griffith Show* has touched our hearts, stirred our souls and, in general pickled us tink…er, tickled us pink. May its precious images flicker across our television screens forever!"

MAYBERRY FEAST—*This* TV Guide *is from 1970.* Reprinted with permission from TV Guide Magazine Group, Inc., publisher of *TV Guide* magazine; Copyright © Volume 17, Issue 30, 1970, TV Guide Inc. *TV Guide* is a trademark of TV Guide Magazine Group, Inc.

SURPRISE, SURPRISE, SURPRISE! (below)—*Yes, Andy Griffith was indeed surprised to be featured on* This Is Your Life *in 1973. On hand (from left to right) are program host Ralph Edwards, Glenn E. Wallich (president of Capitol Records), Capitol sales manager Hal Cook, Ron Howard, Jim Nabors, the guest of honor, personal manager Richard O. Linke, and Ken Berry.* Courtesy of Richard O. Linke.

WHO ARE THESE MASKED MEN?—*This photograph from the 1970s shows Jack Dodson, George Lindsey, and Don Knotts mugging for the camera and looking as if they're about to commit mischief.* COURTESY OF MARY DODSON.

IDLE MINDS?—*Do these look like the kind of qualified mechanics somebody would want to entrust with working on a prized antique automobile?* COURTESY OF MARY DODSON.

SATISFIED CUSTOMER—*Andy Griffith seems pleased with the car work performed by his crew of cut-ups.* COURTESY OF MARY DODSON.

RETURN TO MAYBERRY

TOGETHER AGAIN—*Andy and Don (and Andy and Barney) delighted Mayberry fans with their return to America's hometown in 1986.*

GRINNING GROUP—*Familiar faces make their* Return to Mayberry. *The new face on the far right is Richard Lineback, who played Wally Butler, the somewhat sinister new hotel owner. (But he'll learn.)*

MAYBERRY GIANTS—*Harvey Bullock (left) and Everett Greenbaum, in the midst of preparing their final script for* Return to Mayberry, *visit with Andy Griffith outside the studio where Andy was working on Matlock in November 1985.* PHOTO BY CINDI GRIFFITH.

Harvey Bullock talks about working with Everett Greenbaum: "Both Everett and I had lost our writing partners. We had been friends for years, so it seemed natural that we would get together to write *Return to Mayberry*. I can only say that it's sad that every writer can't have a partner like Everett Greenbaum."

MAYBERRY LEGEND—*As wiry as ever, Barney remained a confident lawman dedicated to duty in* Return to Mayberry.

VOTER POLL—*Ron Howard is surrounded by Barneys on location for* Return to Mayberry, *which was filmed in and around Los Olivos, California, during early 1986.*

CARING PAIR—*An enormous respect for each other continued to bond Ron Howard and Andy Griffith in their work on* Return to Mayberry.

LOOKING GOOD—*Barney's still campaigning for law and order in Mayberry.*

FOCUSED ON MAYBERRY—*Gomer doesn't know it yet, but he's about to take a monster of a photo in* Return to Mayberry.

SCOUTING THE SCENE—*Andy Griffith and Don Knotts survey the situation for their next scene in* Return to Mayberry.

DOWN FROM THE HILLS—*The Darling family made their* Return to Mayberry *and maybe the boys are looking to add to their vocabulary by visiting with Helen Crump Taylor. On location in Los Olivos are, from left to right, Rodney Dillard, Aneta Corsaut, Mitch Jayne, Maggie Peterson, Doug Dillard, and Dean Webb. Photo by Jack Dodson.*

Mitch Jayne comments: "Return to Mayberry was the nicest thing Andy could have done for anybody. It told people that he had never forgotten the place, or the people who had loved him for creating it. He wanted to say goodbye to it in the best way he could come up with, because like all of us, he was moving on. I found my eyes watering, when in the last scene we filmed, he lifts his glass to all the people gathered there and says 'To old friends.' That's how Andy Griffith feels about all of us."

GOT ICE CREAM?—*If you've got cake, you're going to need ice cream and here's the man to call. (And yes, ice cream is now Otis's only indulgence...just not rum raisin.)* PHOTO BY JACK DODSON.

Author Lee Pfeiffer comments: "Audiences often thought that this ensemble cast were merely playing themselves, when nothing could be further from the truth. In fact, they were brilliant actors creating characters that have become integral to American popular culture. So enduring is the show's legacy that I have no doubt that in the year 2040, someone will be creating an eightieth anniversary tribute book."

HOW DO YOU DO, MR. MORRIS?—*At the wrap party for* Return to Mayberry, *Andy Griffith seems to agree that Howard is still a very likable "nut" after all these years.* COURTESY OF BEVERLY SWEENEY.

KEEPERS OF
THE FLAME—
*Cindi and Andy
Griffith pause to
pose on "Main
Street" during
filming of* Return
to Mayberry.
COURTESY OF
BEVERLY SWEENEY.

THAT'S A WRAP—*Andy Griffith and
music director Earle Hagen visit during
the wrap party.* COURTESY OF BEVERLY
SWEENEY.

DARLINGS AND A BASS—*A-pickin' and a-grinnin' are, clockwise from bottom left, Doug Dillard, Rodney Dillard, Dean Webb, Howard Morris, Mitch Jayne, Denver Pyle, and Maggie Peterson.* PHOTO BY JACK DODSON.

JUST CLOWNING AROUND—*On the set of* Return to Mayberry, *Cindi and Andy Griffith pose with a colorful performer who definitely is no Bozo in Mayberry. (Guess who?)* PHOTO BY JACK DODSON.

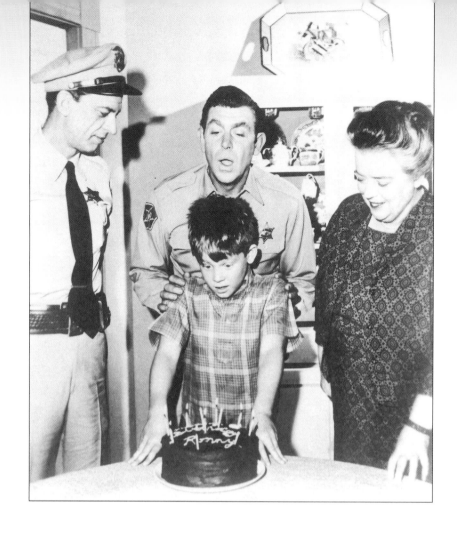

READY TO BLOW—*Don Knotts, Andy Griffith, and Frances Bavier help Ronny Howard celebrate his eleventh birthday in 1965.*

And speaking of celebrating milestones, Ron Howard shares his feelings: "The first thing that happens when you say *Andy Griffith Show* Fortieth Anniversary is just a kind of a feeling that's like when you might look back and remember that favorite summer that you had had in childhood, that one year that was your favorite in elementary school or the camp that you went to and have never forgotten. For me, it represents eight years, but, as corny as it sounds, my recollections are such fond ones that I truly have this warm spot in my heart for the whole experience, and I'm so grateful for that. I'm also one of the few child actors to be able to look back and feel that way. I hope it never goes away. I hope it endures."

FAST FORWARD— *Still taking the cake, Ron Howard has help celebrating his thirty-second birthday in front of the Courthouse set during filming of* Return to Mayberry.

MR. AND MRS.
BARNEY FIFE AND
THE BEST MAN—
When Thelma and Barney
finally get married in
Return Mayberry *in*
1986, a lingering injustice
is finally resolved and a
nation of fans rejoices.
Twenty years earlier,
Barney told Andy about
Thelma Lou, "She's the
only girl I ever loved,
Ange. She's the only girl I
ever will *love." And now*
we can rest with a satisfied
mind that Barney and
Thelma do indeed live
"happily ever after."

ANDY (toasting
Mayberry at Barney
and Thelma Lou's
wedding reception):
"There's something
about Mayberry and
Mayberry folk that
never leaves you. No
matter where life
takes you, you
always carry in your
heart the memories
of old times…and
old friends. Here's to
all of us…old
friends."

The last word here goes to Don Knotts, talking about Andy Griffith and the Mayberry experience: "Andy is probably my closest friend. We just had a great relationship professionally and personally. We have a lot of fun together. We struck up a friendship and began to enjoy laughing together way back before the *Griffith* show when we were in *No Time for Sergeants*. He was a joy to work with and so knowledgeable when you came to a script. He was just fantastic. So, all the way around, you couldn't work for a better guy. That's all there is to it. I really think a part of the reason we came off good on the show is because we were having such a good time. It was a defining experience for me. I've never had an experience since to compare with it."

"Say, 'Amen.'"

"Amen."

MUSIC MEN—*Writer Everett Greenbaum, Andy Griffith, and director Bob Sweeney enjoy a musical moment on the set of the Courthouse.*

𝒮ERIES GUIDE
The Andy Griffith Show

CENTRAL CAST

These actors appear in at least two episodes. See the Episode Summaries that follows for appearances by key guest actors.

Andy Griffith — **Andy Taylor**
Don Knotts — **Barney Fife**
Ron Howard — **Opie Taylor**
Frances Bavier — **Aunt Bee Taylor**
Howard McNear — **Floyd Lawson**
Hal Smith — **Otis Campbell**
Betty Lynn — **Thelma Lou**
Aneta Corsaut — **Helen Crump**
Jim Nabors — **Gomer Pyle**
George Lindsey — **Goober Pyle**
Jack Burns — **Warren Ferguson**
Jack Dodson — **Howard Sprague**
Paul Hartman — **Emmett Clark**
Hope Summers — **Clara Edwards Johnson**
Denver Pyle — **Briscoe Darling**
Margaret Ann Peterson — **Charlene Darling**
The Dillards (Doug Dillard, Rodney Dillard, Mitch Jayne, and Dean Webb) — **The Darling boys**
Hoke Howell — **Dud Wash**
Howard Morris — **Ernest T. Bass** and **voice of Leonard Blush**
Elinor Donahue — **Ellie Walker**
Ken Berry — **Sam Jones**
Arlene Golonka — **Millie Hutchins**
Buddy Foster — **Mike Jones**
Bernard Fox — **Malcolm Merriweather**
James Best — **Jim Lindsey**
Jack Prince — **Rafe Hollister** and others
Dick Elliot — **Mayor Pike**
Parley Baer — **Mayor Roy Stoner**
Joyce Jameson — **Fun Girl Skippy**
Jean Carson — **Fun Girl Daphne**
Joanna Moore — **Peggy McMillan**
Will Wright, Tol Avery, and Jason Johnson — **Ben Weaver**

Cheerio Meredith — **Emma (Watson) Brand**
Olan Soule — **John Masters**
Delos Jewkes — **Glen Cripe**
Renée Aubry — **Choir member**
The Country Boys (Roland White, LeRoy Mack McNees, Clarence White, Eric White, and Billy Ray Latham) — **Local musicians**
Richard Keith (Thibodeaux) — **Johnny Paul Jason**
Dennis Rush — **Howie Pruitt/Williams**
David A. Bailey — **Trey Bowden** and **Fred Simpson**
Sheldon Golomb (Collins) — **Arnold Bailey**
Clint Howard — **Leon**
Joy Ellison — **Mary Wiggins** and others
Ronda Jeter — **Karen Burgess/Folker, Sharon Porter/McCall**
Rance Howard — **Various characters**
Burt Mustin — **Judd Fletcher, Jud, Jubal, Old Man Crowley,** and **Burt**
Joe Hamilton — **Chester Jones, Choney,** and **Jase**
Roy Engel — **Various loafers**
Charles P. Thompson — **Asa Breeney, Asa Bascomb,** and **Doc Roberts**
Norman Leavitt, Trevor Bardette, and Cliff Norton — **Wally**
Frank Ferguson — **Charlie Foley**
William Keene — **The Rev. Hobart M. Tucker**
Warren Parker — **Mr. Meldrim** and **Harlan Fergus**
Fred Sherman — **Fred Goss**
Mabel Albertson — **Mrs. Sprague**
Alberta Nelson — **Flora Malherbe**
Maudie Prickett — **Edna Sue Larch**

and others
Josie Lloyd — **Lydia Crosswaith, Juanita Pike,** and **Josephine Pike**
Mary Lansing — **Martha Clark** and **various townspeople**
George Cisar — **Cyrus Tankersley** and others
Harry Antrim — **Fred Walker**
Jonathan Hole — **Orville Monroe**
Dorothy Neumann — **Rita Campbell**
Florence MacMichael — **Hilda May**
Ruth Thom — **Myrtle** and **various townspeople**
Ruth McDevitt — **Ethel Pendleton**
Phil Chambers — **Jason**
Larry Hovis — **Gilly Walker**
Vince Barnett — **Elmo**
Richard X. Slattery — **Captain M.L. Dewhurst**
Ken Lynch — **Various state policemen**
Roy Jenson — **Various state policemen**
Allan Melvin — **Various heavies**
Bob McQuain — **Joe Waters** and others
Colin Male — **Announcer in opening credits**

Other actors appearing in more than one episode in various roles include Amzie Strickland, Sam Edwards, Margaret Kerry-Willcox, Barbara Perry, Mary Jackson, Janet Stewart, Claudia Bryar, Dabbs Greer, Lewis Charles, Mike Steen, Stanley Farrar, Byron Foulger, James Seay, Forrest Lewis, Jon Lormer, Owen Bush, Jim Begg, Willis Bouchey, Mary Treen, Sara Seegar, Tom Jacobs, and, of course, Mr. Schwamp.

Danny Thomas Productions —
  Production company
Sheldon Leonard —Executive
  producer
Aaron Ruben —Producer and director
Bob Ross —Producer
Richard O. Linke —Associate
  producer
Bob Sweeney —Director
Lee Philips —Director
Alan Rafkin —Director
Don Weis —Director
Howard Morris —Director
Coby Ruskin —Director
Jeffrey Hayden —Director
Earl Bellamy —Director
Dick Crenna —Director

Peter Baldwin —Director
Earle Hagen —Music director
Lee Greenway —Makeup
Frank E. Myers —Production manager
Edward H. Hillie —Production
  manager
Ronald Jacobs —Assistant to producer
Sid Hickox —Director of photography
Joe Gluck —Supervising editor
Ruth Burch —Casting
Hazel Hall —Script continuity
Rosemary Dorsey —Script continuity
Reggie Smith —Prop master

Arthur Stander
Jack Elinson and Charles Stewart
David Adler (Frank Tarloff)
Jim Fritzell and Everett Greenbaum
Harvey Bullock and Ray Allen
Bill Idelson and Sam Bobrick
John Whedon
Fred S. Fox
Fred Freeman and Lawrence Cohen
Ben Joelson and Art Baer
Ben Gershman and Leo Solomon
Dick Bensfield and Perry Grant
Joe Bonaduce
Michael Morris and Seaman Jacobs
Sid Morse
Jin Parker and Arnold Margolin
Aaron Ruben
Bob Ross

Episode Summaries

  This listing of the 249 episodes of *The Andy Griffith Show* is compiled in the order of their original prime-time broadcasts on CBS-TV from 1960 to 1968. The order that the episodes were actually filmed sometimes varies slightly from the broadcast order.

  The authors of this book (and other chroniclers or Mayberry) have used predominantly the filmed order for previous books and listings because the filmed order is the way that most stations have traditionally followed for the syndicated reruns.

  In January 2000, TV Land became the exclusive national cable home for *The Andy Griffith Show* and opted to follow the original broadcast order for its reruns of the show. (Most local stations continue to use the filmed order for their syndicated reruns of *The Andy Griffith Show.*)

  Given both TV Land's choice and our own decision to follow the original broadcast chronology of Mayberry in the rest of this book, our using the original broadcast order for these episode summaries seems appropriate. No matter the order, though, one thing is certain: They're still the same 249 wonderful episodes!

SEASON ONE (1960-61)

Episode 1: "The New Housekeeper," October 3, 1960. Aunt Bee joins the Taylor household after Rose departs for marriage. Cheerio Meredith as Emma Brand, Frank Ferguson as Wilbur Pine, and Mary Treen as Rose. In real life as a boy, Ron Howard had a pet dog named Gulliver just as Opie does. A favorite episode of Betty Lynn and of Rance and Jean Howard. Written by Jack Elinson and Charles Stewart; directed by Sheldon Leonard.

THE LOVE OF MAYBERRY—*"The New Housekeeper" immediatley connects for a home run.*

Taylor as Talbot. First appearance of Orville Monroe. Written by Jack Elinson and Charles Stewart; directed by Don Weis.

Episode 4: "Ellie Comes to Town," October 24, 1960. Walker's Drugstore gets a new pharmacist, Ellie Walker, who is strict about dealing prescriptions out to Emma Brand. First appearance of Ellie Walker. Written by Charles Stewart and Jack Elinson; directed by Don Weis.

Episode 5: "Irresistible Andy," October 31, 1960. Andy erroneously arrives at the notion that Ellie is trying to hook him into marriage. Robert Easton as Pete Johnson. For the first of more than three dozen occasions, Barney wears the old salt-and-pepper suit. Written by David Adler (Frank Tarloff); directed by Don Weis.

Episode 6: "Runaway Kid," November 7, 1960. Opie won't break his promise to rat on young runaway George "Tex" Foley (Pat Rosson). Written by Arthur Stander; directed by Don Weis.

Episode 7: "Andy the Matchmaker," November 14, 1960. Andy connives to pair Barney with Miss Rosemary. Amzie Strickland as Miss Rosemary,

Barney's first girlfriend. The Snappy Lunch is mentioned by name for the only time. Written by Arthur Stander; directed by Don Weis.

Episode 8: "Opie's Charity," November 28, 1960. Andy can't understand why Opie won't donate to a charity. Stuart Erwin as Tom Silby, Lurene Tuttle as Annabelle Silby. Written by Arthur Stander; directed by Don Weis.

Episode 9: "A Feud Is a Feud," December 5, 1960. Andy brings peace between two feuding farming families in order that their children can marry. Arthur Hunnicut as Jedidiah Wakefield, Chubby Johnson as Mr. Carter, Claude Johnson as Josh Wakefield, and Tammy Windsor as Hannah Carter. Written by David Adler (Frank Tarloff); directed by Don Weis.

Episode 2: "The Manhunt," October 10, 1960. Andy and Barney outsmart the state police in capturing an escaped criminal. Ken Lynch as Capt. Barker, Lillian Culver as Barney's mother, and Norman Leavitt as Cal. First episode where Andy carries a gun; first telephone call to operator Sarah; first time Barney accidentally fires his gun. First appearances of Mayor Pike, Otis Campbell, and Burt Mustin as Judd. Also, this episode is the only time Barney's mother is seen. Winner of the Writers Guild of America award for best writing in a comedy or variety series. Favorite episode of Richard O. Linke and Ronald Jacobs. Written by Charles Stewart and Jack Elinson; directed by Don Weis.

Episode 3: "The Guitar Player," October 17, 1960. Andy assists Mayberry's top guitar picker in landing a spot in Bobby Fleet's Band with a Beat. James Best as Jim Lindsey, Henry Slate as Bobby Fleet, and Dub

BARNEY CAN RECITE IT, HAND'S DOWN—*Rule number one of the Sheriff's Rules: " An officer of the law shall enforce the law and order without regard to personal welfare and safety." Barney knows this rule so well when "Ellie Comes to Town," don't be surprised in a few years when he can do just as well with the Preamble of The Constitution of the United States of America (Opie's Ill-Gotten Gain," Episode 103).*

Episode 10: "Ellie for Council," December 12, 1960. Ellie becomes the first women in the history of Mayberry to run for public office. Frank Ferguson as Sam. First appearances of Hilda May and Rita Campbell and the first appearance of Forrest Lewis as an unnamed townsperson. Written by Jack Elinson and Charles Stewart; directed by Bob Sweeney.

Episode 11: "Christmas Story," December 19, 1960. Gruff Ben Weaver wants Andy to lock a man up over the Christmas holiday. Will Wright as Ben Weaver, Sam Edwards as Sam Muggins, Margaret Kerry-Willcox as Bess Muggins, and Joy Ellison as Effie Muggins. First appearance of Ben Weaver, first filmed episode directed by Bob Sweeney, and the only Christmas episode. Elinor Donahue's

Chambers as Jason, Pat Colby as Bill Matthews, Marlene Willis as Lucy Matthews, and Sara Seegar as Mrs. Buntley. First appearance of Floyd the Barber (but not Howard McNear). Written by Arthur Stander; directed by Don Weis.

Episode 13: "Mayberry Goes Hollywood," January 2, 1961. A producer decides to film on location in Mayberry and the townsfolk overreact. Dan Frazier as Mr. Harmon and Josie Lloyd as Juanita Pike. First appearance of Howard McNear as the barber (but his name is Floyd Colby, not Lawson). Written by Benedict Freedman and John Fenton Murray; directed by Bob Sweeney.

Episode 14: "The Horse Trader," January 9, 1961. Andy dumps the town cannon on an antique dealer. Casey Adams (Max Showalter) as Ralph Mason. Written by Jack Elinson and Charles Stewart; directed by Bob Sweeney.

Episode 15: "Those Gossipin' Men," January 16, 1961. A shoe salesman has a field day when the men of Mayberry mistake him for a talent scout. Jack Finch as Wilbur Finch. This is the only time Floyd's son is seen and the first time that Barney plays his harmonica. Final appearance of Orville Monroe. Written by Charles Stewart and Jack Elinson; directed by Bob Sweeney.

Episode 16: "The Beauty Contest," January 23, 1961. Andy has to choose the town's most beautiful female. Lillian Bronson as Irma Bishop, Josie Lloyd as Josephine Pike, Elvia Allman as Henrietta Swanson, and starring Joy Ellison as Miss Mayberry, Junior, Mary Wiggins. Written by Jack Elinson and Charles Stewart; directed by Bob Sweeney.

THREE CHEERS FOR THE HOLIDAYS—*Ellie, Opie, and Andy celebrate Christmas.*

favorite episode. Written by David Adler (Frank Tarloff); directed by Bob Sweeney.

Episode 12: "Stranger in Town," December 26, 1960. A stranger knows everything about everyone in Mayberry. William Lanteau as Ed Sawyer, Walter Baldwin's only appearance as Floyd the Barber, Phil

Episode 17: "Alcohol and Old Lace," January 30, 1961. Andy and Barney discover two old ladies are making moonshine in their greenhouse. Gladys Hurlbut as Clarabelle Morrison and Charity Grace as Jennifer Morrison. Jack Prince's first appearance but not as Rafe Hollister.

Written by Charles Stewart and Jack Elinson; directed by Gene Reynolds.

Episode 18: "Andy, the Marriage Counselor," February 6, 1961. Andy must settle the bickering of a married couple. Jesse White as Fred Boone, Claudia Bryar as Jennie Boone, and Norman Leavitt as Gil. Written by David Adler (Frank Tarloff); directed by Gene Reynolds.

A LIGHT MOMENT—*Andy Griffith has a good time visiting with Country Boys LeRoy Mack McNees and Billy Ray Latham and actor Hugh Marlowe.* COURTESY OF LEROY MACK MCNEES.

Episode 19: "Mayberry on Record," February 13, 1961. A record producer believes Mayberry musicians have the makings for an album, but Andy suspects skullduggery. Hugh Marlowe as Mr. Maxwell, The Country Boys as country boys. Written by John Fenton Murray and Benedict Freedman; directed by Gene Reynolds.

Episode 20: "Andy Saves Barney's Morale," February 20, 1961. Barney arrests half the town on minor offenses, and Andy drops the charges but must then make the townspeople understand that Barney was just doing his job. Burt Mustin as Judd Fletcher, Joe Hamilton as Chester Jones. Last

appearance of Hilda May. Written by David Adler; directed by Bob Sweeney.

Episode 21: "Andy and the Gentleman Crook," February 27, 1961. A smooth-talking conman wins his way into everyone's heart except for Andy. Dan Tobin as "Gentleman" Dan Caldwell. Written by Ben Gershman and Leo Solomon; directed by Bob Sweeney.

Episode 22: "Cyrano Andy," March 6, 1961. Andy again plays matchmaker for Barney, this time with Thelma Lou, but she uses Andy to make Barney envious. First appearance of Thelma Lou. Written by Jack Elinson and Charles Stewart; directed by Bob Sweeney.

Episode 23: "Andy and Opie, Housekeepers," March 13, 1961. While Aunt Bee is away, Andy and Opie make a big mess. After it is cleaned up, they realize that they need to mess it up again in order that Aunt Bee can know how much they missed her. First appearance of Hope Summers, not as Clara, but as Bertha Edwards. Written by David Adler (Frank Tarloff); directed by Bob Sweeney.

Episode 24: "The New Doctor," March 27, 1961. Barney convinces Andy that Ellie and the new physician are "two young people lost in a world of pills" and have matrimony in mind. George Nader as Dr. Robert Benson. Written by Charles Stewart and Jack Elinson; directed by Bob Sweeney.

Episode 25: "A Plaque for Mayberry," April 3, 1961. O 'tis a

great day when historians discover a Mayberrian is related to a hero of the Revolutionary War. Andy is first heard to say, "You beat everything, you know that?" Isabel Randolph as Mrs. Bixby and Carol Veazie as Harriet Wicks. Written by Leo Solomon and Ben Gershman; directed by Bob Sweeney.

Episode 26: "The Inspector," April 10, 1961. An inspector from the state frowns upon Andy's unorthodox methods of keeping the peace. Tod Andrews as Ralph Case, Willis Bouchey as Mr. Brady, and Jack Prince as Luke Reimer. Written by Jack Elinson and Charles Stewart; directed by Bob Sweeney.

Episode 27: "Ellie Saves a Female," April 17, 1961. Ellie does a beauty makeover on a farm girl to the chagrin of a crusty old farmer. R.G. Armstrong as Mr. Flint and Edris March as Frankie Flint. Written by David Adler (Frank Tarloff), directed by Bob Sweeney.

MAKING A MESS OF THINGS—*What will Aunt Bee say when she sees what has been done by "Andy and Opie, Housekeepers"? She'll say, "Land sakes alive, look at this house. Just look at it. If it wasn't for me, this house wouldn't be fit to live in."*

Episode 28: "Andy Forecloses," April 24, 1961. Ben Weaver forces Andy to toss a poor young couple out of one of his rental houses. Sam Edwards as Lester Scobey, Margaret Kerry-Willcox as Helen Scobey, and Joy Ellinson as Mary Scobey. First mention of waitress Juanita by name. Written by Leo Solomon and Ben Gershman; directed by Bob Sweeney.

HEARTH ACHE—*Jim Lindsey and Andy play the fire out of "Midnight Special."* COURTESY OF BART BOATWRIGHT COLLECTION.

Episode 29: "Quiet Sam," May 1, 1961. Barney believes a reclusive farmer may actually be a criminal in hiding. William Schallert as Sam Becker, The Country Boys as country boys. Written by Jim Fritzell and Everett Greenbaum (their first); directed by Bob Sweeney.

Episode 30: "Barney Gets His Man," May 8, 1961. Barney nabs a criminal, who escapes and returns to Mayberry for revenge. Barney Phillips as Eddie Brooke, Bob McQuain as Sgt. Johnson, and Mike Steen as Sgt. Miller. Written by Leo Soloman and Ben Gershman; directed by Bob Sweeney.

Episode 31: "The Guitar Player Returns," May 15, 1961. Hitting hard times, Jim Lindsey returns to Mayberry, and Andy tries to get him back with his band. Herb Ellis as Bobby Fleet. Final appearance of Ellie Walker and Jim Lindsey. Written by Charles Stewart and Jack Elinson; directed by Bob Sweeney.

Episode 32: "Bringing Up Opie," May 22, 1961. Aunt Bee makes an edict that Opie can't hang around the Courthouse because it's not a fit environment for youngsters. Written by Jack Elinson and Charles Stewart; directed by Bob Sweeney.

SEASON TWO (1961-62)

Episode 33: "Opie and the Bully," October 2, 1961. Opie contends with a boy who is strong-arming him for his milk money. Terry Dickinson as Sheldon the bully. Written by David Adler (Frank Tarloff); directed by Bob Sweeney.

Episode 34: "Barney's Replacement," October 9, 1961. A lawyer learns the ropes of deputying, and Barney thinks his job is in danger. Hope Summers as Clara Johnson and Mark Miller as Bob Rogers. Written by Jack Elinson and Charles Stewart; directed by Bob Sweeney.

Episode 35: "Andy and the Woman Speeder," October 16, 1961. A beautiful woman speeds through town and has Barney, Floyd, and Opie eating out of her hand in order that she can beat Andy's charges. Jean Hagen as Elizabeth Crowley. Written by Charles Stewart and Jack Elinson; directed by Bob Sweeney.

Episode 36: "Mayberry Goes Bankrupt," October 23, 1961. An old-timer uncovers a city bond, as Mayberry finds that it may owe him a fortune. Andy Clyde as Frank Myers and Warren Parker makes first appearance as bank president Harlan Fergus. Written by Jack Elinson and Charles Stewart; directed by Bob Sweeney.

Episode 37: "Barney on the Rebound," October 30, 1961. A new girl in town tricks Barney into a marriage proposal but has no intentions of marrying him. Jackie Coogan as George Stevens and Beverly Tyler as Melissa Stevens. Written by Charles Stewart and Jack Elinson; directed by Bob Sweeney.

Episode 38: "Opie's Hobo Friend," November 13, 1961. A good-natured tramp has a malingering influence on Opie. Buddy Ebsen as David Browne. Written by Harvey Bullock (his first and favorite); directed by Bob Sweeney.

Episode 39: "Crime-free Mayberry," November 20, 1961. Phony FBI agents set the town up for a bank robbery. Edmon Ryan as "Fred Jenkins" and George Petrie as "Joe Layton." Written by Paul Henning; directed by Bob Sweeney.

Episode 40: "The Perfect Female," November 27, 1961. Andy dates Thelma Lou's cousin, gets a little boastful, and becomes an easy target in a shooting match. Gail Davis as Karen Moore. Written by Jack Elinson and Charles Stewart; directed by Bob Sweeney.

Episode 41: "Aunt Bee's Brief Encounter," December 4, 1961. A

IN GOOD HANDS—*Director Bob Sweeney was at the helm of every episode filmed in the second season (and for most of the episodes in the first season and for all but two episodes of the third season).*

handyman makes a mark of the Taylors while flirting with Aunt Bee. Edgar Buchanan as Henry "Goldbrick" Wheeler, Doodles Weaver as George Bricker, and George Cisar as Sheriff Mitchell. Written by Leo Solomon and Ben Gershman; directed by Bob Sweeney.

Episode 42: "The Clubmen," December 11, 1961. The Esquire Club looks over Andy and Barney before extending membership to one of them. George Neise as Roger Courtney. Ross Elliott, Bob McQuain, and Brad Olson also appear. Written by Fred S. Fox and Iz Elinson; directed by Bob Sweeney.

Episode 43: "The Pickle Story," December 18, 1961. Aunt Bee prepares "kerosene cucumbers" that Andy, Barney, and Opie must dispose of one way or another. One of Don Knotts's favorite episodes. Written by Harvey Bullock; directed by Bob Sweeney.

Episode 44: "Sheriff Barney," December 25, 1961. Barney gets a shot at sheriffing in Mayberry after a town

expresses interest in hiring him as top gun. Dabbs Greer as Councilman Dobbs and Ralph Dumke as Mayor Purdy. First appearance of Rafe Hollister. Written by Leo Solomon and Ben Gershman; directed by Bob Sweeney.

Episode 45: "The Farmer Takes a Wife," January 1, 1962. A farmer plows Mayberry in search of a bride; he digs Thelma Lou. Alan Hale, Jr., as Jeff Pruitt. First time to hear Barney say "Nip it in the bud!" Pruitt calls Barney "little buddy." Written by Charles Stewart and Jack Elinson; directed by Bob Sweeney.

Episode 46: "The Keeper of the Flame," January 8, 1962. A farmer accidentally burns his barn down and blames Opie's club. Everett Sloane as Jubal Foster, Flip Mark as leader of the Wildcats, and Terry Dickinson as a Wildcat. Written by Jack Elinson and Charles Stewart; directed by Bob Sweeney.

Episode 47: "Bailey's Bad Boy," January 15, 1962. A spoiled teen vows revenge on Andy for keeping him in Mayberry after a wreck. Bill Bixby as Ronald Bailey, Jon Lormer as Fletch Dilbeck, and John Graham as Arthur Harrington. Written by Leo Solomon and Ben Gershman; directed by Bob Sweeney.

Episode 48: "The Manicurist," January 22, 1962. Floyd employs a manicurist and the women of Mayberry revolt. Barbara Eden as Ellen Brown. Final appearance of

Mayor Pike. Written by Charles Stewart and Jack Elinson; directed by Bob Sweeney.

Episode 49: "The Jinx," January 29, 1962. When Mayberrians label a townsperson a jinx, the man's self-confidence is shaken until Andy comes up with a solution. John Qualen as Henry Bennett and Clint Howard as little cowboy, though without a name or trademark sandwich. Written by Jack Elinson and Charles Stewart; directed by Bob Sweeney.

Episode 50: "Jailbreak," February 5, 1962. When Barney lets a criminal escape, he and Andy search Mayberry for the man and his partner. Ken Lynch as Mr. Horton, Allan Melvin as Clarence "Doc" Malloy, and Fred Sherman as Fred Goss. First episode of Allan Melvin. Written by Harvey Bullock; directed by Bob Sweeney.

ALL GUSSIED UP—*Mayor Pike appears to be ready for a manicure.* COURTESY OF GILMORE-SCHWENKE ARCHIVES.

Episode 51: "A Medal for Opie," February 12, 1962. Opie wants a medal at the annual footraces so badly that he can almost taste victory. Written by David Adler (Frank Tarloff); directed by Bob Sweeney.

Episode 52: "Barney and the Choir," February 19, 1962. Tone-deaf Barney believes he's the perfect fit for a void in the choir. Olan Soule makes first appearance as choir director John Masters. One of Don Knotts's favorite episodes. Written by Charles Stewart and Jack Elinson; directed by Bob Sweeney.

Episode 53: "Guest of Honor," February 26, 1962. Mayberry gives the key to the city to a pickpocket who takes his time enjoying the riches of Mayberry. Jay Novello as Sheldon Davis. Written by Jack Elinson and Charles Stewart; directed by Bob Sweeney.

Episode 54: "The Merchant of Mayberry," March 5, 1962. Andy and Barney draw the wrath of Ben Weaver as they help a hapless salesman find his niche. Sterling Holloway as Bert Miller and Bob McQuain as Joe Waters. First episode of Mary Lansing. Written by Leo Solomon and Ben Gershman; directed by Bob Sweeney.

Episode 55: "Aunt Bee the Warden," March 12, 1962. Otis serves time at "the Rock," (a.k.a. the Taylor house) with Aunt Bee (a.k.a. Bloody Mary) as the "beast" in charge. Written by Jack Elinson and Charles Stewart; directed by Bob Sweeney.

Episode 56: "The County Nurse," March 19, 1962. Andy helps a county nurse drive home her point to Rafe Hollister, who needs a tetanus shot. Julie Adams as Mary. Written by Jack Elinson and Charles Stewart; directed by Bob Sweeney.

Episode 57: "Andy and Barney in the Big City," March 26, 1962. Barney has his eyes on a jewel thief in a hotel in Raleigh. Les Tremayne as C.J. Hasler, Allan Melvin as Detective Bardoli, and Arte Johnson as the front-desk clerk. Written by Harvey Bullock; directed by Bob Sweeney.

Episode 58: "Wedding Bells for Aunt Bee," April 2, 1962. Aunt Bee feigns romance with the man at the cleaners in order that Andy can feel free to find a wife. Fred Sherman as Fred Goss. Frances Bavier's favorite episode. Written by Harvey Bullock; directed by Bob Sweeney.

SHOWING BRASS—*Andy helps Bert Miller (Sterling Holloway) turn his sidewalk stand into a well-oiled vending site, much to the dismay of a tarnished Ben Weaver in "The Merchant of Mayberry."*

WHEN DUTY CALLS—*Otis achieves excellent marks with Andy in "Deputy Otis."*

Boswell, Roy Roberts as J. Howard Jackson, and Robert Brubaker as Roger Milton. Written by Jack Elinson and Charles Stewart; directed by Bob Sweeney.

Episode 62: "Cousin Virgil," April 30, 1962. Barney's inept cousin can't seem to do anything right until Andy hits upon a key idea. Michael J. Pollard as Virgil and Rance Howard as the bus driver. Written by Phillip Shuken and Johnny Greene; directed by Bob Sweeney.

Episode 63: "Deputy Otis," May 7, 1962. Andy agrees to let Otis be a temporary deputy when Otis's brother comes to visit. Stanley Adams as Ralph Campbell and Amzie Strickland as Verlaine Campbell. Written by Fred S. Fox and Iz Elinson; directed by Bob Sweeney.

SEASON THREE (1962-63)

Episode 64: "Mr. McBeevee," October 1, 1962. Andy has a hard time believing Opie's story about an adult friend. Karl Swenson as Mr. McBeevee. Written by R. Allen Saffian (Ray Allen) and Harvey Bullock; directed by Bob Sweeney.

Episode 65: "Andy's Rich Girlfriend," October 8, 1962. Andy stops dating Peggy because he believes her high social status is above him. Joanna Moore as Peggy McMillan. First appearance of Peggy McMillan. Written by Jim Fritzell and Everett Greenbaum; directed by Bob Sweeney.

Episode 66: "Andy and the New Mayor," October 15, 1962. Mayberry's new mayor doesn't care for Andy's style of sheriffing. Roy Engel as Jess Morgan, Helen Kleeb as Mrs. Morgan, Janet Stewart as Mrs. Ambrose, and Parley Baer in his first appearance as Mayor Roy Stoner. Written by Harvey Bullock and R. Allen Saffian (Ray Allen); directed by Bob Sweeney.

Episode 67: "Andy and Opie—Bachelors," October. 22, 1962. Peggy McMillan pays so much close attention to Andy and Opie that Floyd convinces Andy that Peggy is thinking matrimony. Written by Jim Fritzell and Everett Greenbaum; directed by Bob Sweeney.

Episode 68: "The Cow Thief," October 29, 1962. "It's moulage time" as the mayor brings in outside help when a rash of cattle thefts hits Mayberry. Malcolm Atterbury as Luke Jenson, Jon Lormer as Tate Fletcher, and Ralph Bell as William Upchurch. Written by R. Allen Saffian (Ray Allen) and Harvey Bullock; directed by Bob Sweeney.

Episode 69: "Barney Mends a Broken Heart," November 5, 1962. After Andy and Peggy have a spat, Barney fixes things up by bringing in "fun girls"

Episode 59: "Three's a Crowd," April 9, 1962. Andy dates the county nurse but just can't seem to find any space to be alone with her. Sue Ane Langdon as Mary Simpson. Written by Jack Elinson and Charles Stewart; directed by Bob Sweeney.

Episode 60: "The Bookie Barber," April 16, 1962. Floyd's new barber uses the barbershop as a front for his bookie business. Herb Vigran as Bill Medwin. Written by Ray Allen Saffian and Harvey Bullock; directed by Bob Sweeney.

Episode 61: "Andy on Trial," April 23, 1962. A newspaper publisher seeks revenge on Andy for a ticket by having a reporter uncover his failures as a lawman. Ruta Lee as Jean

THINKING OF BRIGHT IDEAS—*Director Bob Sweeney and Andy Griffith ponder how to shoot the pivotal scene where Andy discovers there is a "Mr. McBeevee." Sitting at left is script supervisor Hazel Hall. This photograph was taken on July 30, 1962.*

Skippy (Joyce Jameson) and Daphne (Jean Carson). Josie Lloyd as Lydia Crosswaith and Michael Ross as Al. First appearance of the fun girls from Mt. Pilot. Written by Aaron Ruben; directed by Bob Sweeney.

Episode 70: "Lawman Barney," November 12, 1962. Barney stands up to two roadside vendors who make fun of his badge. Allan Melvin as Neal, Orville Sherman as Matt, and Norman Leavitt as Wally. First appearance of Wally. Written by Aaron Ruben; directed by Bob Sweeney.

ITS A MAD MAUDE WORLD—*Big Maude (Reta Shaw) comforts Naomi (Jean Carson) as the situation doesn't sit well with a frazzled Floyd in "Convicts-at-Large."*

FISHIN' BUDDIES—*As much as she might like to, Peggy can't worm out of a day of fishing with Andy and Opie.*

Episode 71: "The Mayberry Band," November 19, 1962. Andy sneaks a few jazzmen into the town band to fool the mayor into allowing the group to perform in Raleigh. Joseph Sirola as Freddy Fleet and William Eben Stephens as Phil Sunkel. Written by Jim Fritzell and Everett Greenbaum. Directed by Bob Sweeney.

Episode 72: "Floyd, the Gay Deceiver," November 26, 1962. Floyd poses as a wealthy widower with Andy as his son when his lonely hearts club friend pays a visit. Doris Dowling as Madeline Grayson. Written by Aaron Ruben; directed by Bob Sweeney.

Episode 73: "Opie's Rival," December 3, 1962. Opie becomes envious when Andy begins spending time with nurse Peggy McMillan. Written by Sid Morse; directed by Bob Sweeney.

Episode 74: "Convicts-at-Large," December 10, 1962. A trio of female convicts takes Floyd and Barney hostage at a cabin. Reta Shaw as Big Maude Tyler, Jean Carson as Jalene Naomi Connors, Jane Dulo as Sally, and Willis Bouchey as Chuck O'Malley. Howard McNear's last episode before his stroke. He returns in "Andy Saves Gomer" (Episode 118). Written by Everett Greenbaum and Jim Fritzell; directed by Bob Sweeney.

Episode 75: "The Bed Jacket," December 17, 1962. The mayor takes advantage of Andy and swaps a bed jacket for his fishing rod to allow Andy to give Aunt Bee the perfect birthday gift. Hope Summers as Clara Johnson and Dabbs Greer as a sales clerk. Written by Harvey Bullock and R. Allen Saffian (Ray Allen); directed by Bob Sweeney.

Episode 76: "The Bank Job," December 24, 1962. Barney takes a crack at the Mayberry bank vault just before robbers get the same idea. Charles Thompson as Asa Breeney, Clint Howard as Leon, Al Checco as Ollie, and Lee Krieger as Mort. First broadcast appearance of Gomer Pyle and of Leon with a name and sandwich. Written by Jim Fritzell and Everett Greenbaum; directed by Bob Sweeney.

ENDEARING SINGER—*Rafe Hollister (Jack Prince) sings solo after Barney drops out of the sing-along (the song's not in his key).*

Episode 77: "One-Punch Opie," December 31, 1962. Opie is forced to confront a new kid in town who is bullying Opie and his pals. Scott McCartor as Steve Quincy. First appearance of Richard Keith (Thibodeaux) as Johnny Paul. Leon also appears. Written by Harvey Bullock; directed by Bob Sweeney.

Episode 78: "Barney and the Governor," January 7, 1963. Barney gives the governor's driver a parking ticket and the governor heads to Mayberry. Carl Benton Reid as the Governor and Rance Howard as the governor's chauffeur. Written by Bill Freedman and Henry Sharp; directed by Bob Sweeney.

Episode 79: "Man in a Hurry," January 14, 1963. A businessman has car trouble in Mayberry on a Sunday morning and is stranded for the day. Robert Emhardt as Malcolm Tucker.

First appearance of Rev. Hobart M. Tucker. First episode filmed with Gomer. Favorite episode of Aneta Corsaut and Doug Dillard and of fans in many polls. Written by Everett Greenbaum and Jim Fritzell; directed by Bob Sweeney.

Episode 80: "High Noon in Mayberry," January 21, 1963. An ex-con whom Andy shot and had sent to the pen comes to town with a little payback. Leo Gordon as Luke Comstock. Dub Taylor appears. Written by Jim Fritzell and Everett Greenbaum; directed by Bob Sweeney.

Episode 81: "The Loaded Goat," January 28, 1963 A goat that fills up on dynamite gets kid-glove treatment from Andy and Barney. Forrest Lewis as Cy Hudgins and Bing Russell (father of Kurt Russell) as Mr. Burton. Written by Harvey Bullock; directed by Bob Sweeney.

Episode 82: "Class Reunion," February 4, 1963. Andy and Barney reunite with high school sweethearts at their class reunion. Peggy McCay as Sharon DeSpain, Barbara Perry as Mary Lee, Molly Dodd as Ramona Wiley Bektoris, and Paul Smith as Harry Bektoris. *The Cutlass* was named after Jim Fritzell's high school yearbook, while the Mayberry colors of orange and blue are from Everett Greenbaum's high school in Buffalo, New York. Written by Everett Greenbaum and Jim Fritzell; directed by Charles Irving.

Episode 83: "Rafe Hollister Sings," February 11, 1963. A backwoods farmer tries out for a singing competition. Kay Stewart as Martha Hollister, Isabel Randolph as Mrs. Jeffries, and Ottola Nesmith as Mrs. Dennis. Last appearance of Rafe Hollister. Andy and Opie sing "The Crawdad Song." Written by Harvey Bullock; directed by Charles Irving.

Episode 84: "Opie and the Spoiled Kid," February 18, 1963. A bratty youngster attempts to teach Opie the finer points of being spoiled. Ronnie Dapo as Arnold Winkler and Harlan Warde as Simon Winkler. Written by Jim Fritzell and Everett Greenbaum; directed by Bob Sweeney.

READY, WILLING, AND…—*Gomer, the easy-going worker at Wally's.*

TRUCK STOP—*Charlene Darling has her eyes on Andy as the boys (Rodney, Dean, Doug, and Mitch) are all keyed up.* COURTESY OF PHIL BOWLING COLLECTION.

Episode 85: "The Great Filling Station Robbery," February 25, 1963. Andy disagrees when evidence points to a young man being the culprit in a series of break-ins. Willis Bouchey as Mr. Carter and Pat Colby as Jimmy Morgan. Written by Harvey Bullock; directed by Bob Sweeney.

Episode 86: "Andy Discovers America," March 4, 1963. After being critical of Opie's teacher, Andy gets Opie and his pals excited about studying History. First appearance of Miss Helen Crump and Howie Pruitt. President Dwight D. Eisenhower's favorite episode. Written by John Whedon; directed by Bob Sweeney.

Episode 87: "Aunt Bee's Medicine Man," March 11, 1963. A fast-talking salesman gets Aunt Bee and her friends tipsy on his tonic. John Dehner as Colonel Harvey. Written by John Whedon; directed by Bob Sweeney.

Episode 88: "The Darlings Are Coming," March 18, 1963. A family of mountaineers descend upon Mayberry, and Mr. Darling's daughter yearns for Andy. First appearance of the Darlings. Hoke Howell as Dud Wash. A studio jug player did the jugging for Briscoe. In later episodes, Briscoe's jugging is silenced altogether. Favorite episode of all of the Dillards and of Maggie Peterson. Written by Everett Greenbaum and Jim Fritzell; directed by Bob Sweeney.

Episode 89: "Andy's English Valet," March 25, 1963. Andy takes on an English handyman after the bicycling tourist mounts up a wad of fines. First appearance of Malcolm Merriweather (Bernard Fox). Bob McQuain as Fletch Roberts. Written by Harvey Bullock; directed by Bob Sweeney.

Episode 90: "Barney's First Car," April 1, 1963. A sharp old lady pawns off a lemon on naive car buyer Barney. Ellen Corby as Mrs. Myrt "Hubcaps" Lesch and Allan Melvin as Jake. A favorite episode of Andy Griffith, Don Knotts, and Betty Lynn. Won Writers Guild of America Award for best writing in a comedy or variety series. Written by Jim Fritzell and Everett Greenbaum; directed by Bob Sweeney.

Episode 91: "The Rivals," April 8, 1963. Barney gets obtuse after Thelma Lou tries to mend Opie's broken heart

Episode 95: "The Big House," May 6, 1963. Barney's schooling of a pair of criminals fails, as they escape the Mayberry jail. Billy Halop as Tiny, Jack Lambert as Doc, Richard Angarola as Morley, and George Kennedy as a detective. Written by Harvey Bullock; directed by Bob Sweeney.

OUTSTANDING!—*Don Knotts picked up his third Emmy for playing Barney Fife on May 26, 1963.*

LOOKS LIKE A CUTE CONTEST—
It's neck and neck to see who can look cuter in "Dogs, Dogs, Dogs." Let's just give a Mister Cooky Bar to both of them.

and the lad develops a crush on her. Written by Harvey Bullock; directed by Bob Sweeney.

Episode 92: "A Wife for Andy," April 15, 1963. Barney combs the whole town as he attempts to find a suitable mate for Andy. Barbara Perry as Lavinia, Janet Waldo as Amanda, and Rachel Ames as Rosemary. Janet Stewart also appears. Written by Aaron Ruben; directed by Bob Sweeney.

Episode 93: "Dogs, Dogs, Dogs," April 22, 1963. When Opie finds a dog and then a whole pack of hounds converge on the Courthouse, Andy and Barney try to find homes for the dogs. Robert Cornthwaite as Mr. Somerset and Roy Barcroft as Clint Biggers. Written by Everett Greenbaum and Jim Fritzell; directed by Bob Sweeney.

Episode 94: "Mountain Wedding," April 29, 1963. Because he won't recognize Andy's power as justice of the peace, Ernest T. Bass gets one more chance to capture Charlene Darling's heart. Dub Taylor as the preacher. First appearance of Ernest T. Bass. Written by Jim Fritzell and Everett Greenbaum; directed by Bob Sweeney.

SEASON FOUR (1963-64)

Episode 96: "Opie the Birdman," September 30, 1963. Opie raises three young songbirds after he accidentally shoots their mother. The birds' names, Winken, Blinken, and Nod, are derived from the Eugene Field poem "Wynken, Blynken, and Nod." Favorite episode of Aaron Ruben. Written by Harvey Bullock; directed by Dick Crenna.

Episode 97: "The Haunted House," October 7, 1963. Andy, Barney, and Gomer check out the Remshaw House after Opie hits a baseball through a window of the haunted house. Ronnie

Dapo as Opie's friend and Nestor Paiva as Big Jack Anderson. Written by Harvey Bullock; directed by Earl Bellamy.

Episode 98: "Ernest T. Bass Joins the Army," October 14, 1963. Ernest T. hopes to enlist in the Army in order to get a uniform to impress his girl. Allan Melvin as Sergeant Pratt and Paul Smith as the Army doctor. Written by Jim Fritzell and Everett Greenbaum; directed by Dick Crenna.

Episode 99: "The Sermon for Today," October 21, 1963. A visiting preacher's sermon has the Mayberry folks banding together in a hurry for a big concert. David Lewis as Dr. Harrison Everett Breen. Written by John Whedon; directed by Dick Crenna.

Episode 100: "Briscoe Declares for Aunt Bee," October. 28, 1963. Briscoe Darling mistakenly believes Aunt Bee has taken a liking to him because of her kind manners, and he vows to win her heart. Written by Everett Greenbaum and Jim Fritzell; directed by Earl Bellamy.

Episode 101: "Gomer the House Guest," November 4, 1963. Gomer gets fired from the filling station and lives at the Taylor house for a few days and drives everybody crazy. Trevor Bardette as Wally. Written by Jim Fritzell and Everett Greenbaum; directed by Earl Bellamy.

Episode 102: "A Black Day for Mayberry," November 11, 1963. A secret gold shipment coming through town is treated to a rousing welcome by all of Mayberry. Rance Howard as a Treasury agent, Ken Lynch as an FBI agent, Doodles Weaver as Regis, and Clint Howard as Leon. Favorite episode of Clint Howard. Written by John Whedon; directed by Jeffrey Hayden.

Episode 103: "Opie's Ill-Gotten Gain," November 18, 1963. When Opie gets straight A's, Andy rewards him, but it turns out that Opie didn't make the grades. Barney recites the Preamble to the *U.S. Constitution* "by heart." Written by John Whedon;

directed by Jeffrey Hayden.

Episode 104: "A Date for Gomer," November 25, 1963. Gomer goes on a blind date with Thelma Lou's shy but nice cousin. Mary Grace Canfield as Mary Grace Gossage. Written by Everett Greenbaum and Jim Fritzell; directed by Dick Crenna.

Episode 105: "Up in Barney's Room," December 2, 1963. Mrs. Mendelbright throws Barney out of his apartment, while he suspects a conman is after her savings. Enid Markey as Mrs. Mendelbright and J. Pat O'Malley as Oscar Fields. Written by Jim Fritzell and Everett Greenbaum; directed by Jeffrey Hayden.

Episode 106: "Citizen's Arrest," December 16, 1963. When Gomer arrests Barney for an illegal U-turn, Barney locks himself in jail. Favorite episode of Jim Nabors. Written by Everett Greenbaum and Jim Fritzell; directed by Dick Crenna.

Episode 107: "Opie and His Merry Men," December 30, 1963. Opie, Johnny Paul, Whitey, and Howie hang around a hobo who thinks lawmen have unfairly persecuted him. Douglas Fowley as the hobo. Written by John Whedon; directed by Dick Crenna.

Episode 108: "Barney and the Cave Rescue," January 6, 1964. Barney organizes the rescue efforts after a cave-in traps Andy and Helen. Written by Harvey Bullock; directed by Dick Crenna.

Episode 109: "Andy and Opie's Pal," January 13, 1964. When Opie's new friend finds a father figure in Andy, Opie turns jealous. First appearance of David A. Bailey as Trey Bowden.

Written by Harvey Bullock; directed by Dick Crenna.

Episode 110: "Aunt Bee the Crusader," January 20, 1964. Aunt Bee sides with a farmer who protests against being evicted from his land. Charles Lane as Mr. Frisbie. Written by John Whedon; directed by Coby Ruskin.

Episode 111: "Barney's Sidecar," January 27, 1964. Barney beefs up the patrol with a motorcycle and sidecar that he buys at auction. At age fourteen, writer Everett Greenbaum bought a bushel basket full of pieces from a World War I-era Harley Davidson. Written by Jim Fritzell and Everett Greenbaum; directed by Coby Ruskin.

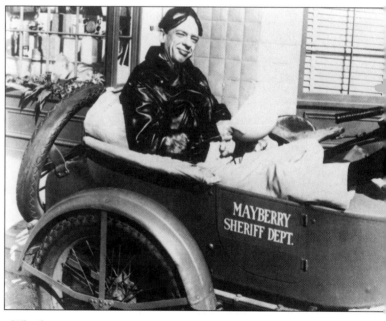

ANDY SAID IT BEST—*"You know, I've a great mind to take the motorcycle away from him and leave him the sidecar and fill it up with sand and give him a bucket and shovel and let him play in it on weekends."*

Episode 112: "My Fair Ernest T. Bass," February 3, 1964. Ernest T. gets a high-society makeover when Andy preps him for a soiree at Mrs. Wiley's house. Jackie Joseph as Ramona Ankrum and Doris Packer as Mrs. Wiley. First appearance of Mr. Schwamp. President Kennedy was assassinated during the rehearsal day for this episode. Written by Everett Greenbaum and Jim Fritzell; directed by Earl Bellamy.

Episode 113: "Prisoner of Love," February 10, 1964. A female prisoner stirs passions as she spends a night in jail. Susan Oliver as Angela Carroll. Written by Harvey Bullock; directed by Earl Bellamy.

Episode 114: "Hot Rod Otis," February 17, 1964. After Otis purchases a vehicle, Andy and Barney fret about the potential for an accident. Andy, Barney, and Otis are the only characters who appear in this episode. Written by Harvey Bullock; directed by Earl Bellamy.

Episode 115: "The Songfesters," February 24, 1964. Barney gets a shot at stardom singing solo in the choir, but Gomer's emergence as a top vocalist causes a problem. Reta Shaw as Eleanora Poultice, Barbara Griffith as choir member Sharon, Delos Jewkes as Glen Cripe, and Renée Aubry as a choir member. Written by Jim Fritzell and Everett Greenbaum; directed by Earl Bellamy.

Episode 116: "The Shoplifters," March 2, 1964. Thievery at Weaver's Department Store causes Barney to spring into action and as a dummy. Tol Avery as Ben Weaver and Lurene Tuttle as shoplifter. Last appearance of Clint Howard as Leon. Won the Writers Guild of America Award for Episodic Comedy Writing. Written by Bill Idelson and Sam Bobrick (their first); directed by Coby Ruskin.

Episode 117: "Andy's Vacation," March 9, 1964. Andy takes a week's break from the office but Barney keeps bothering him with minor details, including letting a prisoner break out of jail. Allan Melvin as the escaped prisoner and Dabbs Greer as husband who fights with wife (Mary Dodd).

Written by Everett Greenbaum and Jim Fritzell; directed by Jeffrey Hayden.

Episode 118: "Andy Saves Gomer," March 16, 1964. Gomer tries to pay Andy back for saving him from a fire, but he nearly smothers Andy and his family in the process. Howard McNear returns after suffering a stroke. Written by Harvey Bullock; directed by Jeffrey Hayden.

Episode 119: "Bargain Day," March 23, 1964. Aunt Bee buys a load of beef but has no place to store it. Frank Ferguson appears as Mr. Foley for the first time. Written by John Whedon; directed by Jeffrey Hayden.

Episode 120: "Divorce, Mountain Style," March 30, 1964. Charlene Darling breaks up with Dud and sets her sights on Andy. Bob Denver as Dudley D. Wash. Written by Jim Fritzell and Everett Greenbaum; directed by Jeffrey Hayden.

Episode 121: "A Deal Is a Deal," April 6, 1964. Opie and his pals have problems unloading their cases of crummy Miracle Salve until Barney gets a bright idea. George Petrie as Lenny and Charles Lewis as Lenny's partner. Written by Bill Idelson and Sam Bobrick; directed by Jeffrey Hayden.

STORIED CHARACTER BUILDERS— *This 1998 photo of legendary writers/actors/ longtime pals Bill Idelson and Everett Greenbaum was taken on the set of the TV series* American Pie. PHOTO BY ELLEN IDELSON. COURTESY OF BILL IDELSON.

Episode 122: "Fun Girls," April 13, 1964. "Fun girls" Daphne and Skippy get Andy and Barney into big-time trouble with Helen and Thelma Lou. First appearance of Goober and the only episode with both Gomer and Goober. Goober takes off on Cary Grant and others. Written by Aaron Ruben; directed by Coby Ruskin.

Episode 123: "The Return of Malcolm Merriweather," April 20, 1964. Malcolm Merriweather makes himself so useful around the Taylor house that Aunt Bee feels unwanted. Written by Harvey Bullock; directed by Coby Ruskin.

Episode 124: "The Rumor," April 27, 1964. Barney spreads an untruth that Andy and Helen are engaged, so a big surprise party is planned. Rance Howard as friend at party. Written by Everett Greenbaum and Jim Fritzell; directed by Coby Ruskin.

Episode 125: "Barney and Thelma Lou, Phfftt," May 4, 1964. Barney's poor treatment toward Thelma Lou causes her to date Gomer as a ruse to stir Barney's jealousy. Written by Bill Idelson and Sam Bobrick; directed by Coby Ruskin.

Episode 126: "Back to Nature," May 11, 1964. Barney and Gomer get lost in the woods as they and Andy take a group of boys camping. Among the campers are Opie, Johnny Paul Jason, Howie Pruitt, and Trey Bowden. Willis Bouchey as Fletch. Written by Harvey Bullock; directed by Coby Ruskin.

Episode 127: "Gomer Pyle, U.S.M.C.," May 19, 1964. Gomer joins the Marines, and Andy makes sure that he adjusts to his new environment. Frank Sutton as Sgt. Carter and Frank Albertson as Col. Watson. Last appearance of Gomer Pyle. Written and directed by Aaron Ruben.

SEASON FIVE (1964-65)

Episode 128: "Opie Loves Helen," September 21, 1964. Opie gets a crush on his teacher, Miss Crump. Written by Bob Ross; directed by Aaron Ruben.

Episode 129: "Barney's Physical," September 28, 1964. Barney needs to grow an inch and add a few pounds to pass new physical requirements for lawmen. When producer Aaron Ruben

left *The Andy Griffith Show* later this season, he was given a plaque from the cast and crew. Engraved upon it was the numeral "5," for five years of service—just like the five engraved on the back of Barney's watch in this episode. Written by Bob Ross; directed by Howard Morris.

Episode 130: "Family Visit," October 5, 1964. Aunt Bee's sister, brother-in-law, and nephews come to stay for the weekend with the Taylors. James Westerfield as Uncle Ollie and Maudie Prickett as Nora. Written by Jim Fritzell and Everett Greenbaum; directed by Howard Morris.

Episode 131: "The Education of Ernest T. Bass," October 12, 1964. Ernest T. Bass goes to school and learns to love Miss Crump. Written by Everett Greenbaum and Jim Fritzell; directed by Alan Rafkin.

Episode 132: "Aunt Bee's Romance," October 19, 1964. An old flame stirs embers in Aunt Bee's heart, but Andy despises the cad. Wallace Ford as Roger Hanover. Floyd and Andy discuss Calvin Coolidge, Mark Twain, and the weather. Written by Harvey Bullock; directed by Howard Morris.

Episode 133: "Barney's Bloodhound," October 26, 1964. Barney gets the idea that he can train Blue the mutt to be a police dog. Arthur Batanides as Ralph Neal. Howard Morris supplies the voices of the radio announcer and singer Leonard Blush. Written by Bill Idelson and Sam Bobrick; directed by Howard Morris.

Episode 134: "Man in the Middle," November 2, 1964. Andy tries to mend a spat between Barney and Thelma Lou and finds himself feeling the wrath of Helen. Written by Gus Adrian (Jim Fritzell) and David Evans; directed by Alan Rafkin.

BLUE PRINT— *Barney's tracking technique may not appear to make a lot of scents, but never underestimate the abilities of "Barney's Bloodhound."*

Episode 135: "Barney's Uniform," November 9, 1964. Barney won't be caught out of uniform because a bully says he'll get him once he appears in street clothes. Allan Melvin as Fred Plummer and Yuki Shimoda as Mr. Izamoto. Written by Bill Idelson and Sam Bobrick; directed by Coby Ruskin.

Episode 136: "Opie's Fortune," November 16, 1964. Opie discovers a wallet with fifty dollars and has to wait one week to see if anyone calls to claim it. Jon Lormer as Parnell Rigsby and Mary Jackson as Mrs. Rigsby. Written by Ben Joelson and Art Baer; directed by Coby Ruskin.

Centennial Pageant, so Aunt Bee sets her heart on the part. Written by Harvey Bullock; directed by Gene Nelson.

Episode 139: "The Darling Baby," December 7, 1964. The Darlings come to Mayberry looking for a suitable young mate for Charlene's baby girl.

Barney starts fooling with a "magic" lamp and fortune-telling cards he bought at an auction. Written by Richard M. Powell; directed by Howard Morris.

Episode 142: "Otis Sues the County," December 28, 1964. After Otis takes a spill in the Courthouse, a lawyer gets him to make a claim against the county. Jay Novello as Neil Bentley and Bartlett Robinson as Mr. Roberts. Written by Bob Ross; directed by Howard Morris.

NICE CAR—*Floyd might be racing around town before long when "Goober Takes a Car Apart." As Floyd says, "You know, Andy, I just might buy this car."*

Written by Jim Fritzell and Everett Greenbaum; directed by Howard Morris.

Episode 140: "Andy and Helen Have Their Day," December 14, 1964. Andy and Helen head for the lake for a picnic, but Barney keeps getting in the way. Howard Morris as George the TV repairman, Colin Male (the announcer of *The Andy Griffith Show*) as Game Warden Peterson. Goober takes off on Cary Grant. Written by Bill Idelson and Sam Bobrick; directed by Howard Morris.

Episode 137: "Goodbye, Sheriff Taylor," November 23, 1964. When Andy considers a new job in Raleigh, Barney takes over for a day and creates havoc. First time to see Goober in his beanie. Written by Fred Freeman and Lawrence J. Cohen; directed by Gene Nelson.

Episode 138: "The Pageant," November 30, 1964. The role of Lady Mayberry is up for grabs in the

Episode 141: "Three Wishes for Opie," December 21, 1964. Count Istvan Teleky grants wishes after

Episode 143: "Barney Fife, Realtor," January 4, 1965. Barney tries his hand at selling houses and persuades Andy to list his for sale. Dabbs Greer as Harry Sims, Amzie Strickland as Lila Sims, Dennis Rush as Howie Williams, and Harlan Warde as Mr. Williams. Written by Bill Idelson and Sam Bobrick; directed by Peter Baldwin.

Episode 144: "Goober Takes a Car Apart," January 11, 1965. Goober assembles an entire vehicle in the Courthouse and Andy just about loses all his bearings. Larry Hovis as Gilly Walker, Wally Englehardt as Sheriff Jackson, and Buck Young as Deputy Joe Watson. Tom Jacobs speaks up as a Mayberry citizen. Written by Bill Idelson and Sam Bobrick; directed by Peter Baldwin.

Episode 145: "The Rehabilitation of Otis," January 18, 1965. When Barney tries psychology on Otis to cure his drinking habit, Otis leaves town. Frank Cady as Luke. Written by Lawrence J. Cohen and Fred Freeman; directed by Peter Baldwin.

Episode 146: "The Lucky Letter," January 25, 1965. Barney believes a chain letter has jinxed him just as he heads for the firing range to requalify for his position. Written by Richard M. Powell; directed by Theodore J. Flicker.

FOUR CHAIRS, WAITING—*Relaxing on the set are Don Knotts, director Alan Rafkin, Andy Griffith, and George Lindsey.* COURTESY OF THE GEORGE LINDSEY COLLECTION OF COLLIER LIBRARY, UNIVERSITY OF NORTH ALABAMA.

Episode 147: "Goober and the Art of Love," February 1, 1965. After Barney gets a date for Goober, he then schools him in the ways of woo by spying on Andy and Helen. Josie Lloyd as Lydia Crosswaith. Written by Fred Freeman and Lawrence J. Cohen; directed by Alan Rafkin.

Episode 148: "Barney Runs for Sheriff," February 8, 1965. Barney challenges Andy for the top law position in Mayberry. Written by Richard M. Powell; directed by Alan Rafkin.

Episode 149: "If I Had a Quarter-Million," February 15, 1965. Barney stumbles across a cool quarter-million dollars and uses the dough to try and catch the thief who lost it. Hank Patterson as a hobo, Al Checco as "Hennessey," Robert Brubaker as Frank Brewster, and Byron Foulger as Fred. Written by Bob Ross; directed by Alan Rafkin.

Episode 150: "TV or Not TV," March, 1, 1965. Bogus movie-makers hit town to make a film about Andy, but their true intentions are to rob the bank. George Ives as Allen Harvey, Barbara Stuart as Pat Blake, and Gavin McLeod as Gilbert Jammel. Written by Art Baer and Ben Joelson; directed by Coby Ruskin.

Episode 151: "Guest in the House," March 8, 1965. When a beautiful friend of the family stays with the Taylors, Helen finds good reason to be jealous. Jan Shutan as Gloria and George Spence as Frank. Written by Lawrence J. Cohen and Fred Freeman; directed by Coby Ruskin.

Episode 152: "The Case of the Punch in the Nose," March 15, 1965. Barney uncovers an unsolved case from yesteryear that causes hard feelings among the best of friends. Written by Bill Idelson and Sam Bobrick; directed by Coby Ruskin.

Episode 153: "Opie's Newspaper," March 22, 1965. Opie and Howie's little paper gets the scoop on all the local gossip, causing a panic attack in Andy, Aunt Bee, and Barney. Final appearance of Howie Pruitt. Written by Harvey Bullock; directed by Coby Ruskin.

Episode 154: "Aunt Bee's Invisible Beau," March 29, 1965. Aunt Bee invents a romance to encourage Andy to get serious about matrimony. Woodrow Chambliss as Orville Hendricks and Bobby Diamond as Evan Hendricks. Written by Art Baer and Ben Joelson; directed by Theodore J. Flicker.

Episode 155: "The Arrest of the Fun Girls," April 5, 1965. When Andy and Barney jail the "fun girls," Helen and Thelma Lou suspect infidelity. Written by Richard M. Powell; directed by Theodore J. Flicker.

Episode 156: "The Luck of Newton Monroe," April 12, 1965. A hapless salesman gets a chance to prove himself at other vocations as Andy lends a helpful hand. Don Rickles as Newton Monroe. Written by Bill Idelson and Sam Bobrick; directed by Coby Ruskin.

Episode 157: "Opie Flunks Arithmetic," April 19, 1965. Andy overreacts when Opie gets low grades in math. Final appearance by Don Knotts as a regular cast member on the show. Written by Richard Morgan; directed by Coby Ruskin.

Episode 158: "Opie and the Carnival," April 26, 1965. Opie is foiled by a crooked shooting gallery contest as he tries to win a prize for Andy. Billy Halop as George and Lewis Charles as Pete. Written by Fred Freeman and Lawrence J. Cohen; directed by Coby Ruskin.

Episode 159: "Banjo-Playing Deputy," May 3, 1965. An unemployed musician and friend of Aunt Bee's family tries his hand as deputy. Jerry Van Dyke as Jerry Miller, Sylvia Lewis as Flossie, Herbie Faye as Flossie's manager, Lee Van Cleef as Skip, and Robert Carricart as Frankie. Floyd and Andy once again discuss what Calvin Coolidge said. Written by Bob Ross; directed by Coby Ruskin.

SEASON SIX (1965-66)
Now filmed in color.

Episode 160: "Opie's Job," September 13, 1965. Opie and another boy vie for a job at the local grocery store. Norris Goff (Abner Peabody of radio's *Lum and Abner*) as Mr. Doakes and John Bangert as Billy Crenshaw. This was the first episode broadcast in color. Written by Art Baer and Ben Joelson; directed by Larry Dobkin.

Episode 161: "Andy's Rival," September 20, 1965. When Helen has to spend long hours on a school project with a good-looking teacher, Andy gets impatient. Charles Aidman as Frank Smith. Written by Laurence Marks; directed by Peter Baldwin.

Episode 162: "Malcolm at the Crossroads," September 27, 1965. Malcolm Merriweather and Ernest T. Bass pair off for a fistfight after Malcolm takes over Ernest T.'s job at the school crosswalk. First appearance of Warren Ferguson. The final appearances of Ernest T. Bass and Malcolm Merriweather. Written by Harvey Bullock; directed by Gary Nelson.

Episode 163: "Aunt Bee, the Swinger," October 4, 1965. Aunt Bee hits the ground running in romance, but neither she nor her suitor cares to confess that they're making time much too fast. Charles Ruggles as John Canfield. First episode *filmed* in color. Written by Jack Elinson; directed by Larry Dobkin.

Episode 164: "The Bazaar," October 11, 1965. The menfolk of Mayberry come down hard on Andy after a stubborn Warren jails the women's charity bazaar members for playing bingo. Amzie Strickland, Mary Lansing, Claudia Bryar, Sam Edwards, Joe di Reda, and Pam Ferdin appear. Written by Ben Joelson and Art Baer; directed by Sheldon Leonard.

Episode 165: "A Warning From Warren," October 18, 1965. Warren insists that his powers of ESP have

TALENTED DUO—*Art Baer (left) enjoys a conversation with writing partner Ben Joelson.* COURTESY OF ART BAER.

informed him that Andy and Helen are in danger. Written by Fred Freeman and Lawrence J. Cohen; directed by Alan Rafkin.

Episode 166: "Off to Hollywood," October 25, 1965. Andy, Opie, and Aunt Bee take a trip to Hollywood when Andy gets paid for the rights to produce his story as a movie. Owen Bush as Mr. Jason and Maudie Prickett as Edna Sue Larch. Written by Bill Idelson and Sam Bobrick; directed by Alan Rafkin.

Episode 167: "Taylors in Hollywood," November 1, 1965. The Taylors visit the set of *Sheriff Without a Gun* and see how the make-believe-world of movie-making works. Gavin McLeod as Bryan Bender, Hayden Rorke as A.J. Considine, Eddie Quillan as the bellhop, Ross Elliott as Al Saunders, June Vincent as the actress, and Herb Vigran as keeper of the gate. Written by Bill Idelson and Sam Bobrick; directed by Alan Rafkin.

Episode 168: "The Hollywood Party," November 8, 1965. Andy goes out with a pretty actress and the news reaches Helen back in Mayberry. Ruta Lee as Darlene Mason and Sid Melton as Pat Michaels. Written by Lawrence J. Cohen and Fred Freeman; directed by Alan Rafkin.

Episode 169: "Aunt Bee on TV," November 15, 1965. Aunt Bee scores big on a TV game show, but her friends grow weary of her tale about the big event. William Christopher as

Mr. Heathcote and Jack Smith as himself. Written by Fred Freeman and Lawrence J. Cohen; directed by Alan Rafkin.

Episode 170: "The Cannon," November 22, 1965. Warren finds good use of the old cannon after crooks rip off an exhibit from the state museum. Robert Karnes as George Archer, Sally Mansfield as Stella, J. Edward McKinley as Governor Handley, and Byron Foulger as Harry Bosworth. Written by Jack Elinson; directed by Alan Rafkin.

Episode 171: "A Man's Best Friend," November 29, 1965. Opie and his pal trick Goober into believing his hound really can talk. Michel Petit as Tommy. Favorite episode of George Lindsey. Written by Art Baer and Ben Joelson; directed by Alan Rafkin.

Episode 172: "Aunt Bee Takes a Job," December 6, 1965. Aunt Bee goes to work at a print shop, never knowing that her employers are printing up fake twenty-dollar bills. Milton Frome as Ralph Kingsley, James Milhollin as Arnold Finch, Jason Johnson as Ben Weaver, Herbie Faye as Mr. Clark, and Maggie Magennis as Violet Rose

Shumaker. Written by Bill Idelson and Sam Bobrick; directed by Alan Rafkin.

Episode 173: "The Church Organ," December 13, 1965. When the All Souls Church organ expires, an excellent used one seems to be the perfect remedy, but a bare collection plate makes buying the organ seem like an impossible dream. Woodrow Chambliss as Harlan Robinson. Written by Paul Wayne; directed by Lee Philips.

Episode 174: "Girl-Shy," December 20, 1965. A sleep-walking Warren turns into a Casanova around Helen and endangers his job. Written by Bill Idelson and Sam Bobrick; directed by Lee Philips.

Episode 175: "Otis, the Artist," January 3, 1966. Warren treats Otis's drinking problem with mosaic art therapy. Written by Fred Freeman and Lawrence J. Cohen; story by Bob Ross; directed by Alan Rafkin.

Episode 176: "The Return of Barney Fife," January 10, 1965. Barney and Thelma Lou meet again at their class reunion, where Barney hopes their flame might burn again. Don Knotts wins an Emmy for actor in a supporting role in a comedy. Final appearance of Thelma Lou. Ted Jordan as Gerald Whitfield, Alberta Nelson as Nettie Albright, and Barbara Perry as Floss. Written by Sam Bobrick and Bill Idelson; directed by Alan Rafkin.

IT'S WATERMELON EATIN' TIME IN MAYBERRY!— *Hearty-eatin' men Andy and Opie are a festival of color as they gobble delicious fruit.*

Episode 177: "The Legend of Barney Fife," January 17, 1966. Warren's hero worship of Barney is tested when the duo tackles an escaped convict. Frank Cady as Farley Upchurch and Ted White as Avery Noonan. Written by Harvey Bullock; directed by Alan Rafkin.

Episode 178: "Lost and Found," Jan. 24, 1966. Aunt Bee finds some lost jewelry for which she has already received her insurance claim. Jack Dodson makes his first appearance as Ed Jenkins (not Howard Sprague). Arthur Malet as a vagrant. Written by John L. Greene and Paul David; directed by Alan Rafkin.

Episode 179: "Wyatt Earp Rides Again," January 31, 1966. A descendant öf Wyatt Earp challenges Andy to a showdown on Mayberry's Main Street. Pat Hingle as Fred Gibson and Richard Jury as Clarence Earp. Last appearance of Warren Ferguson. Written by Jack Elinson; directed by Alan Rafkin.

Episode 180: "Aunt Bee Learns to Drive," February 7, 1966. Andy worries himself sick after Aunt Bee takes up driving with Goober as her instructor. Written by Jack Elinson; directed by Lee Philips.

Episode 181: "Look Paw, I'm Dancing," February 14, 1966. Opie dreads going to a dance because of fear of failure. Last appearance of Johnny Paul Jason. Written by Ben Starr; directed by Lee Philips.

Episode 182: "The Gypsies," February 21, 1966. A gypsy clan curses Mayberry with a drought after Andy makes them quit selling their wares in town. Vito Scotti as Murrillos and Jamie Farr as Sylvio. Written by Roland MacLane; directed by Alan Rafkin.

Episode 183: "Eat Your Heart Out," February 28, 1966. While Goober has eyes for waitress Flora, she only has eyes for Andy. Alberta Nelson as Flora Malherbe for the first time. Written by

Art Baer and Ben Joelson; directed by Alan Rafkin.

Episode 184: "A Baby in the House," March 7, 1966. When the Taylors baby-sit an infant for a few days, Aunt Bee is heartbroken to find the baby doesn't care for her. Alvy Moore as a salesman and Ronnie Dapo as Pete. Written by Bill Idelson and Sam Bobrick; directed by Alan Rafkin.

Episode 185: "The County Clerk," March 14, 1966. Andy and Helen fix Howard up with a lady friend, much to his mother's dismay. First appearance of Howard Sprague. Mabel Albertson as Mrs. Sprague, Jim Begg as bridegroom, and Nina Shipman as Irene Fairchild. Written by Bill Idelson and Sam Bobrick; directed by Alan Rafkin.

Episode 186: "The Foster Lady," March 21, 1966. Aunt Bee becomes a commercial TV star when she is chosen to be the Foster Furniture Polish Lady. Robert Emhardt as Willard Foster and Ronnie Schell as director Jim Martin. Actual crew members from *The Andy Griffith Show* (director of photography Sid Hickox, hair stylist Eva Kryger, and crewman Burt Taylor) appear as members of the commercial camera crew. Written by Jack Elinson and Iz Elinson; directed by Alan Rafkin.

Episode 187: "Goober's Replacement," March 28, 1966. When Flora fills in for Goober at Wally's, her feminine charms dramatically increase business. Maudie Prickett as Edna Larch and Cliff Norton as Wally. Written by Stan Dreben and Howard Merrill; directed by Alan Rafkin.

Episode 188: "The Battle of Mayberry," April 4, 1966. Opie's research establishes that the Battle of Mayberry was not the heroic victory the townspeople thought it was. Clinton Sundberg as Farley Upchurch, Arthur Malet as loafer, and Norm Alden as Tom Strongbow. Written by Paul David and John L. Greene; directed by Alan Rafkin.

Episode 189: "A Singer in Town," April 11, 1966. Aunt Bee and Clara talk a pop singer into recording their composition, "My Hometown." Jesse Pearson as Keevy Hazelton, Joel Redlin as Ferdie, and Byron Foulger as Leroy. Written by Stan Dreben and Howard Merrill; directed by Alan Rafkin.

SEASON SEVEN (1966-67)

Episode 190: "Opie's Girlfriend," September 12, 1966. Helen's niece vies with Opie in a battle of the sexes. Mary Ann Durkin as Cynthia. Written by Budd Grossman; directed by Lee Philips.

Episode 191: "The Lodge," September, 19, 1966. Howard's heart is set on admission into the lodge, but someone doesn't want him in. Written by Jim Parker and Arnold Margolin; directed by Lee Philips.

Episode 192: "The Barbershop Quartet," September 26, 1966. The fourth man in Mayberry's barbershop quartet is a petty thief, whom Andy must bring along for the big competition. Hamilton Camp as Jeff Nelson, Blackie Hunt as Wally, Ken Mayer as Sheriff Blake Wilson, Burt Mustin as Jud-Burt, and Harry Arnie as hobo Kelly. Written by Fred S. Fox; directed by Lee Philips.

Episode 193: "The Ball Game," October 3, 1966. Andy gets the cold shoulder after he calls Opie out at home plate during a championship baseball game with Mt. Pilot. Favorite episode of Ron Howard and Rance Howard. Written by Sid Morse; story by Rance Howard; directed by Lee Philips.

Episode 194: "Aunt Bee's Crowning Glory," October 10, 1966. Aunt Bee can't bear to tell a visiting pastor that she's been wearing a wig ever since she met him. Ian Wolfe as Reverend Leighton. Written by Ronald Axe; directed by Lee Philips.

Episode 195: "The Darling Fortune," October 17, 1966. A lick of good luck and the Omen of the Owl find the Darling menfolk in town in search of wives. Helen gets their attention. The Darlings get back on the truck for the final time. Written by Jim Parker and Arnold Margolin; directed by Lee Philips.

Episode 196: "Mind Over Matter," October 31, 1966. Goober thinks he needs critical attention after he barely hurts his back in a minor accident. Written by Ron Friedman and Pat McCormick; directed by Lee Philips.

Episode 197: "Politics Begin at Home," November 7, 1966. Aunt Bee tosses her hat into the ring for town council and runs against Howard, but Andy has already agreed to support Howard. Written by Fred S. Fox; directed by Lee Philips.

Episode 198: "The Senior Play," November 14, 1966. The school principal forbids Helen and the high school seniors from producing an unorthodox senior play. Leon Ames as Mr. Hampton., Mary Jackson as Miss Vogel, Cynthia Hull as Estelle, and Chuck Brummitt as Homer. Goober takes off on Cary Grant and others. Written by Sid Morse; directed by Lee Philips.

Episode 199: "Opie Finds a Baby," November 21, 1966. Opie and Arnold secretly try to raise an infant that they find on the Courthouse steps. Jack Nicholson as Mr. Garland, Janie Kelly as Mrs. Garland, and James McCallion as Dr. Bailey. Sheldon Golomb makes his first appearance as Arnold Bailey. Written by Stan Dreben and Sid Mandel; directed by Lee Philips.

Episode 200: "Big Fish in a Small Town," November 28, 1966. Of all folks, indoorsman Howard hooks and lands the legendary silver carp, Old Sam. Old Sam was named after writer Sam Bobrick. A favorite episode of Jack Dodson. Written by Bill Idelson and Sam Bobrick; directed by Lee Philips.

NO WONDER ANDY'S SO WISE— *This owl doesn't know how fortunate he is not to have been around while the Darlings were in town. Omen of the Owl notwithstanding, he's a prime candidate for that Darling favorite, hoot owl pie.*

Episode 201: "Only a Rose," December 5, 1966. Aunt Bee's got a sure winner on her hands for the annual garden club competition, but then Opie accidentally breaks off the bloom. John Reilly as Billy and Richard Collier as Mr. Simmons. Written by Jim Parker and Arnold Margolin; directed by Lee Philips.

Episode 202: "Otis the Deputy," December 12, 1966. When they realize that Andy has been taken captive, Otis and Howard search for the hideout of a couple of robbers. Joe Turkel as Fred and Charles Dierkop as Larry. Final appearance of Otis Campbell. Written by Jim Parker and Arnold Margolin; directed by Lee Philips.

Episode 203: "Goober Makes History," December 19, 1966. Goober becomes hard to face with the knowledge he seems to have grown along with his new beard. Sandy Kenyon as Bill Lindsey. Written by Paul David and John L. Greene; directed by Lee Philips.

Episode 204: "A New Doctor in Town," December 26, 1966. The townspeople have no faith in a young physician who has set up practice in Mayberry. William Christopher as Dr. Thomas Peterson. Written by Ray Brenner and Barry E. Blitzer; directed by Lee Philips.

Episode 205: "Don't Miss a Good Bet," January 2, 1967. Andy warns his friends not to invest in a scheme when a visitor claims to hold the map to the long-lost Ross's Raiders treasure. Roger Perry as George Jones. Written by Fred S. Fox; directed by Lee Philips.

Episode 206: "Dinner at Eight," January 9, 1967. Andy chows down on spaghetti, spaghetti, and more spaghetti after Goober passes along misinformation. Emory Parnell as Uncle Edward. A favorite episode of George Lindsey. Written by Budd Grossman; directed by Lee Philips.

Episode 207: "A Visit to Barney Fife," January 16, 1967. Andy spends time with Barney in Raleigh as they crack a string of supermarket holdups. Richard X. Slattery as Capt. M.L.

Dewhurst, Betty Kean as Ma Parker, and Margaret Teele as Agnes Jean Parker. Written by Bill Idelson and Sam Bobrick; directed by Lee Philips.

Episode 208: "Barney Comes to Mayberry," January 23, 1967. Barney tries to wind down in Mayberry for a few days and gets carried away with an old schoolmate who has become a movie star. Diahn Williams as Teena Andrews and Patty Regan as Renée. Written by Sid Morse; directed by Lee Philips.

Episode 209: "Andy's Old Girlfriend," January 30, 1967. Helen grows jealous after Andy gets lost in the woods with his old high school flame. Joanna McNeil as Alice Harper. Written by Sid Morse; directed by Lee Philips.

Episode 210: "Aunt Bee's Restaurant," February 6, 1967. It appears to be Aunt Bee's lucky day when she goes into partnership on a Chinese restaurant in Mayberry. Keye Luke as Charlie Lee and Lloyd Kino as Jack Lee. Written by Ronald Axe and Les Roberts; directed by Lee Philips.

Episode 211: "Floyd's Barbershop," February 13, 1967. After Howard buys the barbershop, he thinks it necessary to raise Floyd's rent. Dave Ketchum as Harry Walker. Written by Jim Parker and Arnold Margolin; directed by Lee Philips.

Episode 212: "The Statue," Feb. 20, 1967. The people of Mayberry agree to commission a monument for Seth Taylor, but then discover he was not the citizen that they thought he was. Dal McKennon as Brian Jackson. Written by Fred S. Fox; directed by Lee Philips.

Episode 213: "Helen, the Authoress," February 27, 1967. Helen's entry into children's book publishing has Andy feeling like an underachiever. Keith Andes as Roger Bryant, Elaine Joyce as Mavis Neff, and Laurie Main as Robling Flask. Aneta Corsaut's favorite episode with Helen Crump. Written by Doug Tibbles; directed by Lee Philips.

Episode 214: "Goodbye Dolly," March 6, 1967. Opie cares for the milkman's horse and the animal quits eating. Tom Tully as Walt Simpson. Written by Michael L. Morris and Seaman Jacobs; directed by Lee Philips.

Episode 215: "Opie's Piano Lesson," March 13, 1967. Opie has his hands full trying to play football and practice the piano at the same time. Rockne Tarkington as Coach Flip Conroy and Richard Bull as Mr. Jackson. Written by Leo and Pauline Townsend; directed by Lee Philips.

Episode 216: "Howard, the Comedian," March 20, 1967. After Howard displays his comedic wit on a TV program, his friends mistakenly think he is poking fun at them. Dick Haynes as Colonel Tim. Written by Michael L. Morris and Seaman Jacobs; directed by Lee Philips.

Episode 217: "Big Brother," March 27, 1967. Howard agrees to mentor a high school student and then flips for the boy's older sister, and in doing so neglects the boy and his own career goals. Elizabeth MacRae as Betty

HAPPY PAIR—*Andy and Helen are bound to have much to look forward to.*

Parker, Peter Hobbs as John Tracy, and Scott Lane as Tommy Parker. Written by Fred S. Fox; directed by Lee Philips.

Episode 218: "Opie's Most Unforgettable Character," April 3, 1967. Opie struggles to pen a composition on his most unforgettable character, his father. Joy Ellison as Betsy. Written by Michael L. Morris and Seaman Jacobs; directed by Lee Philips.

Episode 219: "Goober's Contest," April 10, 1967. Goober invents a cash give-away game to drive up business at Wally's and then discovers that he has made a big mistake. Rob Reiner as Joe and Owen Bush as Mr. Hammond. Last appearance of Floyd the Barber. Written by Ron Friedman and Pat McCormick; directed by Lee Philips.

SEASON EIGHT (1967-68)

Episode 220: "Opie's First Love," September 11, 1967. Opie's first big date turns sour when his girlfriend drops him for another guy. Suzanne Cupito (Morgan Brittany) as Mary Alice Carter, Joy Ellison as Iris, Owen Bush as Doyle Perkins, and David Alan Bailey as Fred Simpson. Written by Doug Tibbles; directed by Lee Philips.

Episode 221: "Howard the Bowler," September 18, 1967. Howard has his sights on a perfect game at the bowling alley when the electricity goes off during a match with Mt. Pilot. First appearance of Emmett Clark. Norman Alden as Hank. Written by Dick Bensfield and Perry Grant; directed by Lee Philips.

Episode 222: "A Trip to Mexico," September 25, 1967. Two of Aunt Bee's best friends accompany her to Mexico after she wins a contest. Ruth Thom as Myrtle and José Gonzalez-Gonzalez as a shopkeeper. Vince Barnett appears for the first time as Elmo. Written by Dick Bensfield and Perry Grant; directed by Lee Philips.

Episode 223: "Andy's Trip to Raleigh," October 2, 1967. Andy works on business with a lady lawyer in Raleigh, but Helen doesn't buy his explanations. Whitney Blake as Lee Drake. Written by Joseph Bonaduce; directed by Lee Philips.

Episode 224: "Opie Steps Up in Class," October 9, 1967. When Opie becomes chums with a boy from a wealthy family, Aunt Bee and Andy try to put on a ritzy front. Joyce Van Patton as Laura Hollander, Sandy Kenyon as George Hollander, and Don Wyndham as Billy Hollander. Written by Joseph Bonaduce; directed by Lee Philips.

Episode 225: "Howard's Main Event," October 16, 1967. Howard stands up to a bully, Millie's ex-boyfriend, despite the fact that he doesn't know much about how to defend himself. Allan Melvin as Claude Plaunt. First appearance of Arlene Golonka as Millie Hutchins. Written by Earl Barrett and Robert C. Dennis; directed by Lee Philips.

Episode 226: "Aunt Bee the Juror," October 23, 1967. Aunt Bee sits on a jury in a case of robbery and is the lone voice who believes the accused man is not guilty. Jack Nicholson as Marvin Jenkins, Rhys Williams as Judge Cranston, Henry Beckman as Mr. Gilbert, Jim Begg as Charles Keyes, and Tol Avery and Emory Parnell as jurors. This episode has the most actors with specific speaking parts. Written by Kent Wilson; directed by Lee Philips.

Episode 227: "Tape Recorder," October 30, 1967. Opie and Arnold tape a private conversation between a crook and his attorney and find the whereabouts of stolen loot. Herbie Faye as Eddie Blake and Jerome Guardino as Myles Bentley. Written by Michael L. Morris and Seaman Jacobs; directed by Lee Philips.

Episode 228: "Opie's Group," November 6, 1967. Opie is invited to play in a rock 'n' roll band, much to Andy and Aunt Bee's dismay. Jim

Kidwell as Clifford, Gary Chase as Jesse, Joe Leitch as Wilson, and Kay Ann Kemper (Kay Lenz) as Phoebe. Written by Doug Tibbles; directed by Lee Philips.

Episode 229: "Aunt Bee and the Lecturer," November 13, 1967. A visiting lecturer falls for Aunt Bee because of her resemblance to his deceased mate. Edward Andrews as Professor Hubert St. John. Written by Michael Morris and Seaman Jacobs; directed by Lee Philips.

Episode 230: "Andy's Investment," November 20, 1967. Andy moonlights as owner of a laundry operation in order to prepare for Opie's college education. Ken Lynch as Inspector Rogers, Maudie Prickett as Edna Sue Larch, and Jesslyn Fax as Mrs. LeGrande. Written by Michael Morris and Seaman Jacobs; directed by Alan Rafkin.

Episode 231: "Howard and Millie," November 27, 1967. Howard proposes to Millie but a long train ride brings them to another destination. Written by Joseph Bonaduce; directed by Peter Baldwin.

Episode 232: "Aunt Bee's Cousin," December 4, 1967. Andy finds that Aunt Bee's fast-talking cousin is not as prosperous as he might seem. Jack Albertson as Bradford J. Taylor and Ann Morgan Guilbert as Ella. Written by Dick Bensfield and Perry Grant; directed by Lee Philips.

Episode 233: "Suppose Andy Gets Sick," December 11, 1967. Deputy Goober turns Mayberry upside down as he fills in for an ailing Andy. Written by Jack Raymond; directed by Peter Baldwin.

Episode 234: "Howard's New Life," December 18, 1967. Howard ditches life in Mayberry for adventures on an exotic Caribbean island. The voice belonging to the narrator of the travelogue show on TV is that of writer Bill Idelson. Harry Dean Stanton as the general store owner and Sir Lancelot as "the man." Written by

Dick Bensfield and Perry Grant; directed by Lee Philips.

Episode 235: "Goober the Executive," December 25, 1967. Goober buys out Wally and learns what it's like to manage a business for himself. Dave Ketchum as Harry Walker and Bo Hopkins as George. Written by Seaman Jacobs and Michael L. Morris; directed by Lee Philips.

Episode 236: "The Mayberry Chef," January 1, 1968. Aunt Bee returns before the TV cameras as chef on a cooking show, but Andy and Opie's appetites pay the price. Don Keefer as Carl Phillips and Jack Bannon as Mr. Sabol. Written by James L. Brooks; directed by Lee Philips.

Episode 237: "Emmett's Brother-in-Law," January 8, 1968. Emmett closes down his Fix-It Shop and turns to the lucrative vocation of insurance sales. Dub Taylor as Ben Beacham. Mary Lansing plays Martha Clark for the first time. Written by James L. Brooks; directed by Lee Philips.

Episode 238: "Opie's Drugstore Job," January 15, 1968. Opie accidentally breaks a bottle of expensive perfume at his new job at the drugstore and keeps it a secret from his employer. Robert F. Simon as Mr. Crawford. Written by Kent Wilson; directed by Lee Philips.

Episode 239: "The Church Benefactors," January 22, 1968. A committee at church must decide between repairing the church building or purchasing new choir robes. Written by Earl Barrett and Robert C. Dennis; directed by Lee Philips.

Episode 240: "Barney Hosts a Summit Meeting," January 29, 1968. When Barney steers American and Russian diplomats to Mayberry as the perfect site for a summit, Aunt Bee saves the day. Richard X. Slattery as Capt. Dewhurst, Michael Higgins as Mr. Clifford, Ben Astar as Mr. Vasilievich, Alan Oppenheimer as Mr. Ruskin and, Paul Fix as Mr. McCabe. Final appearance of Barney Fife. Written by Aaron Ruben; directed by Lee Philips.

Episode 241: "Goober Goes to an Auto Show," February 5, 1968. Goober becomes reacquainted with an old pal in Raleigh and, finding the man apparently to be a big success, feels as though he's a failure. Noam Pitlik as Roy Swanson, Patty Regan as the manicurist, and Don Sturdy (Howard Hesseman) as the sandwich man. Trivia buffs note the Coors beer truck that passes the Raleigh gas station several years before that brand of beer was available in North Carolina. Written by Joseph Bonaduce; directed by Lee Philips.

Episode 242: "Aunt Bee's Big Moment," February 12, 1968. Aunt Bee decides she wants to learn how to fly an airplane. John McLiam as Mr. MacDonald. Written by Dick Bensfield and Perry Grant; directed by Lee Philips.

Episode 243: "Helen's Past," February 19, 1968. Helen is put on the hot seat by school board members after Andy digs up some seemingly bad news from her past. Ruth McDevitt as Ethel Pendleton and Peter Hobbs as Mr. Lockridge. Written by Doug Tibbles; directed by Lee Philips.

Episode 244: "Emmett's Anniversary," February 26, 1968. Emmett considers purchasing an expensive fur for his wife's anniversary present. Ronnie Schell as Bernie. Final appearance of Flora. Written by Dick Bensfield and Perry Grant; directed by Lee Philips.

Episode 245: "The Wedding," March 4, 1968. Howard lets his hair down and throws a big bash at his house after his mother marries and moves away. Iggie Wolfington as George Watson and Teri Garr as a girl who turns down Goober for a date. Written by Joseph Bonaduce; directed by Lee Philips.

Episode 246: "Sam for Town Council," March 11, 1968. Emmett and Sam Jones run head to head for a position on the town council. First appearance of Sam Jones. Don Sturdy (Howard Hesseman) as Harry. Written by Dick Bensfield and Perry Grant; directed by Lee Philips.

Episode 247: "Opie and Mike," March 18, 1968. Opie proves a good role model for young Mike but finds Mike's admiration too much to take. Buddy Foster as Mike Jones, Diane Quinn as Heather Campbell, Kellie Flanagan as Claudia Campbell, and Russell Schulman as Edgar Watson. Written by Doug Tibbles and Bob Ross; directed by Lee Philips.

Episode 248: "A Girl for Goober," March 25, 1968. A computer matchmaking service pairs Goober with a female intellectual. Nancy Malone as Dr. Edith Gibson, Tod Andrews as Mr. Franklin, and Margaret Ann Peterson as Doris. Written by Bruce Howard and Bob Ross; directed by Lee Philips.

Episode 249: "Mayberry R.F.D.," April 1, 1968. When Sam Jones invites a friend from Italy to stay with him, the man brings his father and sister along. Gabrielle Tinti as Mario Vincente, Bruno della Santina as Papa Vincente, Letitia Roman as Sophia Vincente, and Almira Sessions as Mrs. Fletcher. Written by Bob Ross; directed by Peter Baldwin.

Learn more about Mayberry:

To find out more about *The Andy Griffith Show,* contact *The Andy Griffith Show*
Rerun Watchers Club (TAGSRWC) at 9 Music Square South, PMB 146,
Nashville, TN 37203-3286